CW00763570

'Left liberals have for some time continually painted a twisted, racist picture of working-class life and culture. Yet in this fascinating and true-to-life text based on ethnographic research, Dr Luke Telford, shows in real life this is not the case. By immersing himself in a forgotten northern community, he traces the words and feelings of the working class to the deindustrialisation of the area and loss of respectable, well-paid work coupled with the rise of inadequate and unrewarding jobs in the exploitative and degenerative commercial sector. This, he argues, sets the scene for the discontent and political anger. A magnificent text and must read for anyone wanting to learn about working class politics!'

Dr Daniel Briggs, Professor in Criminology,
Universidad Europea

'Luke Telford offers a fresh and engaging perspective on rising political dissatisfaction and nationalist sentiment. Drawing on rich empirical data and sophisticated social theory, this book thoroughly unpicks the thorny issue of English nationalism whilst cutting through populist discourse. Heartfelt and honest, this wonderfully written book gives voice to the frustrations of those left behind by capitalism, and is essential reading for anyone interested in navigating the turbulence of Brexit'.

Dr Justin Kotzé, Senior Lecturer in Criminology and
Criminal Justice, Teesside University

English Nationalism and its Ghost Towns

In order to understand today's nationalism, we need to address the historical decline of working-class communities, the sense of loss brought by deindustrialisation and how working-class people have been denied a voice in society and politics. Discontent has manifested strongly in these deprived post-industrial areas, often branded as communities that have been left behind under neoliberal globalisation. Whilst more and more people are voicing their discontent with a system that fails to provide social security and economic stability, many researchers have branded them merely as racists, xenophobes and ill educated. Although prejudices are likely to play a part in all political outcomes, today's dissatisfaction across the West cannot be reduced to mere emotion and intolerance.

This book therefore utilises on-the-ground research with working-class individuals in a Leave voting locale in Britain, exploring their discontent with politicians, the Labour Party, the European Union, immigration, refugees and the prolonged calls for a second referendum. It situates this sentiment towards society and politics within the decline of capitalism's post-war era and the loss of well-paid industrial jobs, increase in non-unionised service employment and the hollowing out of community spirit.

Dr Luke Telford is a lecturer in criminology at Staffordshire University. Luke's main interests include the rise of nationalism, deindustrialisation, labour markets, the shift from post-war capitalism to neoliberalism, consumerism and ultra-realist theory. Luke is a co-author of *Lockdown: Social harm in the Covid-19 era* (Palgrave Macmillan, 2021) and the e-book *Researching the COVID-19 pandemic: A critical blueprint for the social sciences* (Policy Press, 2021).

English Nationalism and its Ghost Towns

Luke Telford

Routledge
Taylor & Francis Group

NEW YORK AND LONDON

Cover image: Cover image taken by Luke Telford

First published 2022
by Routledge
605 Third Avenue, New York, NY 10158

and by Routledge
4 Park Square, Milton Park, Abingdon, Oxon, OX14 4RN

Routledge is an imprint of the Taylor & Francis Group, an informa business

© 2022 Taylor & Francis

The right of Luke Telford to be identified as author of this work has been asserted by them in accordance with sections 77 and 78 of the Copyright, Designs and Patents Act 1988.

All rights reserved. No part of this book may be reprinted or reproduced or utilised in any form or by any electronic, mechanical, or other means, now known or hereafter invented, including photocopying and recording, or in any information storage or retrieval system, without permission in writing from the publishers.

Trademark notice: Product or corporate names may be trademarks or registered trademarks, and are used only for identification and explanation without intent to infringe.

Library of Congress Cataloging-in-Publication Data
Names: Telford, Luke, author.
Title: English nationalism and its ghost towns / Luke Telford.
Description: New York, NY : Routledge, 2022. | Includes
    bibliographical references and index.
Identifiers: LCCN 2021054219 | ISBN 9781032056715 (pbk) |
    ISBN 9781032056722 (hbk) | ISBN 9781003198666 (ebk)
Subjects: LCSH: Cities and towns. | Industries. | Nationalism.
Classification: LCC HT151 .T39 2022 | DDC 307.76—dc23/
    eng/20211216
LC record available at https://lccn.loc.gov/2021054219

ISBN: 978-1-032-05672-2 (hbk)
ISBN: 978-1-032-05671-5 (pbk)
ISBN: 978-1-003-19866-6 (ebk)

DOI: 10.4324/9781003198666

Typeset in Garamond
by Apex CoVantage, LLC

Contents

Acknowledgements   viii
Foreword   ix

Introduction   1

1   History   13

2   Neoliberalism   32

3   The quest to understand nationalism   51

4   The industrial age   66

5   Absent futures   89

6   Nationalism   106

7   The past, present and future   137

Index   155

Acknowledgements

All individual achievements are collective efforts. As this book is based upon my PhD studies, my greatest gratitude is expressed to Dr Anthony Lloyd because his impact on both my professional and intellectual growth is incalculable. He offered persistent encouragement and intellectual guidance. He perpetually challenged my views of our social world, and he is a prescient scholar. I also thank Dr Justin Kotzé, my second supervisor, as Justin offered invaluable support and encouragement. I owe much to Emeritus Professor Steve Hall. Since I met Steve during my postgraduate studies, Steve has offered guidance, support and encouragement and his intellect never ceases to amaze me. A big thanks also goes to Professor Daniel Briggs, since Dan also provided guidance and had a big impact on helping improve my narrative. My thanks also goes to other academics who have helped shape the book's arguments, including Professor James Treadwell, Professor Simon Winlow, Dr Mark Bushell, Dr Anthony Ellis, Dr Thomas Raymen, Dr Oliver Smith and Dr Jonathan Wistow.

My gratitude is expressed to the research participants for giving up their time to speak to me. My thanks go to the NINE DTP ESRC for funding the PhD project that underpins this book. I also thank my employer, Staffordshire University, for giving me the time and space to think about our social world and engage in writing projects like this book. Not a day goes by where I don't think that I am immensely privileged to be able to do so. My gratitude is also expressed to Routledge and my editor Lewis Hodder. I can't thank Lewis enough for believing in this book from day 1 and offering guidance throughout the process.

I owe everything to my mam, Judith, and beautiful fiancée, Gemma. Without my mam's unwavering support, particularly in my troubled teenage years, I would not be writing this. Indeed, Gemma has lived and breathed this book with me and put up with bouts of long working hours. I love you both more than you will ever know. I also thank my dad, nanna and grandad for their support. Finally, I thank my little brother and legend, Jack—time away from writing and watching football instead was always a refreshing and enjoyable break.

Foreword

Since the United Kingdom voted to leave the European Union in June 2016 and Donald Trump was elected as president of the United States in November 2016, journalists, commentators and academics have rushed to explain this seemingly sudden lurch to the political right. These trends have been characterised as the return of fascism, authoritarianism, nationalism and populism. For some, media-savvy charlatans have conned the uneducated. For others, a racist underbelly has been revealed through anti-immigrant sentiment, colonial nostalgia and a nationalist sense of superiority. Some suggest those left behind by neoliberalism and globalisation have reminded the elites that they still exist. Political and cultural fault lines have hardened, and debate has often been reduced to opposing sides shouting past each other, unable or unwilling to listen and understand the other side whilst remaining convinced of one's own righteousness. These political, social, economic and cultural developments represent an important and historical moment that has called into question many conventional wisdoms. Does nationalism represent a rejection of globalisation? Are we seeing the beginning of a shrinking world? Is this the re-emergence of fascism? Are we set for an authoritarian future? Are capitalism and liberalism now no longer in sync? Have we reached the nadir of neoliberalism? Where are we going?

Much of the analysis that I have read over the last five years somehow simultaneously agrees that it's a complex issue and then posits a mono-causal explanation. The Brexit vote was down to a lack of education. Trump won because he appealed to an underlying racism. Cambridge Analytica and Facebook are to blame. And so on. The reality is that these issues are complex and there is no single underlying explanation. In this excellent new book, Luke Telford demonstrates the value of understanding where we have come from in order to both make sense of the present and look to where we are heading. His analysis takes into account the fields of political economy and culture, global trends and regional variations, communities, jobs and individual lives. His arguments are persuasive. If we want to understand nationalist sentiment, we have to situate it within the context of people's lives. Political views and opinions don't exist in a vacuum or appear from nowhere. They are shaped by the influences and experiences across the life course and rooted in place and time.

His work provides a refreshing methodological and theoretical approach to the messy complexity of our times. We can't empirically verify a mono-causal explanation and posit a key variable as the most important factor behind any given political trend or development. Meanwhile, we can't rely on old ideas and explanations; we have to look for new ways to make sense of what's happening in the world today. A world that has changed significantly over recent decades and is on the cusp of further change post-pandemic. As we look forward with an eye on understanding where we are going, Telford's account of political economy and the hollowing out of politics—on both the left and the right—should give us food for thought. Why do people think and vote in the way they do? Perhaps, if we spent more time listening and understanding, situating their lives in a broader context of politics, economics, culture, opportunities and barriers towards stable, secure and meaningful lives, instead of lecturing people about their apparent deficiencies and wrong-headed thinking, we might be able to answer those questions. Until we do that, the fault lines that characterise the United Kingdom, United States and Europe today will only harden.

Dr Anthony Lloyd, Reader in Sociology and
Criminology, Teesside University,
13th July 2021.

Introduction

Ghost town

I walk into the town centre on a Tuesday morning and pass a young woman with long dark hair. She stares at her phone and briefly looks up to see where she is going, before her eyes glance downwards again. Whilst chewing gum is embedded in the grey-brick pavement, cigarettes and broken bottle glass are scattered in other areas. Various bits of rubbish including shopping receipts and plastic bags fly around me as a strong wind permeates the air. The first shop I witness is a closed retail store. Inside, it is empty and dark and a white sign above states 'retail unit to let'. I walk twenty yards and witness another large, empty store. It is not boarded up but the glass door on the left-hand side has been smashed, the doors are dirty and the brown paint on the frame has faded. It looks like it has been closed for a long time. Ripped posters advertising a nearby circus hang off the decaying wood and the faded initials of 'M & S' are etched into the steel board.

The high street is extremely quiet. A row of benches occupies the middle of the town centre with a pathway either side, but they are largely empty. Only a handful of people walk in each direction. A 'Christian band' is playing music to my left but nobody is paying any attention. Most people don't make eye contact and simply walk past. A small, old man, with a black woolly hat on, tattered dark coat and a clear limp comes hobbling out of a public telephone box. The phone doesn't appear to be working, so he tries the other one. He looks harried and concerned and he is getting annoyed because that one doesn't work either. Behind him lies a sizable hotel that has closed down. A board outside advertises 'karaoke and live music', but the lights are turned off and the music has stopped. Inside, the blinds and curtains are closed. Ivy is growing on the building, and hanging baskets containing dead flowers lie adjacent to the closed entrance. It is hard to imagine this place 40 years ago when it was populated by tourists and thriving.

As I look to my left, posters stating, '50% off' are plastered across a shoe shop window. But nobody is in the store. I walk 50 yards and a familiar sight occurs, 'sale, grab a bargain' at a 'discount' store. Standing ten yards ahead is a

DOI: 10.4324/9781003198666-1

pub with an England flag hanging to the right of the entrance. The establishment's current midweek offer is two meals for £7.50, as well as £1 sambuca shots on a Saturday night. A middle-aged man is outside smoking a cigarette, and seagulls fly around him. Behind me, a grey-haired man comes out of the bookies and says to his friend, 'Meet you over there at half past'. He goes back inside. It is 11 am.

Although stores including a unisex hairdresser, jewellery outlet claiming 'we buy gold', and various cafes are open, they are quiet. Characterising Steel Town's high street are boarded up (or closing down stores), charity shops and litter which is scattered across the pavement. As the town centre is bereft of people, a hollowed-out quietness fills the locality. This absence is partially a symptom of Steel Town's current employment conditions and broader economic decline.

Most of the participants believed the town centre was an empty place, deprived of civility and meaningful social interaction. Many stores have closed, replaced by charity and takeaway food stores. Many people were saddened about this, though fatalism and resignation permeated their views. There was no punctual moment that engendered the locality's decline; instead, deindustrialisation combined with the current labour market's absence of stability and security brought a slow-motion social dislocation to Steel Town. As the data reveals, it has not always been like this; many of the older respondents remembered when Steel Town was a relatively prosperous and vibrant place. Anna describes how:

> There is nothing, jobs wise. It is just shopping, but they are closing. There used to be shops all the way down both sides of the high-street—Marks and Spencer, Woolworths, big shops, they have gone. Those that have taken over, there is nobody in them. You go in them shops at any time and there is nobody in them. In the winter, it is very quiet.

Claire offers a similar narrative:

> I used to work on the high-street, it is just *dead* now. Things are closing, it is all charity shops and pound shops—they aren't putting enough money into it. Buildings are left empty for ages, landlords put the rates too high, so people can't afford to open new stores. The high street is *dying*. I worked at a shop last Christmas, and it was dead, nobody was coming in. It is a shame.

Anna and Claire offer a story of decline, perhaps symbolised by the word *dead*, indicating how what remains in Steel Town's high street provides little social substance. As stores either shut down or demand for their services diminishes, fewer and fewer employees are required. This contributes to joblessness and a lack of disposable income for people to spend in the locality, aiding a domino effect that intensifies Steel Town's decline. Dave also elucidates a sense of perpetual deterioration:

> Shops like M & S will stay derelict now because the person who owns it are still getting the rent paid by M & S because they had a long lease on it. If they rented it out to another shop, say it lasted a year or two, then they wouldn't get the rent like they are now. So, it makes business sense for the person who owns it to leave it derelict, which isn't good. They had to pay ten years on it. It has been shut for five years, so it will probably be shut another five years now.

Most respondents were saddened about the closure of Marks and Spencer since it had been on Steel Town's high street since the 1950s. Its closure occurred alongside the abandonment of 'so many good shops', including one of the local butchers which had also existed in Steel Town for over 70 years. Therefore, the closure of these outlets further contributed to feelings that the area had been abandoned. Micky outlines how:

> The only thing in the town is takeaways, pubs or charity shops. That is all the town consists of. There are some plastic shops—where there are pictures on the windows, so it makes it look as though there is a shop, but there isn't. It's just waiting for somebody to buy the place.

'Plastic shops' provide a pseudo-image of civility, sociality and cultural vibrancy, though behind this is abandonment and economic decline. Although there is a degree of geographical variation, many of England's high streets are rather homogenous, populated by empty stores, takeaway outlets, decrepit retail and charity shops, providing little meaningful social sustenance. Scholars suggest that these places are often defined by post-social relations[1]; shop workers are not genuinely interested in customers, they stimulate conversation only to solicit sales and profitability. The remaining pubs and cafes are often quiet, as a brief foray into the high-street illuminated:

> After paying £1.20 to park my vehicle for two hours, I walk into the town centre. A pop up 'money expert' van lies ahead, and two shoppers to my left ignore the worker's request for a moment of their attention. He turns around and asks me, 'Alright mate, do you pay any bills?' I reply 'No', and walk ahead. He does not genuinely care about my economic position but attempts to construct an image of civility to attract customers and facilitate profit maximisation. In other words, the interaction is substanceless and not real.

As we will see, Steel Town and Teesside were once at the forefront of England's workshop of the world, helping to build important global landmarks like the Sydney Harbour Bridge. The locale had a clear function and social purpose. Many of the older respondents talked about elements of this era because it generated fond recollections of a time that has now been lost, like Mary: 'A friend of mine has a shop called Teesside pottery [pseudonymised], and she stamps it with made in Steel Town—that is all we have left now'.

Similarly, Julia suggests Steel Town has:

> Changed a lot over the years. You can walk through, and it is like a *ghost-town*—empty shops, virtual shops, pound shops or charity shops seem to be the mainstay of the town, and pubs. No matter what time of day you go downtown, there are people falling out of the pubs, honestly. Even if it is 11 o clock on the morning, they will always be standing outside the Phoenix Arms [pseudonymised]—smoking, waiting to be let in for a drink.

Although Steel Town's high street was perceived to have died, the respondents' neighbourhoods also contained post-social tendencies. All the participants believed that community life had declined, with many no longer speaking to their neighbours. Valuable aspects of civilised social life including reciprocity, mutuality and an attachment to one's community, appeared to be absent in post-industrial Steel Town. Julia said:

> Most of the time people don't know their neighbours, or who is living on their street. It didn't always used to be like that. I remember the silver jubilee in the late 70s, there was street parties, and everybody knew each other. Everybody is just too busy now. It takes people longer to get to work, the pace of life.

What Julia describes is a structural feeling of fractured post-social relations; residents no longer spending time with people in their neighbourhood, they are mere strangers who possess little knowledge about one another. Ellie also highlighted this post-social arrangement:

> I don't think you get a feeling of community now. You used to see more people; I don't really talk to my neighbours. I remember when I was younger, my mam would come out of the front door and chat to people over the fence. Nowadays, you don't get that. On this street, I know a handful of people to say hello to. People have just moved in next door, they were alright at first, but they go out now and turn the other way and don't say hello—just weird. It is like they don't want to communicate—what is the world coming to?

As this book will demonstrate, whilst a degree of mutual relations and community bonds were once present in Steel Town, these characteristics were absent from the respondents' communities today. Also observe how Ellie outlines one of the 'unwritten rules of post-social engagement',[2] that is, her neighbours tolerate Ellie but keep her at a safe distance to avoid substantive contact. Put another way, the neighbour's presence is acceptable, though they should not venture too close. Matty continues the story on Steel Town's post-social tendencies:

> There's no courtesy anymore, no hiya, opening doors, like that thing where you would be brought up respectful, sense of community, that's gone now. Everybody just seems to be looking after number one. But years and years ago, I remember being a kid, everybody's door was open, but not anymore. It has changed massively, for the worse. It hasn't finished yet; everything is about money now and greed.

Christopher Lasch displayed myriad prescience when he wrote over 40 years ago that civic life was being eroded by competitive individualism, which encourages people to view one another as an enemy to elicit envy from.[3] Lasch claimed that individualism, if left unchecked, would continue to erode the social and collective good, turning society into an interpersonal and hostile battle.[4] Ultimately, Lasch believed that egotistical individualism would erode a sense of community and peoples' ability to forge meaningful relationships, since its core logic is to protect the self against others who would outdo you, given the opportunity.

As the above demonstrates, the world into which the COVID-19 pandemic emerged in March 2020 was one defined by growing social polarisation, inequalities and dissatisfaction, particularly the rise of political discontent via nationalistic sentiments in post-industrial and left behind areas like Steel Town. Given how all encompassing the pandemic has been, it is somewhat difficult to imagine the time before COVID-19 emerged. Donald Trump had won the United States of America Presidential Election in 2016. Nationalist politicians were also on the march across Europe including leader of the National Rally Party Marine Le Pen in France, as well as Matteo Salvini's Lega Nord in Italy.[5] Support from traditional working-class voters in post-industrial areas for social democratic parties had fell to a historical low across the European continent, as historical political allegiances faded from view. Some suggested we had entered a new political age, one defined by new schisms such as age, cultural views on immigration and educational background[6] rather than social class.

However, Britain's vote to Leave the European Union (EU) in 2016—Brexit—was the most class correlated vote in the modern era,[7] whilst the subsequent fall of the Red Wall in December 2019 was driven by working-class voters in Brexit voting locales across the North of England, who had shifted from voting Labour to the Conservatives, often for the first time in their history.[8] Why, after years of economic decline and declining living standards, were the political Left unable to harness peoples' discontent in their former heartlands? Why, after years of social fragmentation and the weakening of civic life, were the Labour Party unable to harness the palpable sense of dissatisfaction that exists in England's post-industrial areas?

Popular accounts of these two political earthquakes in both the media and academia have often claimed voters in economically abandoned towns are ill educated, myopic and culturally regressive, often expressing racist and sexist views and longing for the age of Empire when England waged its imperial might. However, might it be a little bit more complex than this? Might it be a good idea to place how people feel about politics and society within a historical context, shedding light upon the structural conditions within which political dissatisfaction grows and mutates? Indeed, this book is based on in-depth qualitative research with working-class individuals in post-industrial 'Steel Town' in Teesside in the Northeast of England; a Brexit-voting area that also voted for the Conservatives in 2019 for the first time in half a century. It situates Brexit and the eventual collapse of the Red Wall, discontent with politicians, immigration, refugees, identity politics and the prolonged calls for a second vote on EU membership within the shift from post-war capitalism to neoliberalism. It places emphasis upon the importance of the collapse of the post-war settlement, deindustrialisation and current structural conditions in the labour market and surrounding area in explaining the rise of nationalistic views. As we will see, working-class demands for socio-political change have been congealing throughout the neoliberal epoch.

Steel Town, a deindustrialised locality in Teesside populated by working-class people,[9] offers an ideal means to study the rise of nationalism in the context of neoliberal capitalism. Throughout the twentieth century, Steel Town was a popular seaside resort, whilst the local economy was dominated by steelmaking, mining, petrochemicals, shipbuilding and heavy engineering. This sizable industrial sphere meant the area was important to British capital accumulation.[10] As we will encounter, whilst industrial employment was repetitive and hard work, it engendered structural feelings of social purpose and pride because Teesside's industrial workers built important global architecture including the Sydney Harbour Bridge.[11] Relative social stability and economic security formed the basis of social life. As it was not uncommon for employees to spend their working lives at one industrial employer,[12] some workers expressed confidence that their children and grandchildren would follow in their footsteps and obtain remunerative manufacturing work.

Teesside's industry also contained a large petrochemicals base, led by Imperial Chemicals Industry (ICI), who was the largest producer of ammonia in the world.[13] ICI was a core employer in Steel Town, offering sizable pay and pension packages. Around 6,000 people were also employed at Steel Town's core steelworks in the early 1980s, and it was one of the largest sites in Western Europe.[14] With relatively powerful trade unions advancing the working-class and their economic interests through holding their employers to account over exploitative working practices, economic inequality narrowed for the first time in history.[15] Whilst this period contained fixed and rigid gender roles, a sense of security and identity were harnessed as people knew their role in society.[16]

Shifting to neoliberalism in the 1980s, though, engendered rapid social, economic and cultural change with a service sector gradually replacing an industrial economy in Teesside.[17] Between the mid-1970s and turn of the millennium, Teesside's local economy lost 100,000 well-paid industrial jobs and gained 92,000 service sector employment roles.[18] Whilst pockets of remunerative employment exist, many service sector jobs do not provide the financially worthwhile pay and pension packages of the industrial age. The local economy's restricted labour markets in the industrial epoch meant it was unable to cope with the rapid withdrawal of industrial work. Although Teesside does contain some areas that are as affluent as anywhere in England,[19] it also contains locales that are amongst the most deprived, characterised by higher than national average levels of joblessness, family breakdown, crime, and legal and illicit drug misuse.[20] A structural sense of socio-economic decline in Teesside was intensified in 2015 with the closure of the largest remaining steelworks. Over 2,000 people lost their jobs, as well as many more indirectly, further eroding the industrial age's stability and security.

Throughout the neoliberal epoch, remunerative industrial work that equipped many working-class people in places like Steel Town with a sense of social purpose has declined.[21] As this book documents, the work that many working-class people now undertake is menial and characterised by the absence of industrialism's positive symbolism; much of it is rather poorly paid and non-unionised.[22] With the imposition of austerity measures after the 2008 global financial crisis, the welfare state has been hollowed out, contributing to a rise in private indebtedness.[23] Many working-class people now lack the material comfort afforded by both stable work and a functioning welfare state.[24] Economic inequality, already at tectonic levels before the onset of the COVID-19 pandemic, has recently reached a level unseen in human history,[25] with much of the citizenry's living standards declining.

The restructuring of Teesside's socio-economic context has impacted upon the area's previously strong allegiance to social democratic politics. Throughout much of the twentieth century, most localities in Teesside like Steel Town returned a Labour Party Member of Parliament (MP) as their electoral representative.[26] This is an area that once corresponded to the idea that even if a donkey stood for election wearing a red Labour Party rosette, it would win. As we will encounter, the Teesside region lost working-class support throughout the New Labour years as millions of voters became disillusioned with politics and stopped voting.[27] This political malaise intensified in the subsequent years, with many deindustrialised conurbations voicing their support for the United Kingdom Independence Party (UKIP) at the 2015 general election.[28] However, it erupted in 2016 and 2019. Firstly, all the core areas across Teesside voted to leave the EU by a significant margin, whilst at the 2019 general election areas that formed the Red Wall from Wales to the North of England—Steel Town—elected a Conservative MP, often for the first time in half a century, signalling the Labour Party's worst defeat since 1935.[29]

The narrative that the shift towards nationalism is a manifestation of idiocy, mere racism and xenophobia has been hegemonic amongst some politicians, media commentators and a section of academics[30]; many others have claimed that the demands for voter sovereignty and primacy to England's domestic interests are reminiscent of the nation's age of Empire. Although the data in this book demonstrates subjective discontent towards many thorny matters including immigration, dismissing this as mere racism and idiotic is anti-intellectual and not conducive to unearthing the context that underpins such sentiments and opinions. In fact, it might be argued that it disguises neoliberal capitalism from critique, concealing its impact upon shaping English nationalism and aiding the system's hegemon in the face of structural crises—not least the COVID-19 pandemic and impending ecological catastrophe.

Alongside this potentially simplistic narrative, the methodological tools that some researchers have used to understand English nationalism have been of a quantitative dimension, comprising questionnaires, surveys and statistical analysis. Although researchers using these methods have made an important contribution to the debate on political change, highlighting issues like age, education and voting differences across the nation, they tend to search for a single and definitive answer at the expense of complexity, history and contextual conditions. In consequence, they disconnect empirical data from the formative context in which sentiments grow and evolve. This book, therefore, builds upon the lack of qualitative research in deindustrialised areas that have shifted away from Leftist politics towards nationalism, outlining how local people feel against a structural backdrop of industrial collapse, service-based employment and a sense of political abandonment. The chapter outline below documents the content of the book's individual chapters.

Outline of chapters

Chapter 1, 'History', provides the book's historical foundations by exploring Steel Town and Teesside's development under capitalism. It begins with a discussion of the industrial revolution before explicating structural crises like the 1929 Great Depression and the Second World War, demonstrating how—when the political economy changes—Steel Town and Teesside are reconfigured too.[31] The chapter then shifts into capitalism's post-war phase, outlining the social stability and economic security awarded by industrial labour under the class compromise, as well as how a sense of community was harnessed in places like Steel Town. As we will see, elements of this era continue to shape memories and sentiments about the present. It closes with an exploration of how the local economy has been transformed since the 1980s with the shift to neoliberal political economy.

Although Chapter 1 closes with a brief outline of neoliberalism's reconfiguration of Steel Town and Teesside, Chapter 2—'Neoliberalism'—offers a more detailed and theoretical discussion. In particular, it utilises insights from various scholars like David Harvey to explicate how neoliberalism functions in various ways, including as a restorative project to restore class power and wealth to the financial elite.[32] It then focuses on how it has restructured the social world through other changes including the ascent of consumer culture, offering a transient escape from the insecurity of today's working conditions.[33] It then explores the 2008 global financial crash and the hegemonic political response across England—austerity measures. As New Labour were central to this period, it also explores their electoral reign.

This provides a formative context for Chapter 3—'The quest to understand nationalism'. This chapter is split into two core parts. Firstly, it explores the hegemonic perspectives on the rise of English nationalism, particularly Brexit, documenting how academia failed to foresee this historical event.[34] It outlines how much analysis has been rather reductionist, often condemning voters as myopic, racist and longing for the imperial age, whilst much other commentary has been based upon quantitative methods. Although they might award researchers an empirical basis for further exploration, their search for objectivity and a universal explanation of nationalism neglects historical processes and important context. This provides the foundations for the second part of the chapter, a brief exploration of the qualitative methodological approach that underpins the book.

Whilst the book's first three chapters provide the historical context, the next three chapters focus on analysing the empirical data gleaned through the qualitative research. These three chapters theorise evidence to advance our understanding and deploy several ethnographic vignettes to place sentiments within a contextual backdrop of economic decline.[35] Chapter 4, 'The industrial age', outlines Anthony Lloyd's idea of capitalism's *somewhat mythical* golden age.[36] It addresses how the research participants recalled this epoch in Steel Town fondly, offering social stability and economic security. Chapter 4 also identifies how Steel Town became a popular tourist resort in the post-war era and offered various cultural amenities to the local population and 'day trippers'. It closes with an explication of Steel Town's decline, specifically through the closure of both ICI and the steelworks, documenting how it engendered joblessness, mental ill health and impacted adversely on the local town centre.

Chapter 5—'Absent futures'—addresses current labour market conditions in Steel Town. It documents how contrary to neoliberal ideology's sacred ideals of freedom, opportunity, meritocracy and success, many people experience work characterised by the absence of pride, fulfilment and social purpose.[37] Although many people worked hard to obtain a stable job, most respondents could not acquire economically secure work in a local economy defined by deep industrial job loss.[38] It builds upon Mark Fisher's idea that capitalist realism,[39] the negative and depressive sense that nothing can change for the better in society, clouds many workplaces as it had congealed in many of the participants' psyche. The chapter outlines how capitalism has uncloaked its post-war ideological camouflage and returned to its fundamental essence of the maximisation of profitability and market expansion.[40]

As a result, many participants and their family members experienced bouts of unemployment and uncertain employment. Whilst several expressed dissatisfaction with these working conditions, the chapter builds upon recent theoretical work to outline how many people feel politically impotent under neoliberalism.[41] It then outlines how working conditions have also been corroded through overworking and the managerial imposition of targets, atomising and individualising workers.

This is the constitutive context for the book's final data chapter—'Nationalism'. The chapter incorporates the dissatisfaction with industrial collapse, current working conditions and the area's socio-economic decline to display how this culminated in a deeply held belief that politicians do not protect working-class interests but their own careers. It utilises the notion of 'capitalo-parliamentarianism'[42] to suggest that it has been hollowed out in the neoliberal era to serve capital accumulation rather than the working class. Rather than capitalo-parliamentarianism existing as a mechanism to channel peoples' discontent about society and politics, the chapter shows how it was perceived as a tool to facilitate the rich's accumulation of wealth and power. Next, it documents Steel Town's desire for fundamental change, expressed first through the 2016 Brexit vote, outlining how the EU was perceived to be undemocratic and unaccountable.

The chapter then documents how the contextual conditions revealed in Chapters 4, 5 and 6 engendered the demand to reduce immigration. However, this was a nuanced form of discontent, occasionally manifesting in racist remarks that were tethered to Steel Town's decline. The chapter closes with an outline of the liberal left's demands for a second referendum, which occurred from June 2016 to December 2019 with the eventual collapse of the Red Wall and Boris Johnson's promise to implement the Brexit vote.

The book's final chapter—'The past, present and future'—briefly summarises the book's core arguments before discussing the emergence of the COVID-19 pandemic in March 2020. It documents the impact of this upon society, including how it has exploded pre-existing vulnerabilities in both the economy and social inequalities. It also documents the unintentional consequences of the lockdowns, and the lack of political critique directed towards them. This chapter closes with a discussion of the future, speculating on what potentially lies ahead. It discusses the electoral futility of the political Left's focus on identity politics, calling for the Labour Party to focus on *Sameness*. It then outlines various ways for the political Left to remedy their drift away from the working-class, drawing on Modern Monetary Theory, the potential for a state funded job guarantee and a Green New Deal. It briefly outlines the potential consequences if we do not shift away from neoliberalism and implement a Green Industrial Revolution—namely, a future characterised by the bleak and dark horizon of the dystopian fiction movie *Children of Men*. Firstly, though, the book returns to history, outlining how political economic change has historically restructured Steel Town and Teesside.

Notes

1. Winlow, S & Hall, S (2013) *Rethinking Social Exclusion: The End of the Social?* London: SAGE.
2. Winlow, S & Hall, S (2013), p. 123.
3. Lasch, C (1979) *The Culture of Narcissism: American Life in an age of Diminishing Expectations*. London: W.W. Norton & Company.
4. Also see: Raymen, T (2021) *The Assumption of Harmlessness*. In Davies, P, Leighton, P & Wyatt, T (eds.), *The Palgrave Handbook of Social Harm*. London: Palgrave Macmillan, pp. 59–88.
5. Mitchell, W & Fazi, T (2017) *Reclaiming the State: A Progressive Vision of Sovereignty for a Post-Neoliberal World*. London: Pluto Press.
6. Eatwell, R & Goodwin, M (2018) *National Populism*. London: Pelican Books; Goodhart, D (2017) *The Road to Somewhere: The New Tribes Shaping British Politics*. London: Penguin.
7. Winlow, S, Hall, S & Treadwell, J (2017) *The Rise of the Right*. Bristol: Policy Press.
8. Embery, P (2020) *Despised: Why the Modern Left Loathes the Working Class*. Cambridge: Polity.
9. Foord, J, Robinson, F & Sadler, D (1985) The Quiet Revolution: Social & Economic Change on Teesside 1965–1985. A Special Report for BBC North East; Telford, L & Wistow, J (2020) Brexit and the working class on Teesside: Moving beyond reductionism. *Capital & Class*. 44(4): 553–572.
10. Hudson, R (2004) Rethinking change in old industrial regions: Reflecting on the experiences of North East England. *Environment and Planning A*. 37(4): 581–596.
11. Warren, J (2018) *Industrial Teesside, Lives and Legacies: A Post-Industrial Geography*. London: Palgrave Macmillan.
12. Telford, L & Wistow, J (2020).
13. Telford, L & Wistow, J (2020); Warren, J (2018).
14. Lloyd, A (2013) *Labour Markets and Identity on the Post-Industrial Assembly Line*. Farnham: Ashgate; Shildrick, T, Macdonald, R, Webster, C & Garthwaite, K (2012) *Poverty and Insecurity: Life in Low-Pay No-Pay Britain*. Bristol: Policy Press.
15. Piketty, T (2014) *Capital in the Twenty-First Century*. Cambridge: Harvard University Press.
16. Hall, S (2012) *Theorising Crime and Deviance: A New Perspective*. London: SAGE; Hall, S & Winlow, S (2020) Back to the future: On the British liberal left's return to its origins. *International Journal of Media and Cultural Politics*. 16(1): 65–73.

17. Beynon, H, Hudson, D & Sadler, D (1991) *A Tale of Two Industries: Contraction of Coal and Steel in the North East of England*. London: Open University Press; Beynon, H, Hudson, D & Sadler, D (1994) *A Place Called Teesside: Locality in a Global Economy*. Edinburgh: Edinburgh University Press.
18. Shildrick, T, Macdonald, R, Webster, C & Garthwaite, K (2012).
19. Warren, J (2018).
20. English Indices of Deprivation (2019) *The English Indices of Deprivation 2019*. Ministry of Housing, Communities and Local Government. Accessed on 14/07/2021. Available at: https://assets.publishing.service.gov.uk/government/uploads/system/uploads/attachment_data/file/835115/IoD2019_Statistical_Release.pdf; Kotzé, J (2019) *The Myth of the 'Crime Decline': Exploring Change and Continuity in Crime and Harm*. Oxon: Routledge.
21. Raymen, T (2018) *Parkour, Deviance and Leisure in the Late-Capitalist City: An Ethnography*. Bingley: Emerald Publishing Limited; Winlow, S & Hall, S (2005) *Violent Night: Urban Leisure and Contemporary Culture*. Oxford: Berg.
22. Lloyd, A (2018a) *The Harms of Work*. Bristol: Policy Press.
23. Lloyd, A & Horsley, M (2021) Consumer culture, precarious incomes and mass indebtedness: Borrowing from uncertain futures, consuming in precarious times. *Thesis Eleven*. 1–17.
24. Horsley, M (2015) *The Dark Side of Prosperity: Late Capitalism's Culture of Indebtedness*. Farnham: Ashgate Publishing Limited; Horsley, M & Lloyd, A (2020) Mass indebtedness and the luxury of payment means. In Hall, S, Kuldova, T & Horsley, M (eds.), *Crime, Harm and Consumerism*. Abingdon: Routledge, pp. 73–89.
25. Briggs, D, Ellis, A, Lloyd, A & Telford, L (2021) *Researching the Covid-19 Pandemic: A Critical Blueprint for the Social Sciences*. Bristol: Policy Press; Ellis, A, Telford, L, Lloyd, A & Briggs, D (2021) For the greater good: Sacrificial violence and the coronavirus pandemic. *Journal of Contemporary Crime, Harm, Ethics*. 1(1): 1–22.
26. Beynon, H, Hudson, D & Sadler, D (1991).
27. Embery, P (2020).
28. Ford, R & Goodwin, M (2017) Britain after Brexit: A nation divided. *Journal of Democracy*. 28(1): 17–30.
29. Pabst, A (2021) *PostLiberal Politics*. Cambridge: Polity Press.
30. Eatwell, R & Goodwin, M (2018).
31. Lloyd, A (2018a); Warren, J (2018).
32. Harvey, D (2005) *A Brief History of Neoliberalism*. Oxford: Oxford University Press.
33. Raymen, T (2018); Raymen, T & Smith, O (2019) Deviant leisure: A critical criminological perspective for the twenty-first century. *Critical Criminology*. 27: 115–130; Smith, O & Raymen, T (2016) Shopping with violence: Black Friday sales in the British context. *Journal of Consumer Culture*. 17(3): 677–694.
34. Salter, B (2018) When intellectuals fail? Brexit and hegemonic challenge. *Competition & Change*. 22(5) 467–487.
35. Briggs, D (2017) *Dead-End Lives: Drugs and Violence in the City Shadows*. Bristol: Policy Press; Briggs, D (2021) *Climate Changed: Refugee Border Stories and the Business of Misery*. Abingdon: Routledge; Raymen, T (2018).
36. Lloyd, A (2018a).
37. Warren, J (2018).
38. Foord, J, Robinson, F & Sadler, D (1985).
39. Fisher, M (2009) *Capitalist Realism: Is There No Alternative?* Ropley: O Books; Fisher, M (2018) *K Punk*. London: Repeater Books.
40. Winlow, S & Hall, S (2013).
41. Stiegler, B (2019) *The Age of Disruption: Technology and Madness in Computational Capitalism*. Cambridge: Polity Press.
42. Badiou, A (2015) *The Communist Hypothesis*. London: Verso, p. 76.

Chapter 1

History

This is the book's first of three contextual chapters, outlining Steel Town and the wider Teesside region's history. This historical sketch extends to the broader locale of Teesside as the historical development of the wider area during the late nineteenth and early twentieth century had myriad implications for Steel Town.[1] Indeed, it begins with capitalism's Victorian era, highlighting how the area was at the centre of the Industrial Revolution, owing its existence to early capitalists' demands for capital accumulation, market expansion and the maximisation of profitability.[2] The chapter then discusses the early twentieth century's social hardships, including myriad economic inequality, inadequate housing and slum conditions. It then addresses the inter-war years, shedding light on how Steel Town became one of England's most popular coastal resorts because of its proximity to the coast and various cultural amenities.

As the 1929 Great Depression further dislocated the lives of the working classes, social inequalities, unemployment and political discontent continued to accumulate. Whilst austerity was implemented to try address capitalist crises and steady the economy, arguably it was not until the onset of the Second World War in 1939 that people in the Teesside region were paradoxically put to work again, providing a degree of stability and certainty. Therefore, how Teesside was central to the nation's defence efforts abroad will be outlined, demonstrating how its industrial prowess played an important role in deterring enemy attack. Although capitalism failed to provide social and economic security for most during the early twentieth century, victory in the Second World War meant the system had to change; it would have been unacceptable for war heroes to return home to mass unemployment and impoverishment.[3] This chapter analyses how the industrial working class in Teesside witnessed relative socio-economic betterment during the post-war period, branded as the somewhat mythical golden age.[4]

As we will encounter, this did not continue indefinitely; the post-war era encountered structural shocks and neoliberal policies were enacted. The impact of the *great change*[5] in the late 1970s will then be briefly discussed to further elucidate how capitalism's historical development has myriad socio-cultural implications. The chapter's aim is to lay bare the

DOI: 10.4324/9781003198666-2

book's historical foundations, providing context for the social and political dissatisfaction expressed in the second half of the book.

The Victorian era

The industrial revolution has been cast as one of history's most important processes as it transformed England and many of its localities like Teesside.[6] The onset of manufacturing work was geographically variegated due to each area's natural conditions; on 8 June 1850 in Teesside, large quantities of iron ore were discovered by the mining engineer John Marley and ironmaster John Vaughan.[7] Such a discovery ushered in the epoch of: 'heavy industry; the industrial revolution, which set in motion a powerful process of rapid economic development in Teesside'.[8] Capitalists favoured the Teesside region because it possessed conditions for maximising profitability that were unmatched across the country. Limestone and coking coal were secured from Durham, around 25 miles from Teesside, which fuelled the area's blast furnaces.[9] Teesside also possessed flat land in abundance, enabling the formation of the railways to transport raw materials to Teesside's River Tees and then the North Sea to ship them across the globe.

Whilst the locale's ecological conditions enabled the rapid construction of industrial plants, there was a dearth of labour available to provide the required manual labour to fuel the plants.[10] Economic migrants from across the globe thus moved to Teesside in the 1840s and 1850s—many emigrated from the British Colonies and European countries like Ireland because of the Great Hunger.[11] Starvation and disease were prevalent across Ireland because crops, particularly potatoes, were infected on an unprecedented scale. All the while, occupied Ireland still exported what little food was available to England including millions of bushels of grain, countless gallons of butter and thousands of Irish calves in the 'famine years'.[12] One million Irish people died and a further million emigrated to survive. The arrival of migrants generated tensions in the area—namely, involving Irish workers who arrived from Lancashire in the 1840s in Middlesbrough, nine miles from Steel Town. The migrants had to be escorted to work by the police because they were derided by over 350 residents, who eventually attacked them which forced the Irishmen to flee the area.[13]

The onset of the industrial revolution generated Teesside's *great iron rush*. Thirty years after iron ore was discovered in the region, 120 blast furnaces were built in Teesside. The region became the global leader in iron ore production, acquiring the nickname Ironopolis. Prominent politicians visited Teesside to witness its industrial prowess and the consequential bursts of flame and smoke, including former Prime Minister William Gladstone who claimed 'Teesside was a remarkable place, the youngest child of England's enterprise, is an infant, but if an infant, an *infant Hercules*'.[14]

Whilst a mass industrial labour force was put to work, workers' living standards did not increase; instead, wealth was concentrated amongst the capitalists. Such economic insecurity meant industrial workers' pay would principally be given immediately to their wives, and every penny was carefully spent. This financial and social hardship meant men drank regularly and gambled on horse-racing, engendering debt and household friction.[15] Although the area was branded as *Ironopolis*, iron production in Teesside reached its maturity in 1883, since cheaper and better-quality iron ore was imported from elsewhere including Spain.[16] However, the decline of Teesside's iron industry occurred at the same time as the onset of the *great steel age*. Although many men in Steel Town obtained employment in Teesside's steel plants, health and safety conditions were poor. In 1885 at Steel Town's steelworks, 11 men died after a site explosion and many others were injured.[17] Such hazardous conditions were occasionally reinforced by male workers—Smith's Dock opened in Teesside in 1908, employing thousands of men within several years; however, there was a culture of indifference towards safety measures like hard hats and earplugs, which were branded as pointless and feminine.[18]

Whilst the industrial plants provided tough and difficult employment opportunities, they also engendered clouds of thick smoke, potentially impacting detrimentally on industrial worker's health. Although 'even the birds coughed'[19] in many of Teesside's localities, Steel Town's proximity to the coastline meant it offered a transient leisurely relief to Teesside's industrial working class. Branded as 'the lung of the great industrial population of Teesside',[20] Steel Town offered a boating lake and an open-air swimming pool. At the same time, Teesside:

> was a mighty centre of industry. Along the lower reaches of the River Tees innumerable furnaces belched flames and smoke into the sky. Long regimented rows of terraced houses huddled close by. Iron ships filled the docks and lined the quays, while cranes busily emptied their bowels in the seemingly never-ending task of satisfying the ravenous furnaces. Elsewhere, the finished iron and steel was transformed into huge engineering masterpieces, bridges, framed ships and industrial plant.[21]

Although Teesside's vast industrial plants meant it was relatively easy for locals to obtain work, the locale's dependence on manufacturing resulted in higher than national average levels of unemployment during the Great Depression years. However, Steel Town paradoxically burgeoned in popularity with both locals and tourists, becoming one of the most popular coastal resorts in England between the First and Second World Wars.[22]

The inter-war period

Whilst the First World War engendered myriad social distress throughout 1914–1918, Teesside's industrial plants expanded further.[23] In Steel Town, a blast furnace was opened by Dorman Long next to the River Tees in 1918. This site employed 6,000 men within four years and contained an 'enormous cogging mill and the only universal mill in the United Kingdom'.[24] Working here was dirty and dangerous, though it awarded workers feelings of social purpose and an identity because they helped produce the materials for social infrastructure.[25]

Although Teesside's industrial companies yielded sizable profits, heightened competition from abroad meant many had to perpetually alter their market focus. This is what Karl Marx characterised as the *coercive laws of competition*,[26] capitalists occasionally seek to exploit other markets and diversify because of competition from other companies. Indeed, steel was offered cheaper by other businesses, meaning Teesside's ports endured a decline in profitability.[27] Accordingly, Dorman Long restructured their focus and began to build steel bridges; the most famous of which was the Sydney Harbour Bridge. Opening in 1932, it utilised 50,000 tons of Teesside steel.[28] The bridge is regarded as an exemplary piece of architecture, and therefore, the company forged a reputation for the construction of significant landmarks.

Imperial Chemicals Industry (ICI) was born in 1926, as four chemical companies merged in Teesside. This transformed Billingham, 18 miles from Steel Town, from a relatively small locale to a town characterised by industrial work. The rhythm provided by industrial work created feelings of community, obligation and social bonds amongst both employees and residents.[29] Whilst working in Teesside's steel, chemicals, shipbuilding and heavy engineering industries was hard work, relationships amongst colleagues were generally cooperative and supportive.[30] However, there were many scarring effects of social class. Whilst high rates of excessive alcohol consumption, suicide and psychological distress accompanied the industrial age, men were often absent from their children's lives partially because of long working hours.[31] Nevertheless, ICI innovated in both pharmaceutical and chemical processing, inventing important products like Perspex that was exported globally. Although unemployment rose during the inter-war years, ICI's demand for a mass industrial workforce meant it assimilated pockets of Teesside's unemployed.

Such difficult structural conditions were made much worse in the years following the 1929 stock market crash. As global demand and consumption fell to a historical low, joblessness, socio-economic deprivation and psychological despair intensified.[32] A lack of regulation and control over the economic activities of the world's financial elite allowed reckless speculation on financial markets. Most of the political class believed state intervention in a capitalist economy would derail investment, growth and expansion, leading to an economic downturn. Most also claimed the role of government during economic crises is to implement austerity, thus reducing state investment and stagnating wages to inspire confidence in the business world, kickstarting the recovery and economic growth.[33] Indeed, England and many other nations such as the United States followed this economic dogma in the 1930s, engendering the Great Depression.

In this context, world trade dropped by 60% and mass unemployment became the norm across much of the Western world.[34] Although many sizable businesses closed, the poor suffered the most since they did not have savings to fall back onto or a social safety net to mitigate their destitution. Somewhat inevitably, Teesside's dependence on the steel, shipbuilding, mining and petrochemicals industries meant the locale's unemployment rate was more than double the national average.[35] Activity at many industrial sites, particularly within the mining industry, was halted across the region, whilst those fortunate enough to retain their job witnessed their wages fall significantly.[36] Despite this global tumult, Steel Town became a haven for leisure and pleasure in the 1930s. The area offered a cinema, large pier for fishing, ballroom for dancing and an open-air swimming pool.[37] A sizable park was also constructed, possessing both a tennis court and a boating lake; indeed, it is still popular with many residents today. These cultural pleasures meant that around two million people visited Steel Town annually in the 1930s, including over 30,000 visitors on a bank holiday weekend, making it one of the most popular coastal locales in England. Nonetheless, life was difficult for much of the working class; women would often come 'armed with large paper carriers containing food for the day'[38] as they could not afford to buy it in Steel Town.

Whilst ICI managed to survive this period, hope, despair and destitution prevailed across much of northern England. Myriad capitalist crises enabled other ideologies to harness support such as communism and fascism. Both ideologies responded to crises differently. Whilst communism saw it as an inevitable crisis that capitalism could not resolve, fascism was the arm of the bourgeoisie acting in its own self-interest to maintain their class position through crises. Indeed, Oswald Mosley formed the British Union of Fascists (BUF) in 1932. Formerly a Conservative and Labour MP, Mosley was disgruntled with both party's perceived incompetence in addressing capitalism's structural crises.[39] Accordingly, Mosley believed laissez-faire capitalism had failed; a new form of capitalism had to be constructed. Mosley's BUFs were inspired by other fascist parties in Europe including Mussolini's National Fascist Party and Hitler's Nazi Party in Germany, wearing blackshirt uniform and utilising violence to suppress opposers. The BUF also utilised public campaigns to disseminate their ideology across the country.[40] Mimicking Hitler's Nazi Party in Germany, Mosley attempted to harness support from the 'ground up', particularly in socially and economically marginalised areas.[41] Therefore, many believed that Stockton, characterised by high joblessness and deprivation and 15 miles from Steel Town, was susceptible to fascism.

The BUF possessed a headquarters in Stockton, which was utilised to arrange campaigning events around Northern England.[42] One of which was in Stockton high street in September 1933, attracting proponents of the BUF from Teesside, Tyneside and Manchester. In fact, 100–300 advocates gathered at Stockton's Market Cross, though they were jeered by 2,000–3,000 locals.[43] As the fascists attempted to flee Stockton, many of the locals cornered them into nearby Silver Street where they assaulted them. Whilst they often used potatoes with inserted razor blades,[44] the 'Blackshirts were spat at, attacked with staves, sticks and pickaxe handles'.[45] Other reports note how one fascist was knocked unconscious.[46] Eventually, BUF supporters made their way back to their buses, followed by many locals who cheered as the buses drove away. Whilst around 20 supporters of the BUF were injured and hospitalised, no arrests were made as only seven police officers were on duty during the Battle of Stockton.[47]

A local rally including Labour Party councillors and faith group leaders was held by Stockton's local Labour Party a day after the battle to demonstrate solidarity with each other. They also enumerated on the debilitating impact on society if the BUF emerged victorious in the early twentieth century's politico ideological battle. Since the Battle of Stockton occurred before bigger BUF events like the 1936 Battle of Cable Street in London, where violence occurred between the BUF, law enforcement and opposers, the police realised that violence was a possibility at the BUF's campaigning events and were better resourced thereafter.[48] Evidently, Stockton was temporarily at the centre of laissez-faire capitalism's ideological tumult; yet, the Battle of Stockton has largely been forgotten about in Teesside's history.

These ideological conflicts hardened with the onset of the Second World War in 1936. Rearmament meant Teesside's industry could be utilised again, providing jobs, stability and a degree of certainty. As austerity failed to mitigate the Great Depression, it is possible that the Second World War ended this period of prolonged economic downturn, since mobilisation for war increased production, provided employment and stimulated the economy.[49]

Second World War

Rearmament increased industrial employment and unionisation, particularly in the steelworks, mining and chemical industries.[50] Whilst over three million English men served in the British Army, women entered the industrial workforce in increasing numbers. ICI played a pivotal role during the war, building explosives, mortars and aircrafts to power attacks across Europe.[51] Production of synthetic ammonia multiplied, providing the fuel for bombs and explosives, whilst Teesside's steel provided the raw materials for bridges and pillboxes to mitigate the detrimental impact of enemy invasions.[52] Indeed, during the Second World War nearby Middlesbrough won the contract for 'one of the biggest steel orders ever'[53] placed in England.

Teesside's importance to both the national economy and war effort meant many politicians believed it would be stringently attacked during the war. In consequence, in 1939 around 6,000 individuals were evacuated from Middlesbrough.[54] Whilst industrial pollution may have negatively affected the local population's health, it provided a camouflage for the region's towns and industry during the war. ICI's chemical production was thus increased to ensure a 'thick blanket of smoke'[55] filled the sky. A large rump of ICI's chemical site was also disguised with camouflaged netting. Nevertheless, Teesside was England's first industrialised area to be bombed,[56] despite the mechanisms constructed in industrialised locales like Steel Town which 'saw an accumulation of concrete strong points (known as "pillboxes"), machine-gun posts and searchlight emplacements'.[57]

In October 1941, Steel Town witnessed what has been cast as the town's darkest event—an air attack caused 12 fatalities including Steel Town's mayor, and many others were injured.[58] As a point of remembrance to the deceased, a memorial garden now exists on the site. Whilst Steel Town's main steelworks was situated next to the River Tees and thus North Sea, it was subjected to frequent attacks, including in 1941 and 1942 when the steelworks were bombed. This caused 20 fatalities, injured many others and caused myriad infrastructural damage to the steelworks.[59] Despite these attacks, much of Teesside's industry continued to power the war effort—such as the shipyard Smith's Dock who built 87 ships during the Second World War.

As the West joined together with the Soviet Union, they defeated Nazi Germany in September 1945. However, capitalism was in a state of profound crises after a tumultuous period, not least because of the Second World War which generated mass death, anxiety, disease, sicknesses, malnutrition, eviscerated infrastructure and thus pervasive homelessness. This was laissez-faire capitalism's historical 'triple challenge of slump, fascism and war'[60] in which the system's ability to accrue stability, security and relative prosperity for the English working class was discredited.[61] Panic therefore prevailed amongst politicians, suggesting progressive change had to be implemented. Subsequently, a political consensus emerged in the West, that is, capitalism could be saved but only if it placed the socio-economic interests of the working class at the forefront of its modus operandi.[62] Policies to ensure this included, not least, the nationalisation of key industries, further unionisation and industrial expansion in areas like Steel Town in Teesside.

Capitalism's somewhat mythical golden age

After a prolonged period of crises, most politicians emphasised the need to avoid laissez-faire capitalism's 'hell on earth'.[63] As full employment was attained during the Second World War, it was difficult to dispense from peoples' mindset during peacetime.[64] In this context, Clement Attlee's Labour Party won a majority in the 1945 general election, sending shockwaves throughout society and politics. Core industries including the railways and gas were nationalised by 1946, whilst unprecedented employment levels were achieved by 1947.[65] The nation state played a hands-on role in the economy, enforcing sizable taxation levels on the rich. By 1948, the welfare state and National Health Service (NHS) were built. A core plank of the NHS was that it should be free at the point of use, providing health care to all members of society. This was a landmark achievement, branded as the envy of other countries. Whilst Attlee's government restructured capitalism along historically unprecedented progressive lines, some believed he saved capitalism when the opportunity was there to implement revolutionary change.[66] Nonetheless, as ideological change became entrenched in both society and amongst politicians, the main political parties forged a cross party consensus, generally accepting the need for social democratic policies.

Industrial expansion in areas like Teesside and economic growth were central to capitalism's post-war age.[67] Other localities in England also possessed large manufacturing sites; together, they formed 'the workshop of the world'.[68] Given the tumultuous years of the Great Depression, though, Teesside's mining industry never recovered. Pits closed throughout the 1950s and 1960s, culminating in the final closure in 1964.[69] The pit was 720 feet deep and therefore the biggest pit that had existed in Teesside. Its closure signalled the end to Teesside's 100-year history of mining.[70]

Nevertheless, ICI expanded in the post-war epoch, opening another chemical site in 1956 in Wilton, two miles from Steel Town. Cast as 'a great adventure, a great experiment',[71] the Wilton site specialised in organic chemicals and it became the largest global producer of ammonia. Therefore, it generated tens of thousands of remunerative jobs, accruing stability and security to many people in Steel Town and the surrounding locales. As Chapter 4 outlines, many participants once worked at ICI and recalled it fondly. Indeed, as mass production, widespread investment and working-class interests were given primacy, full employment was achieved. This was a core objective of the political class in the post-war period, engendering a sizable period of certainty and stability. However, the abundance of employment undermined employers; attempts to discipline the workforce would often be ineffective as workers could obtain another job relatively easily.[72]

ICI's apprenticeships were often for five years, providing training, stability and longevity. The petrochemicals company offered lucrative support to workers, including housing which meant occupational communities were formed, since employees often lived on the same street.[73] Such a context meant a sense of communal bonds and duty to each other was forged within industrial work. The diktats of the state often facilitated this, including the 1963 Hailsham Report and thus state subsidies. The report outlined how both Labour and the Conservatives were committed to enhancing industrial plants in places like Teesside, suggesting it was an important locale for further development and growth.[74] Therefore, ICI used 60% of the state's regional development grants to expand its two sites in Teesside.[75]

Some suggest these working conditions were not reflective of values like obligation and duty to workers; instead, they represented capitalism's desire to survive after the early twentieth century's social crises.[76] This involved a reciprocal relationship between employers and employees, containing economic stability and social security, whilst allowing governments to intervene in business affairs to provide fairer and more just social outcomes.[77] Perhaps this was a means for capital to obtain commitment from the working class and ensure capitalism's survival. As we will see, when capitalism encounters more structural crises and thus the opportunity emerges to magnify workforce control, productivity and degrade working conditions, it does so and wraps itself in a *new spirit*.[78]

Nevertheless, industrial labour harnessed a culture of reciprocity and togetherness. The manual construction of material objects also created a sense of accomplishment and utility amongst workers cognisant of their importance to economic growth and global export.[79] In this way, industrial work afforded a clear biography and an associated sense of social fulfilment, principally to men. As we will see, the rhythm and solidity of industrial work meant it was not uncommon for sons to follow in their father's footsteps and accrue a manufacturing job.

Mass unionisation was also common in industrial labour markets, substantiating feelings of working-class solidarity and forming a labour movement which accrued substantial bargaining power.[80] This meant capital's attempts to degrade working conditions were often met with strike action. The profit motive was transiently restrained, meaning many industrial workers received an adequate share of their labour. As better rights and wages were implemented, an age of relative affluence enveloped working-class life.[81] Indeed, it was the first and only time in capitalism's longue durée that economic inequality reduced.[82]

Placed in this context, industrial labourers and their families were generally content with social conditions.[83] Wages in Teesside in the 1960s were the third highest in Britain, behind London and Aberdeen.[84] This experiential reality created positivity, optimism and hope that the future contained further relative prosperity. Commodified consumer freedoms aided this sense of optimism, though its core value of competitive individualism permeated the working-class and began to loosen social bonds.[85]

Such consumer freedoms potentially expanded to obtain their allegiance to post-war capitalism; however, it was generally believed that the English working classes 'had never had it so good'.[86] Memories of laissez-faire capitalism's social and economic hardship had faded into the background as:

> Full employment, the growth of trade union power, the establishment of a welfare state and capitalism's shift into a consumerist phase where a measured increase in the spending power of the masses became a vital economic fuel, together created a combination of affluence and security previously unseen in working-class communities.[87]

This era was an anomaly in capitalism's history, cast as the golden age or thirty glorious years,[88] though as Anthony Lloyd highlights this notion is somewhat mythical because it contained various antagonisms.[89] Whilst industrial workers, in particular, harnessed decent working conditions and wages, they did not possess genuine power over how to organise their workplace or society. As we will encounter, racism was also a prominent feature of white working-class culture, suggesting they occupied a position of superiority over other ethnic groups in society.[90] Gender roles were also fixed with the male's job providing a family wage. Although this was sufficient to provide a stable and secure living standard, women's social function was characterised as housebound—cleaning, cooking, rearing the children and attending to their husband's needs.[91] Whilst more and more women entered the workforce in the post-war era, they were generally employed in jobs at the bottom of the labour market, receiving much less pay.

Migrants (principally men) from Pakistan arrived at nearby Middlesbrough in the late 1950s; many moved because of Teesside's industrial prowess and thus they ascertained employment in the steelmaking, shipbuilding and petrochemicals industries.[92] Workers from both Asia and Sub-Saharan Africa also migrated in the 1950s, further filling gaps in the local labour market and thus expanding the area's industrial workforce. As they settled in different areas of Middlesbrough to local white residents, there was a lack of integration. Whilst the local media such as *The Northern Echo* offered stories on the newly arrived migrants lack of cleanliness, residents suggested they were responsible for the town's lack of housing.[93] Law enforcement also intensified these cultural antagonisms, encouraging local dancehalls to not let 'coloured men'[94] in because they would intensify these tensions, potentially erupting in violence.

On 19 August 1961, a young white local resident called John Hunt was fatally stabbed and the murder was associated with the newly arrived immigrants.[95] This resulted in Teesside's worst outbursts of racial antagonisms—namely, race riots across four days which involved the vandalism of many Asian businesses and homes, as well as threats by local white residents towards a Pakistani landlord because he evicted a white tenant. In light of John Hunt's death, around 500 local white residents gathered outside the Taj Mahal café in Cannon Street to voice their dissatisfaction at the newly arrived immigrants. Thereafter, violence between immigrants and white residents ensued; the latter smashed the café's windows and tried to set fire to the property with petrol-soaked cloths. Police officers attempted to defuse the situation by encouraging immigrants to leave Middlesbrough to protect themselves, leading locals to suggest the police were on the side of the immigrant community. Consequently, the police were attacked with a 'barrage of bottles, bricks, piping and guttering that had been ripped from buildings', as well as 'potatoes implanted with razor blades'.[96]

John Hunt's funeral also brought more violent activity, with many white locals vandalising an immigrant's café. As approximately 3,000–5,000 local people were involved in the riots, the police failed to control the troubles. Indeed, the cost of the riots amounted to over £1200, whilst 55 people were prosecuted, and many policemen were injured.[97] Despite these racial antagonisms, the town's mayor dismissed the riot's racial dimensions, and the local media instead focused on the irrational behaviour of 'hooligans'. Nonetheless, the riots attracted media attention across the globe, including in India and Pakistan.

Returning to industrialism, many steelwork sites in both Steel Town and the broader Teesside area degenerated and were abandoned in the 1960s, partially because of the construction of new industrial sites and thus development of alternatives to steel overseas.[98] However, the damaging impact of this decline was mitigated because of the state's focus on providing socio-economic betterment and the local councils' aim to do what is best for Teesside. In this context, several developments occurred which consolidated Teesside as one of the country's leading industrial bases. In 1967, British Steel was established, bringing most of Britain's steelworks under national ownership. The first potash mine in the country—Boulby mine—also opened in 1973, 11 miles from Steel Town. At over 1,300 feet deep, the mine still stands today, employing around 450 workers.

Shortly after British Steel was formed, they outlined a ten-year plan involving a multimillion-pound steelwork site in Steel Town, which was cast as an important area for lengthy investment.[99] Despite outlining five proposals for the steelworks, only two were implemented because of the economy's stagnation. Nevertheless, the plant opened in 1979, and it was one of the largest steelwork sites in the Western world; indeed, by 1984, it employed 7,000 people and generated more social stability and economic security.[100] Therefore, Steel Town became defined by its core characteristics:

> as a Corporate Borough, [Steel Town] was able to apply to the College of Heralds for a coat of arms. It was decided that the design should reflect the industries of the town, both modern and traditional. Ships

and fishes shared the design with steel ingots and a blast furnace; the motto means 'By sea and Iron'.[101]

Whilst the post-war period's somewhat mythical golden age provided around two decades of stability and security, 'by the 1970s blizzard warnings returned'.[102] This included a sizable reduction in the Middle East's oil production, engendering a myriad price increase and a global oil crisis. The stagnation of the domestic economy increased inflation to over 20%, meaning stagflation became a core political issue. Many industrial labourers also voiced their discontent at the insular nature of working-class life, exacerbating the widespread sense that social democratic capitalism was in trouble. Moreover, thousands of people in Billingham signed a petition regarding the pollution emitted by ICI's Billingham plant.

The 1978 winter of discontent served to intensify these blizzard warnings. As public sector workers like binmen and gravediggers went on strike, the dead went unburied and the rubbish went uncollected.[103] Dissatisfaction amongst the citizenry grew, as their lives were perpetually disrupted. The Conservatives suggested the trade unions were responsible for these problems, claiming they held too much bargaining power and influence in labour markets. As will become clear in the upcoming chapters, this glossed over their desire to erode the post-war era's *class compromise* and set the stage for the restoration of wealth and profitability.[104] As Harold Wilson former Labour Party MP and Prime Minister between 1964–1970 and 1974–1976 highlighted, the Conservatives wanted to 'reverse the course of twenty-five years of social revolution'.[105]

Although Labour MP Tony Benn offered a social democratic framework to mitigate the economy's problems including investment in the nation's industry, James Callaghan, Prime Minister between 1976 and 1979 abandoned this approach and requested a loan from the International Monetary Fund (IMF). This was granted on the condition that the state implement austerity measures, including reductions in public expenditure and the temporary suppression of workers' wages.[106] These measures reduced public spending on the welfare state, whilst dwindling the post-war governmental goal of full employment. James Callaghan's structural readjustment failed to resurrect post-war social democratic capitalism, thereby enabling another phase of capitalism to emerge. As the Labour Party failed to address capitalist crises, a renewed version of laissez-faire capitalism—neoliberalism—was taken forward by Margaret Thatcher's election in 1979.

Influential politicians like Thatcher are important, though her core ideas of marketisation, individualism and both market and individual liberty had been fomenting throughout the post-war era. For example, the Mont Pelerin Society was forged in 1947, spearheaded by Milton Friedman and Friedrich Hayek. The society enumerated on how to consolidate individual freedoms in the face of social democracy, since they believed that it was a 'dark age, governed by Keynesian delusions and misguided fantasies of global economic equality'.[107] Although these notions were given little political consideration under capitalism's post-war phase, they were unshackled in the 1980s.

Neoliberalism ascendant

As neoliberalism became hegemonic, power and control shifted back to capital, enabling the privatisation of many state utilities. By the end of the 1980s, England had endured an unprecedented asset sale—British Gas, British Petroleum, British Telecom, British Railways and British Steel had been privatised. Indeed, privatisation subjects a service that should exist for the benefit of the citizenry 'into the icy waters of an untamed market economy in the hope that it will eventually start swimming'.[108] As we shall encounter, though, many utilities such as Steel Town's steelworks develop structural problems, involving debilitating consequences for local people.

Whilst the somewhat mythical golden age fostered a belief of infinite socio-economic betterment, neoliberalism brought about a negative realism; if industrial plants wanted to remain feasible, they had to downsize the workforce and implement reductions in pay. Whilst many mines in the North East were profitable, globally steam coal was oversupplied and therefore many industrial plants were threatened with mass redundancies or closure.[109] Therefore, many industrial disputes erupted, including a national steelworkers' strike in 1980. The strike ensued for over 13 weeks, involving approximately 17,000 Teesside steelworkers. The infamous miners' strike also occurred across 1984–1985. To weaken their solidarity, welfare payments were slashed to striking miners' families and voluntary redundancies were offered. Whilst strikes temporarily lead to a loss of productivity and profitability, capital can endure them longer than employees because they have far more economic power.[110] As the miners were defeated, various antitrade union regulations were implemented such as the introduction of a ballot in the workplace before strikes could occur. As we will see, peoples' employment conditions, particularly in places like Steel Town in Teesside, have further degenerated under neoliberalism.

Rather quickly, neoliberalism abandoned capital controls to ensure the flow of goods and services across national borders to maximise profitability. This put capital in the ascendancy; a historical reversal of capital flow occurred whereby companies shifted their industrial plants to developing countries.[111] Lax laws and regulations in the labour market enabled companies to lower production costs and hyper-exploit the workforce. This ensured capital's expansion, leaving little regard for the concomitant social damage in previously relatively prosperous locales across the West including Teesside.

As the deindustrialisation process intensified, 400,000 steelworkers across Europe were made redundant in around ten years. In the North

East of England, 83 pits closed in the 1980s. Locales that had been characterised by industrial work for over 100 years were eroded very quickly. Between 1974 and 1984, many industrial plants including Swan Hunter Shipyard, Teesside Textiles, Head Wrightson Steelworks and the British Steel Corporation Britannia and Aytron Works were all abandoned.[112] An area 'literally created from scratch',[113] Teesside suffered more than other locales; in 1984, unemployment climbed to 23% whilst in some parts of Middlesbrough it catapulted to 40%.[114] Whilst the Conservative government offered several schemes to help the jobless including Youth Training and Community Enterprise, they merely postponed joblessness.

Whilst Steel Town's steelworks provided employment for thousands of people throughout the 1980s and 1990s, as we will encounter, both of ICI's chemical sites in Teesside declined because the company was faced with competition from abroad. New processes were implemented that did not require a mass industrial labour force, whilst competitors were yielding more profitability with fewer workers, meaning ICI made many workers redundant by shifting some of their plants abroad, concentrating on special chemicals and thereby reducing its manufacturing output in Teesside.[115] ICI's remaining chemical plants were marketised for various companies to take them over. Although various chemical companies like SABIC and Hunstman operate today at ICI's old chemical sites and employ some of ICI's former workers, it is a small proportion of the 43% of Teesside's population that held an industrial job in 1975.[116]

As Teesside's industrial decline occurred gradually throughout the postwar era, deindustrialisation in the 1980s 'merely turned off the life-support system for a patient that was already dead',[117] partially because England's industrial plants were the oldest in the Western world, suffering from deteriorated infrastructure and strained relations between workers and capital. Nevertheless, deindustrialisation combined with the government's abandonment of full employment as a policy goal generated myriad changes to Teesside's labour market—in the 1980s, a factory opened near ICI's Billingham plant and 3,050 people applied for its first 24 job advertisements.[118] The stark reality that 'there is not a job for everyone'[119] intensified in 1987 as Smith's Dock closed. Such rapid restructuring of the local economy engendered social problems, with Thatcher taking her infamous walk through the wilderness in 1987 to witness this change. She meandered through marshland in Thornaby, 12 miles from Steel Town, suggesting the area required a new *raison d'être*.

Many governments throughout neoliberalism have echoed Thatcher's sentiments, implementing various schemes to try and mitigate higher than average levels of unemployment, poverty and socio-economic deprivation.[120] Nevertheless, by the 2000s, Teesside was one of the most deindustrialised locales in the Western world. Pockets of remunerative employment exist, though there is an over dependency on public sector jobs within the NHS, local authorities and education whilst many of the jobs in the service economy contain meagre wages and degrading working conditions. Research in Teesside's leisure, retail and call centres found that employment in these industries often does not offer industrialism's adequate remuneration or positive symbolism.[121] Other research discerned that workers in Teesside's service economy were overworked, often working long hours to adhere to unreasonable targets.[122] Whilst incentives were offered for meeting targets, these included a high-street shopping voucher and not an improvement in working conditions. Employees suggested they obtained little sense of pride or fulfilment from their jobs, since they failed to accrue an identity, social stability and economic security.

As Teesside's industrial labour market dwindled, joblessness and its associated structural problems like poverty intensified. Many localities in Teesside possess rates of joblessness that are double the national average, poor mental and physical well-being, high levels of crime and poor educational outcomes.[123] The Teesside studies research[124] involved, amongst other issues, exploring young peoples' transitions in a deprived area and thus their attempts at obtaining housing and employment. These transitions were complex, characterised by uncertainty and perpetual setbacks. Although they worked hard to find a job, they were faced with a constant low-pay, no-pay cycle, that is, periods of unemployment to short-term and poorly paid jobs. Whilst many did courses such as youth training schemes, they accrued qualifications that held little value in Teesside's labour market. In consequence, some claimed the only way to ascertain work was to fabricate information on their curriculum vitae.

Conclusion

The onset of the industrial revolution in the nineteenth century had significant implications for Teesside, transforming many locales into towns that were dominated by the rhythm of industrial work. This culminated in the *iron rush* and the *great steel age*, exposing how Teesside was a product of capitalism's drive to expand markets and maximise profitability. Whilst laissez-faire capitalism's structural crises in the early twentieth century brought myriad social distress to Teesside, the 1920s was a significant decade for the region as the Sydney Harbour Bridge was built with Teesside steel and ICI was formed. Nevertheless, the Great Depression years magnified unemployment, poverty and inequalities in Teesside, culminating in four in ten people being unemployed in some areas of Teesside.

Structural crises like the Great Depression and the Second World War combined to produce an anomaly phase in capitalism's history from 1945 to 1979; the nationalisation of key industries, unprecedented bargaining power for many trade unions and gradual improvements in industrial workers' pay and livelihoods. Whilst many of Teesside's mines and steelworks were abandoned in the post-war period, successive governments' commitments to putting the interests of the working class at the centre of their agenda meant this decline was managed. Capital's demands for a large labour force led to an increase in economic migrants from the colonies and Sub-Saharan Africa, manifesting in periodic eruptions of anti-migrant sentiments in Teesside.

The ascendancy of neoliberalism in the 1980s restructured the area's economy, away from production towards services. Eruptions of political protests thus occurred, involving a national steelworker strike which included over 17,000 Teesside steelworkers. Much of the employment opportunities in the service economy are contrary to industrial labour, failing to provide the stability, security and longevity that were once stable features of Teesside and Steel Town's labour market. Whilst this change was briefly explored, the next chapter documents neoliberalism in more depth to further outline the book's constitutive context, laying the foundations for the nationalistic sentiments expressed in the book's second half. As political dissatisfaction is central to this book, it will also outline the 2008 global financial crash and the New Labour era, including the party's expansion of immigration from Eastern European countries. As we will encounter, the political discontent expressed in this book has its roots in historical processes, not least New Labour's premiership and the Party's commitment to neoliberalism.

Notes

1. Warren, J (2018).
2. Lloyd, A (2013).
3. Hobsbawm, E (1994) *Age of Extremes: The Short Twentieth Century 1914–1991*. London: Abacus.
4. Lloyd, A (2018a).
5. Hall, S, Winlow, S & Ancrum, C (2008) *Criminal Identities and Consumer Culture: Crime, Exclusion and the New Culture of Narcissism*. Devon: Willan Publishing.
6. Hobsbawm, E (1994).
7. Hornby, C (2004) *A Century in Stone*. VHS. Pancrack Pictures.
8. Foord, J, Robinson, F & Sadler, D (1985), p. 7.
9. Wilkinson, E (1939) *The Town That Was Murdered: The Life Story of Jarrow*. London: Victor Gollancz Ltd.
10. Warren, J (2018).
11. Warwick, T (2019) *A Town of Immigrants: Histories of Migration*. Middlesbrough: Middlesbrough Institute of Modern Art.
12. Kinealy, C (1997) *A Death-Dealing Famine: The Great Hunger in Ireland*. London: Pluto Press.
13. Taylor, D (1993) The Middlesbrough race riot of 1961: A comment. *Social History*. 18(1): 73–79.
14. Hornby, C (2004).
15. Bell, L (1907) *At the Works: A Study of a Manufacturing Town*. London: E Arnold.
16. Currie, D & Sherlock, S (1996) *Now and Then: Cleveland Ironstone Mines*. Stockton-On Tees: Meander Publications.

17. Cockroft, J (1984) *Redcar and Coatham: A History to the End of World War II*. 3rd edition. Redcar: A Sotheran Ltd.
18. Williamson, M (2012) *Life at the Yard: Memories of Working at Smith's Dock South Bank*. Teesside: Teesside Industrial Memories Project.
19. Warren, J (2018), p. 156.
20. Cockroft, J (1984), p. 106.
21. North, G (1975) *Teesside's Economic Heritage*. Cleveland: County Council of Cleveland, p. 1.
22. Huggins, M & Walton, J (2003) *The Teesside Seaside Between the Wars*. Newcastle: North East England History Institute.
23. North, G (1975).
24. Frey, J (1929) Iron and steel industry of the Middlesbrough district. *Economic Geography*. 5(2): 176–182, p. 181.
25. Ellis, A (2016) *Men, Masculinities and Violence: An Ethnographic Study*. Abingdon: Routledge; Kotzé, J (2019).
26. Marx, K (1990) *Capital*. Vol 1. Oxford: Oxford University Press.
27. Nicholas, K (1986) *The Social Effects of Unemployment on Teesside. 1919–1939*. Manchester: Manchester University Press.
28. Gleave, J (1938) The Teesside iron and steel industry. *The Geographical Journal*. 91(5): 454–467.
29. Williamson, M (2008) *Life at the ICI: Memories of Working at ICI Billingham*. Bishop Auckland: Printability Publishing Ltd.
30. North, G (1975).
31. Hobsbawm, E (1962) *The Age of Revolution: Europe 1789–1848*. London: Abacus; Winlow, S (2001) *Badfellas: Crime, Tradition and New Masculinities*. New York: Berg.
32. Horsley, M (2015).
33. Blyth, M (2015) *Austerity: The History of a Dangerous Idea*. New York: Oxford University Press.
34. Hobsbawm, E (1962).
35. Nicholas, K (1986).
36. Warren, J (2018).
37. Sotheran, P (1975) *Redcar in Retrospect*. Redcar: A. A Sotheran Ltd.
38. Huggins, M & Walton, J (2003), p. 25.
39. Copsey, N (1999) *Anti-Fascism in Britain*. London: Palgrave Macmillan.
40. Channing, I (2014) *Blackshirts and White Wigs: Reflections on Public Order Law and the Political Activism of the British Union of Fascists*. Unpublished PhD thesis.
41. BBC Radio 4 (2011) Making History. Broadcast on 18 November 2011. Accessed on 16/03/2021. Available at: www.bbc.co.uk/sounds/play/b015zpdj; Walsh, D (2017) The Battle of Stockton, 1933. *Libcom*. Accessed on 16/03/2021. Available at: https://libcom.org/history/battle-stockton-1933.
42. Walsh, D (2017).
43. Channing, I (2014).
44. Lloyd, C (2011) The Battle of Stockton, 1933. *The Northern Echo*. Accessed on 16/03/2021. Available at: www.thenorthernecho.co.uk/news/9309751.battle-stockton-1933/.
45. Channing, I (2014), p. 99.
46. BBC Radio 4 (2011); Walsh, D (2017).
47. Channing, I (2014).
48. Copsey, N (1999).
49. Stiglitz, J (2010) *Freefall: America, Free Markets, and the Sinking of the World Economy*. New York. W.W. Norton & Company.
50. Cronin, J (1984) *Labour and Society in Britain 1918–1979*. London: Batsford Academic and Educational.
51. Tomlin, D (2002) Cleveland chemical industry. In Anderson, M (ed.), *Aspects of Teesside: Discovering Local History*. Barnsley: Wharncliffe Books, pp. 135–152.

52. Race, M & Hardy, C (1989) *Teesside at War*. Bristol: Archive Publishing Ltd.
53. Race, M & Hardy, C (1989), p. 27.
54. Race, M & Hardy, C (1989).
55. Race, M & Hardy, C (1989), p. 32.
56. Norman, B (2004) *Wartime Teesside Revisited*. Guisborough: Bill Norman.
57. Norman, B (2004), p. 30.
58. Norman, B (2004).
59. Race, M & Hardy, C (1989).
60. Hobsbawm, E (1994), p. 8.
61. Whitehead, P & Crawshaw, P (2014) 'A tale of two economies' the political and the moral in neoliberalism. *International Journal of Sociology and Social Policy*. 34(1/2): 19–34; Whitehead, P (2018) *Demonising the other: The Criminalisation of Morality*. Bristol: Policy Press.
62. Streeck, WG (2016) *How Will Capitalism End?* London: Verso.
63. Driver, S & Martell, L (1998) *New Labour: Politics After Thatcherism*. Malden: Blackwell Publishers Inc, p. 8.
64. Judt, T (2010) *Postwar: A History of Europe Since 1945*. London: Vintage Books.
65. Seymour, R (2017) *Corbyn: The Strange Birth of Radical Politics*. 2nd edition. London: Verso.
66. Bew, J (2017) *Citizen Clem: A Biography of Attlee*. London: Riverrun.
67. Lloyd, A (2013).
68. Hobsbawm, E (1962), p. 317.
69. Hudson, R, Beynon, H & Sadler, D (1994) *A Place Called Teesside: A Locality in a Global Economy*. Edinburgh: Edinburgh University Press.
70. North, G (1975).
71. Warren, J (2018), p. 64.
72. Cronin, J (1984).
73. Hudson, R, Beynon, H & Sadler, D (1994); Williamson, M (2008).
74. HMSO (1963) *The North East: A Programme for Regional Development and Growth*. London: HMSO.
75. Foord, J, Robinson, F & Sadler, D (1985).
76. Hall, S (2012); Harvey, D (2005).
77. Streeck, WG (2016).
78. Boltanski, L & Chiapello, E (2017) *The New Spirit of Capitalism*. London: Verso.
79. Ellis, A (2016); Willis, P (1978) *Learning to Labour*. Farnham: Ashgate Publishing.
80. Hall, S, Winlow, S & Ancrum, C (2008).
81. Goldthorpe, J, Lockwood, D, Bechhofer, F & Platt, J (1969) *The Affluent Worker in the Class Structure*. London: Cambridge University Press.
82. Streeck, WG (2016).
83. Goldthorpe, J, Lockwood, D, Bechhofer, F & Platt, J (1969).
84. Shildrick, T, Macdonald, R, Webster, C & Garthwaite, K (2012).
85. Heath, J & Potter, A (2004) *The Rebel Sell: How the Counterculture Became Consumer Culture*. Toronto: Harper Collins Publishers Ltd.
86. Beynon, H (1973) *Working for Ford*. London: Allen Lane, p. 12.
87. Winlow, S & Hall, S (2006) *Violent Night*. Oxford: Berg, p. 23.
88. Mitchell, W & Fazi, T (2017).
89. Lloyd, A (2018a).
90. Winlow, S, Hall, S & Treadwell, J (2017).
91. Hoggart, R (1958) *The Uses of Literacy*. London: Chatto & Windus; Williamson, M (2009) Gender, leisure and marriage in a working-class community, 1939–1960. *Labour History Review*. 74(2): 185–198.
92. Panayi, P (1991) Middlesbrough 1961: A British race riot of the 1960s? *Social History*. 16(2): 139–153.
93. Taylor, D (1993).

94. Taylor, D (1993), p. 75.
95. Panayi, P (1991); Taylor, D (1993).
96. Taylor, D (1993), p. 77.
97. Panayi, P (1991); Taylor D (1993); Warwick, T (2019).
98. Hudson, R (2004).
99. Warren, K (1976) British steel: The problems of rebuilding an old industrial structure. *Geography*. 61(1): 1–7.
100. Hudson, R, Beynon, H & Sadler, D (1994); North, G (1975).
101. Cockroft, J (1984), p. 106.
102. Whitehead, P & Crawshaw, P (2014), p. 22.
103. Vinen, R (2011) *Thatcher's Britain: The Politics and Social Upheaval of the 1980s*. New York: Simon & Schuster.
104. Harvey, D (2005).
105. Viven, R (2011) *Thatcher's Britain: The Politics and Social Upheaval of the 1980s*. New York: Simon & Schuster, p. 34.
106. Seymour, R (2017).
107. Slobodian, Q (2018) *Globalists: The End of Empire and the Birth of Neoliberalism*. London: Harvard University Press, p. 18.
108. Streeck, WG (2014) *Buying Time: The Delayed Crisis of Democratic Capitalism*. London: Verso, p. 161.
109. Warren, J (2018).
110. Harvey, D (2014) *Seventeen Contradictions and the end of Capitalism*. London: Profile Books Ltd.
111. Varoufakis, Y (2011) *The Global Minotaur: America, the True Origins of the Financial Crisis and the Future of the World Economy*. London: Zed Books.
112. Foord, J, Robinson, F & Sadler D (1985).
113. Kotzé, J (2019), p. 26.
114. Foord, J, Robinson, F & Sadler, D (1985).
115. Hudson, R, Beynon, H & Sadler, D (1994).
116. Warren, J (2018).
117. Viven, R (2011), p. 286.
118. Hudson, R, Beynon, H & Sadler, D (1994).
119. Boltanski, L & Chiapello, E (2017), p. 235.
120. Shildrick, T, Macdonald, R, Webster, C & Garthwaite, K (2012).
121. Winlow, S & Hall, S (2005).
122. Lloyd, A (2018a).
123. English Indices of Deprivation (2019) The English Indices of Deprivation 2019. Ministry of Housing, Communities and Local Government. Accessed on 19/03/2021. Available at: https://assets.publishing.service.gov.uk/government/uploads/system/uploads/attachment_data /file/835115/IoD2019_Statistical_Release.pdf.
124. For example, see: Macdonald, R & Marsh, J (2005) *Disconnected Youth? Growing Up in Britain's Poor Neighbourhoods*. London: Palgrave Macmillan; Shildrick, T, Macdonald, R, Webster, C & Garthwaite, K (2012); Macdonald, R & Shildrick, T (2013) Youth and wellbeing: Experiencing bereavement and ill health in marginalised young people's transitions. *Sociology of Health & Illness*. 35(1): 147–161; Macdonald, R (2013) Poverty talk: How people experiencing poverty deny their poverty and why they blame 'the poor'. *Sociological Review*. 61(2): 285–303; Macdonald, R, Shildrick, T & Furlong, A (2016) Not single spies but in battalions: A critical, sociological engagement with the idea of so-called 'troubled families'. *Sociological Review*. 64(4): 821–836.

Chapter 2

Neoliberalism

It is not controversial to state that neoliberal capitalism has fundamentally transformed society. The sense of stability, security, coherency and longevity that underpinned capitalism's post-war era in Chapter 1 has faded into history; uncertainty, risk and transience now define both social relations and neoliberal labour markets. The relative solidarity and sense of community that were prevalent in the industrial age have been replaced with individualism and fragmentation. Such structural changes have not occurred out of thin air; rather, they form part of a systematic 'restoration' of power and wealth to society's richest members.[1] The deindustrialisation process is a key part of this restoration, enabling capital to shift to low-wage economies to maximise returns on investments. This class project, which has seen working-class people accrue unprecedented private debt and a decline in living standards, has been reproduced by successive governments throughout the neoliberal era, leading to widespread political disillusionment.

The dissatisfaction in Steel Town directed towards politicians, the European Union (EU), immigration, refugees, 'identity politics' and a second referendum does not occur in a vacuum; it is generated under certain structural conditions. This chapter's purpose is to explore the current macro-context in which this research study takes place. Firstly, various debates surrounding neoliberalism's contested nature will be outlined to demonstrate how it functions and impacts upon working-class life, such as suppressing wages and working conditions. As political discontent forms the book's core, this chapter will shift to the consensual response to the 2008 global financial crisis; transformations within the Labour Party vis-a-vis New Labour and their expansion of immigration from Eastern European countries aided by the EU and their four freedoms. Although between 2010 and the emergence of the COVID-19 pandemic austerity had been presented as fiscal common sense, it has caused further social damage in post-industrial Steel Town and Teesside. Outlining these structural trends provides the constitutive context for the literature on the rise of nationalism in the next chapter and the empirical data outlined thereafter.

DOI: 10.4324/9781003198666-3

Turbo charged capitalism

Debates over how neoliberalism operates have occurred for some time. The notion that neoliberalism has retrenched the nation state from social life is prevalent, particularly amongst many left-leaning commentators. In this view, the government plays a minimal role in intervening in markets to address their tendency to produce social inequalities, enabling capital to dispense of its commitments to the workforce and maximise profitability. Therefore, the retrenchment of the nation state allows government actors to further dwindle the citizenry's post-war entitlements, whilst enabling the rich to increase their wealth through the privatisation of state assets and implementation of degrading working conditions.

Recent scholarship, however, has problematised the notion that neo-liberalism has entailed a withdrawal of the state; rather, it depends upon politicians and social institutions to enforce neoliberal values including competitive individualism and profit production.[2] Market obstacles that limit the freedom for capital to augment profit including restrictions on capital's movement and trade tariffs must be either eviscerated or weakened, enabling the 'institutional encasement'[3] of markets and nation states. Global and influential bodies like the IMF, World Trade Organisation and, as we will see, the EU are vital in securing neoliberalism's hegemony, since they enforce the system's logic of marketisation, competition and policies that favour the rich at the expense of the working class. This institutional encasement was a core aim of many of neoliberalism's founding fathers like Fredrich Hayek, as it provided the global economy with a degree of structural protection against citizenries' demands for economic redistribution. Therefore, ensnaring neoliberal ideals in global institutions somewhat dwindles the power of the citizenries' and domestic governments' political demands.[4]

Encasement also elucidates how the market needs the assistance of the law to build a scaffolding of protection to prevent interference from perceived meddlesome and ill-informed ideologies who seek to dwindle capital's power. In effect, this depoliticises the economy; neoliberalism insulates the economy from public contestation, presenting it as non-ideological and a *fait accompli*. Such depoliticised logic has been absorbed in most of the citizenry's psyche; neoliberal capitalism is not thought of as an ideology amongst many but merely the economy.[5]

Neoliberalism's gurus suggest market restrictions—trade barriers and controls—distort the market's freedom, efficiency and ability to self-correct.[6] Social problems like joblessness, rising house prices and high inflation are therefore engendered by too much state interference in the market. The solution to such problems is to borrow insights from laissez-faire capitalism, explicated in the previous chapter; leave the marketplace alone, it will correct itself and generate a more equal social, economic and cultural order. Some argue that this serves to reinforce neoliberalism because if inequalities further increase its proponents can suggest amenable market conditions were not in place and there was too much state interference and regulation.[7]

However, there is often a discrepancy between neoliberal ideology and reality. Some argue that markets do not address social problems but emphasise the importance of competitive individualism and augmenting profitability; values that are likely to intensify inequalities.[8] Of course, markets do not simply exist, they are constructed by nation states. What has happened under neoliberalism is the restructuring of the nation state, away from intervening in markets to protect the working-class and their socioeconomic interests by imposing regulation on capital's activities, to allowing capital-free reign to exploit ordinary people.[9] In effect, nation states now form 'capital's executives',[10] allowing them to do what is required for the benefit of market expansion. With this in mind, neoliberalism depends upon the state to both exist and prosper. As we witnessed in Chapter 1, neoliberalism's ascendency in the United Kingdom was, in part, aided by Margaret Thatcher's government's assault on the trade union movement to liberate capital from their demands for economic redistribution from the social structure's top to the bottom.

Although proponents of neoliberalism suggest the free market and thus economy is the most important domain of social life, other evidence reveals that the *free market* is a smokescreen, glossing over the close ideological relationship between nation states and capital, capital's lobbying efforts and political donations to enforce policies that serve their economic interests.[11] Whilst neoliberalism has consistently emphasised the importance of the free market, full employment, remunerative industrial work and a universal welfare state have subsided. At the same time, wealth amongst the richest members of society has increased at an unprecedented rate; the world is now home to more billionaires than ever before, many of which live in England's capital—London—a playground for the world's super rich.[12] Meanwhile, post-industrial locales like Steel Town are left to languish, characterised by joblessness and the associated social problems like the high prevalence of mental ill health and criminal activity.[13]

Although neoliberalism has encased the global economy in transnational institutions, restructuring it to service capital's interests, it is therefore also a class project that *restores* capital's wealth after their profit margins dwindled in capitalism's post-war period.[14] Nation states including in the United Kingdom and capital have often worked in tandem, dwindling economically stable and secure labour markets to restore their hegemony. As mentioned, since the 1980s Steel Town's labour market has shifted from industrial prowess to one characterised by uncertain and insecure jobs that fail to offer social fulfilment.[15] Part of this process has been dependent upon the erosion of trade unions' power, since they are a central structural obstacle to limiting profit production. As we will see, the erosion of their power has thus denied many workers an institutional bargaining tool to fight back against heightened exploitation.[16]

Although collectivism amongst employees has declined throughout neoliberalism, competitive individualism has become endemic, particularly in deindustrialised and economically abandoned areas like Steel Town.[17] This has been aided by neoliberalism's claims to offer a meritocracy; a notion that energises most people but legitimises structural inequality, masking social class, race and gender's role in determining peoples' life chances.[18] The ideology of meritocracy purports that no matter where you are in the social world you can achieve ostentatious wealth with hard work and determination, providing legitimacy to preserve neoliberalism. In this way, those who occupy industrially ruinated zones—Steel Town in Teesside—who often labour in non-unionised and degrading jobs—can still climb to the top of the system if they abide by its logic.

However, reality is much more complex—research has displayed how criminal markets offer the only stable and secure apprenticeships in some areas of the North East including conurbations close to Steel Town.[19] Despite being involved in forms of organised crime, socio-economic deprivation and thus impoverishment was common, though they believed the good life awaited them in the near future. Whilst members of the discarded working-class scoured criminal markets to attain wealth and prestige, most encountered a state of inertia, languishing in often petty forms of crime and in and out of prison. Whilst they dreamt of neoliberalism's commodified objects of pleasure like expensive sport vehicles and designer clothing, a life of intimidation, fear, anxiety and illicit drug misuse was endemic.

As capital no longer requires a large industrial workforce in areas like Steel Town for its functioning, the post-war governmental commitment to full employment has been abandoned; a degree of unemployment and underemployment is now accepted by the nation state.[20] Before the COVID-19 pandemic emerged, 3% unemployment in England was deemed normal and acceptable, though a myriad structural issue is underemployment since millions of workers are reliant on short-term and low-paid employment contracts. Whilst these workers often search for alternative employment provisions, demand outstrips supply, enhancing capital's power and control over the workforce. As we will see in Chapter 7, the COVID-19 pandemic and its implications for the future threaten to intensify unemployment.[21]

Placed in this context, a global reserve army of labour has emerged under neoliberalism—latest estimates stand at 2.4 billion people.[22] Although the levels of joblessness differ geographically, in Teesside many areas have a higher than national average unemployment rate, since industrial employment has not been sufficiently replaced.[23] The national hotel chain Premier Inn has a site in Teesside, and it recently received 500 applications for six jobs within six hours.[24] As we will see, this oversupply of workers under-mines the sense of unity amongst employees, which prevailed in indus-trial labour markets, since it makes disciplining the workforce far easier. Although the reserve army of labour weakens employees' battles against the incursion on their working conditions, today's workers no longer require a reserve army to fundamentally undermine their sense of collectivism; rather, social instability and economic insecurity combined with posses-sive individualism fragments workplaces and foments anxiety and stress.[25] Keeping workers in a subjective state of socio-economic insecurity aids their conformity to their employer's demands as having a decent job is now cast as a privilege; employees must be grateful they possess one.[26]

Indeed, the stable and secure working conditions of capitalism's post-war epoch have now faded into history; workers must be both flexible and adaptable. Therefore, neoliberal ideology claims people have new opportu-nities to construct their biographies and experience a working world that was unattainable under post-war capitalism.[27] This is particularly the case for women, who have entered the workforce in unprecedented numbers under neoliberalism. Of course, equal opportunities between all genders at work are socially desirable and progressive, though neoliberalism's version of gender equality is rather hollow.[28] We might argue that it has meant women are now exploited as much as men, whilst ensuring the hegemon of a system that has presided over the biggest reallocation of wealth in history from the bottom of the social hierarchy to the top. Moreover, an unprecedented amount of both men and women now work in poorly paid employment, often working unsociable hours. Therefore, as we will see, it is not uncommon for couples to work several jobs to *get by*, eroding the traditional family unit. The longitudinal Teesside studies found that many couples who both worked often relied upon welfare payments, since their joint income did not provide a reasonable standard of living. This economic uncertainty engendered household distress, thereby weakening the family base.[29]

People living in the neoliberal era have been detached from their col-lective history, not least community ties and social class. In consequence, people search consumer markets for the mechanisms that enable them to gauge meaning, semblance and an identity. A hyper-consumerist phase has thus emerged under neoliberalism, operating as the 'opiate of the people'[30] and thereby providing solace from the bleakness of social reality, particu-larly insecure labour markets. As the economy has shifted from produc-tion to services, consumer spending and the stimulation of new desires is central to economic growth, fuelling the system's expansionary logic. Whilst workers' collective bargaining power in post-industrial locales like Teesside has declined,[31] real wages have stagnated for several decades. The system has historically responded to crisis-ridden conditions by imposing more capitalist measures, and therefore, English consumers have taken on unprecedented private debt through credit cards, overdrafts and loans in order to provide the economic fuel for consumer capitalism.[32]

In essence, debt has proliferated from 2000 onwards as more and more people have their desires stoked for consumerism's commodified items to form their identity. Whilst private indebtedness is prevalent in disadvantaged localities, it has seeped into the middle class with some estimates suggesting consumer debt in the United Kingdom is £1.5 trillion.[33] Obtaining credit is relatively straight forward because of the drive for profitability amongst creditors; credit limits are often imposed, but the consumer's request to increase their debt is easily approved. Indebtedness amongst individuals in Teesside intensified their mental health problems such as stress and anxiety, whilst fomenting a sense of guilt, shame and often suicidal thoughts.[34] Nevertheless, private indebtedness has generated a pseudo spectacle of material wealth and rising living standards, enabling the citizenry to live a standard of life beyond their annual incomes.

Although consumer capitalism posits ideals such as freedom, positivity and self-expression, behind this ideological veil lies a conformity to consumerism's central tenets of egotistical individualism and a need to disassociate oneself from the masses.[35] Consumerism therefore forms neoliberalism's cultural partner, encouraging people to escape into consumer markets to alleviate their stress and worries rather than join together to pursue social change.[36] Whilst consumerism exists as a core background force, people solicit its symbols for their core sense of being in the world—recent research on performance enhancing drugs like Botox in locales not too distant from Steel Town exposed how people expressed a deep-seated desire to develop their image and outcompete other people.[37] Whilst it provided transient satisfaction, their deep sense of lack was not ameliorated but intensified, further compelling them back into consumer markets. This is because 'Capitalism co-opts subjective desire and the hope for future satisfaction and fills the non-essential void with unquenchable desires and drives which releases and stimulates libidinal drives towards ephemeral objects of pseudo-satisfaction'.[38]

Such a dynamic is elucidated by steroid users in a post-industrial conurbation in Teesside—which now possesses one of the highest rates of steroid consumption in England. The users displayed a deep commitment to individualism, competition and self-improvement,[39] viewing their body as a product to enhance and thereby elicit envy from other people and attain cultural recognition. The degree of relative solidarity and commonality that was once prevalent in the post-war epoch is often absent from these locales; other individuals are viewed as a hostile competitor to outdo in what potentially constitutes a social Darwinianist cultural battle.

When young people are thrust into these sociocultural conditions, it is not surprising that large amounts are anxious, depressed, insecure and sometimes suicidal.[40] Ensnared in a 24/7 world of fast food, Xbox and digital communications, many young people live in a *claustrophobic cloud;* they want to escape society and enact a subjective distance from other people. Whilst the temporary delights bestowed upon the younger generation are cast as new freedoms, 'depressive hedonia'[41] appears to define their psychic state. Embodying an inability to do anything but unsuccessfully try and find gratification in consumer markets, many young people are more anxious than psychiatric ward patients in the aftermath of the Second World War.[42] However:

> even in the face of debt, foreclosure, unemployment, austerity and a general proleterianisation of our lives, there are still lots of goodies— YouTube, Facebook, lots of different kinds of music, sports on television, cheap imported clothes, abundant snack food, and that these goodies, these little nuggets of pleasure, attach us to capitalism.[43]

The ability of neoliberal capitalism to colonise our hopes, dreams and lives was made clear with the 2008 global financial crisis. Whilst the event transiently lacerated the system and enabled people to imagine a different world, it embarked upon the age of austerity and further fomented political discontent. As highlighted, this book argues that situating dissatisfaction with liberal politicians, the EU, immigration and refugees within a broader contextual backdrop is of fundamental importance in adequately understanding today's nationalism. Therefore, the next section turns to New Labour's political reign to demonstrate the reasons behind the political consensus in the immediate years after the crash, situating the next chapter's focus on the literature on nationalism within a political and economic context. Whilst this book so far has painted a historical picture, the next part brings the book firmly into a more contemporary moment.

Political sterility

As neoliberalism transformed society—deindustrialising many locales in England such as Teesside and consolidating a new service economy— the Labour Party's core support group of industrial workers numerically declined. The Party therefore struggled to adapt to this new reality and suffered at election time, being out of power for nearly two decades. The election of Tony Blair as the Party's leader in 1994 breathed new life into the Party, as he sought a new direction; to move away from its historical constitution and appeal to England's middle class. Essentially, Blair suggested that for the Labour Party to appeal to the masses and win an election it must modernise and come to terms with globalisation, a service economy and hyper-consumerism. Recasting the Party as 'New Labour', Blair changed its focus and cast it into uncharted waters.[44]

Blair achieved electoral success, winning successive general elections in 1997, 2001 and 2005. He appealed to people that the Labour Party had historically struggled to attract support from, and he kept the previously dominant Conservative party out of power for a considerable length of time. However, this was arguably the era in which ideological commitment and thus fidelity to a political ideal were relegated to history. New Labour was cast as a political party that would govern for all age groups, all workers including steelworkers in Steel Town and the CEO of a global corporation, offering a political struggle without any clear fault lines. In essence, they were not interested in Labour's historical connection to the industrial working class and its social democratic commitments to full employment; rather, empty platitudes such as looking to the future and modernisation were cast as essential electoral components.[45] In this way, New Labour suggested that what politically matters is *what works*. By offering pliable rhetoric, New Labour tended to offer soundbites rather than substantive ideas on how to organise society.

Lying beneath New Labour's political discourse of opportunity, self-improvement and the future was a commitment to reproducing neoliberalism. In effect, the Party pushed beyond Thatcher's idea that there was no other choice but to cement neoliberalism, presenting it as simple common sense.[46] As the system was presented as inevitable, history's macro-ideological conflicts were relegated to capitalism's post-war era. A positive vision on how to socially and economically organise society receded from view; neoliberalism was cast as the only viable form of political economy, anything else would fail. What this did was naturalise neoliberalism whilst all alternatives like social democracy were discredited.

New Labour also instigated the onset of unprecedented net migration levels, particularly from Eastern European countries. By 2007, Cyprus, Lithuania, Slovakia, Estonia, Hungary, Romania, Malta, Latvia and Bulgaria became part of the EU.[47] Wages and working conditions in these nations tend to be much worse than Western states, offering little means to forge a stable and secure livelihood. The unprecedented influx of migrants from these EU states was enabled by the EU's 'four freedoms': the freedom of movement for capital, labour, commodities and services. This means people from EU states can migrate across the continent to work in England, despite the impact it might have on intensifying community divisions and social fragmentation.[48] Indeed, 13,000 immigrants were expected to arrive in the United Kingdom each year; however, across 2004–2006 around 560,000 migrants from the EU accession states entered the United Kingdom.[49] Many of these newly arrived migrants were Polish and under the age of 25. Some of these individuals in an impoverished area of the Northeast have been racially abused, with some local residents telling them they are both not welcome and to go home.[50]

In 2004, the number of Eastern European migrants living in the United Kingdom stood at 170,000, though by 2013 it reached 1.24 million.[51] This mass movement of migrants from the EU, believed to be 'one of the largest in British history',[52] engendered myriad ethnic change in some areas of England. Migrants were also classified as either being in tier one—highly skilled, tier two—skilled and tier three—low skilled. Under New Labour's reign, many poorly paid and non-unionised jobs in the service economy like restaurant workers were rebranded as highly skilled. Employers have been found to actively seek out migrants from Eastern Europe, since they are less likely to complain about exploitative working conditions and often work very long and unsociable hours.[53]

Improved working conditions relative to Eastern European countries and the potential for socio-economic betterment attracts many to come to England, though they often work under hyper-exploitative working conditions.[54] Many migrants work in jobs that are dangerous and where underpayment is common such as within the meat-processing industry. Bereft of the knowledge on England's history of trade unionism and collectivism, many migrants possess no knowledge of their working rights and often depend upon payday loans to make ends meet.[55] Whilst they often view economically uncertain and insecure employment as a means to get a foot in the door and move up the social structure, opportunities for better pay and working conditions are non-existent. Some evidence suggests that trade unions have sometimes attempted to ameliorate these working practices, though employers respond by moving migrants to different sites in another locale or compel them to sign work contracts where they are not eligible for sickness or holiday pay. The four freedoms enshrined into the EU are 'Tailor-made for the interests of global capitalism',[56] shifting power back to capital by enabling them to further undermine working conditions. Although Eastern European migrants are attracted principally for economic reasons, those fleeing the Middle East and North Africa as refugees are often compelled to do so because of domestic issues like terrorism and war.

On the other hand, New Labour did invest in the welfare state, Sure Start centres, and enacted a national minimum wage. However, some commentators believe this was more about a desire to retain power rather than an authentic political and ideological commitment to help the nation's most disadvantaged social groups.[57] Opinion polls across the country demonstrated that the NHS was viewed fondly by most people and therefore underfunding or introducing mass privatisation would have been unpopular. At the same time, New Labour cosied up to capital, slashing inheritance and corporation tax whilst regularly holding meetings with them to advance their interests.[58] Under New Labour's premiership, income inequality catapulted, reaching its highest level on record.[59] Despite the harmful social effects of inequality including high levels of mental distress, crime and precarious employment, the party adopted a laissez-faire approach to the exploitative practices of the rich, elucidated by ex-New Labour cabinet minister Peter Mandelson who suggested they were 'intensely relaxed about people getting filthy rich'.[60]

Ultimately, this was a party that governed for capital's interests and thereby sought to abandon its historical focus on bettering the structural conditions of the working classes. The revision of Clause IV symbolised this, as the act ensured the party focused on implementing the collective ownership of the means of production throughout much of the twentieth century.[61] Others also believed it embodied a commitment to full employment and tackling the gap between the rich and poor.[62] Whilst New Labour cemented neoliberalism, they provided a new political discourse including entrepreneurship, meritocracy and opportunity. This was no longer about identifying a structural enemy in society, as Blair himself admitted: 'forget the past, no more bosses versus workers. You are on the same side. The same team'.[63]

Such rhetoric, however, covered up capitalism's production of inequalities, enabling Blair to depoliticise social, economic and cultural problems.[64] By the mid-2000s, the term working class was ditched from the Labour Party's political lexicon, espousing instead hardworking people. The ability of politics to inspire and make people dream of a better world faded, as the 'umbilical cord'[65] between working-class people in areas like Steel Town and the Labour Party was severed. Nationally, the party lost nearly five million working-class votes in the New Labour era. Whilst a Labour MP represented Steel Town throughout New Labour's reign, in 2010 the Liberal Democrats emerged victorious in the town whilst voter turnout had fallen to 62.5%. This story is similar to the surrounding area. For instance, Middlesbrough continued to elect a Labour MP, but turnout had fallen from 65% in 1997 to 48.8% in 2005, whilst Middlesbrough South and East Cleveland returned a Labour MP throughout New Labour's premiership, but turnout fell from 76% in 1997 to 63.6% in 2010. Perhaps, this growing voter disillusionment embodied how:

> The Left failed to defend a vision of a better world, an egalitarian world of common production, by and for the collective people. Instead, it accommodated capital, succumbing to the lures of individualism, consumerism, competition and privilege, and proceeding as if there were no alternative to states that rule in the interests of markets.[66]

The 2008 global financial crash, which many believe is an important contributor to today's nationalism,[67] laid bare the political consensus between the Left and Right members of Parliament. Proponents of neoliberalism believed history's ideological battles and financial crises had been relegated to a previous era, though other marginal economists foresaw the crisis but were denied a voice in popular debate.[68] The absence of an alternative narrative that equipped the citizenry with a structural understanding of the crash, such as the role of private debt,[69] meant the event permeated a sense of shock throughout the social body. Essentially playing out in theatrical and cinematic fashion, people watched the crisis unfold as the blame was directed towards widespread immoralism in the financial sector. Although New Labour had naturalised neoliberalism, the financial crisis lacerated the system and provided space to imagine a different social world.

However, most politicians forged a political consensus, failing to challenge neoliberalism and pursue a new political project.[70] Instead, they formed the system's administrators, suggesting neoliberalism had to be saved. In this way, the idea of pushing beyond the system was regarded as an insult to the consumer freedoms, market dynamism and innovation of neoliberal political economy. Political discontent erupted with the immediate rise of the Occupy movement, galvanised around the idea of 'we are the 99%'. Whilst the movement did not harness any protests in places like post-industrial Steel Town, it eventually subsided because of internal divisions and a lack of an alternative vision; they were against neoliberalism but not for anything.[71] Whilst an initial burst of optimism prevailed society, this was eventually replaced by fatalism and resignation as neoliberalism continued by default.

Most politicians suggested the only viable response was myriad state intervention in the form of a rescue package. Although this *consensual* response served to cover up the possibility of a different political economy, some suggest this is slightly myopic as neoliberalism was ideologically hegemonic.[72] There was also widespread social anxiety, with many people worried about their employment, losing lifelong savings, pensions and a potential inability to withdraw money from cash machines.[73] Embodying the biggest state intervention since the 1929 Great Depression, the nation state acted as a neoliberal variant of Keynesianism and rescued the banks which cost several trillion pounds.[74] The profoundly unjust nature of this intervention did not compel the Labour Party to rethink its political priorities and pursue a different form of political economy; instead, and much like post-war capitalism's crises in the 1970s, the Conservative Party ushered the system into a new dawn with the age of austerity.

Post-crash austerity

The Conservative Party and Liberal Democrats formed a coalition government in 2010. They announced an age of austerity but attempted to diminish the impending debilitating social impact by suggesting we are all in this together. The coalition government and Labour Party claimed that austerity measures were a difficult fiscal choice, but they argued that balancing the budget was an economic imperative because of an out-of-control deficit. Austerity has failed throughout history and caused myriad social distress in the process; yet, it was cast as sensible fiscal policy. Whilst austerity would socially injure those at the bottom of the social structure the most, particularly in already struggling locales like Steel Town, the Labour Party offered a message of *negativity*; under their power, the measures would not be as punitive.[75] This was a way to depoliticise capitalist crises and preserve neoliberal hegemony.[76]

Across England austerity measures dealt a hammer blow to the public sector, involving reductions in local council's annual budgets and the privatisation of public assets. Between 2013 and 2015, over 600,000 relatively well-paid public sector jobs were lost.[77] Punitive cuts have also been inflicted upon Sure Start centres, public libraries and domestic abuse support services. The legal aid system, previously regarded as one of the best in the world for ensuring society's most impoverished groups receive adequate legal representation, has endured unprecedented cuts.[78] Austerity has also further dwindled young peoples' prospects of acquiring a decent job and forging a secure livelihood. Whilst student fees have trebled, maintenance grants to help working-class kids from deprived backgrounds to go to university have been replaced by financial loans. The Future Jobs programme and Connexions, which helped young people find employment, have also been left to do more with less. These structural conditions mean half of those under 30 have not purchased a home and laid down roots such as getting married or rearing children.[79]

The Welfare Reform Act 2012 brought unprecedented changes to the welfare state, hitting deindustrialised and relatively deprived Teesside the hardest.[80] Perhaps this is a process where 'communities in older industrial Britain are being meted out punishment in the form of welfare cuts for the destruction wrought to their industrial base'.[81] The introduction of workfare programmes signifies this, whereby welfare recipients often must work full time hours each week for a large company to receive their payments. The governmental commitment to retrenching the welfare state has meant that vulnerable people have had their benefits sanctioned for arriving late at the job centre. The government's private contractors also found severely disabled people fit to work. In this context, suicides and the consumption of anti-depression medication has increased exponentially, with nearby Middlesbrough being branded as England's suicide capital in 2018. The locale now also contains some of the most deprived places in England, with food insecurity being a core problem.[82]

An unprecedented rise in food bank usage therefore occurred in the age of austerity, with many families compelled to choose whether to heat their home or buy food. Recent research in Stockton, 15 miles from Steel Town, found that food bank users were often in cyclical forms of employment; in and out of insecure work and joblessness and therefore they endured mental ill health.[83] Relatedly, other research in Teesside found that impoverished young people often relied on the welfare state to survive, generating nihilistic sentiments and feelings of a lack of social purpose.[84] As many of these people struggled to pay the bills, it had a detrimental impact on their mental and physical well-being.

Indeed, the impact of austerity has been delineated in myriad empirical studies, particularly upon socially disadvantaged groups such as problematic drug users.[85] However, whilst neoliberal values like individualism and competition have further congealed at society's core, empathy and sympathy directed towards society's most vulnerable have dwindled.[86] This is even though recent work in Teesside demonstrated how problematic drug users often endure overdoses, premature deaths and a lack of governmental support.[87] Using heroin for a considerable period meant many had damaged their mental and physical health, with physical impairment and diseases like hepatitis being common. With remunerative employment difficult to obtain, many were resigned to a life of acquisitive crime, prison and despair.

Perhaps it is not controversial to claim that austerity has been utilised by capital as a class instrument to enhance their wealth, power and social influence, particularly through the privatisation of state functionaries. Therefore, it has formed a neoliberal structural adjustment programme[88]; state ran services including within the NHS and criminal justice system have been underfunded and privatised. Recent work in Teesside in the criminal justice system shed light on how the transient privatisation of the probation service meant employees spent less time with offenders, detrimentally impacting on their ability to forge relationships.[89] The probation services historical tendency to operate for the social good had been replaced with an emphasis on efficiency, performance targets and the maximisation of profitability. Decreases in income and corporation tax for society's most wealthy have also occurred, embodying 'distant echoes; nothing is more constant in depression or recession than the belief that more money for the affluent, not excluding one-self, will work wonders as to recovery'.[90]

Whilst there has been an emphasis on fiscal pragmatism, balancing the budget and annual growth rates, the social harms generated by an increase in inequality under austerity have been neglected. The inadvertent harms of austerity and inequality include a rise in substance misuse, violence, particularly knife crime and alarming levels of psychological distress.[91] Somewhat inevitably, the age of austerity also intensified debilitating social conditions in deindustrialised and left-behind Steel Town and the broader Teesside region. Teesside possesses higher than national average levels of both short-term and long-term unemployment, welfare claimants and employed people generally earn less than the national average.[92] Nearby Southbank, six miles from Steel Town, is one of England's most destitute towns, enduring the 'deep scars of industrial ruination'[93] which encompasses poor educational outcomes, long-term joblessness, high levels of crime, depopulation and poor housing stock.

Deindustrialisation, a lengthy economic process to restore capital's dwindling returns on investment in the post-war period, has also continued in Teesside. Steel Town's core steelworks, open since 1979, encountered financial problems throughout neoliberalism, steadily laying off workers and enduring several rounds of privatisations. Such structural difficulties meant that it was threatened with closure in 2010, leading to it being transiently mothballed. Indeed, the site had failed to update its facilities with the passage of time, largely because it did not implement British Steel's five core proposals outlined in Chapter 1. This meant it did not have the structural capability to transform steel into the finished product to sell on the global market. The steel slabs were therefore transferred to sites elsewhere, increasing production costs. Whilst Sahaviriya Steel Industries (SSI) took over the site in 2011 after agreeing a multimillion-pound deal, they regarded it as a short-term solution because they did not intend to deal with the site's underlying deficiencies.[94] As China's steelmaking plants also undercut the price of Steel Town's steel on the global market, the site was cast as both unviable and threatened with closure. This was immediately packaged by the local media as a catastrophe, stating that nearly two centuries of industrial history were under threat. Local residents responded with a 'Save our Steel' campaign, supported by Anna Turley and Tom Blenkinsopp (two former local Labour Party MPs). The campaign involved several protests in the local area, as well as a special race meeting at Steel Town's racecourse to raise money for the cause.

Bolstered by their 2015 general election victory, the Conservative government failed to offer a rescue package and the site closed. Over 2,000 remunerative and unionised industrial jobs were lost, including many more in the local supply chain. As we will see, the closure also impacted detrimentally upon local businesses, suppliers and the families of the former steelworkers. A small part of the site, which specialises in the rolling of beams, was managed by a different company and it is still open today, though only around 400 people work there. Teesside's other remaining steelworks is in Skinningrove, 11 miles from Steel Town, employing around 300 workers. However, the site has often been threatened with closure and features frequently in the local and national news. In this context, Steel Town's steelwork's closure in 2015 marked the end of the area's industrial prowess.[95] Along the banks of the River Tees lies this industrial past, since many sites still stand today but have been abandoned. 'Dorman Long' or 'British Steel' remains sketched into the site's architecture, but the lights have been turned off; they form industrial ghosts intruding upon the present.

Although Steel Town and the surrounding area have principally elected an MP from the Labour Party at most general elections, as mentioned, this has changed in recent years.[96] Middlesbrough South and East Cleveland, home to a Labour MP since 1997, elected a Conservative in both 2017 and 2019. Whilst UKIP finished third in the 2015 general election in Steel

Town, the town also voted to Leave the EU in 2016. Moreover, Steel Town formed part of the collapse of the Red Wall in December 2019, returning a Conservative MP for the first time since 1964. However, voter turnaround stood at 62%, and therefore, non-voting is a core issue in the area. As we will encounter, this political discontent is nuanced and has been congealing for several decades.

Whilst Steel Town contains one of the least ethnically diverse populations in the country, nearby locales like Middlesbrough possess large numbers of different ethnic groups.[97] This includes higher than national average levels of asylum seekers, in particular from Sub-Saharan Africa and the Middle East, who often make a traumatic journey overseas to escape war and conflict. Indeed, deindustrialised and deprived areas like Middlesbrough often become core dispersal sites for asylum seekers, since housing is cheap. As previously mentioned, racial troubles were prominent in Middlesbrough in the post-war era, though racial antagonisms erupted again in 2015 and 2016. Regarded as the red door controversy, asylum seekers' household doors were painted red, meaning they were 'easy targets for racially motivated vandalism and abuse'[98] by some locals. Whilst this was not a deliberate intention by the company responsible, it was branded as irresponsible and myopic. Such racial problems were discussed in the national media, which involved some local people expressing racist sentiments in the online coverage forums.[99]

Conclusion

Neoliberalism's arrival in the late 1970s fundamentally transformed the social world and localities like Steel Town. As it restructured the nation state away from regulating capital in order to limit the harmful impact of unrestrained profit production, neoliberalism has successfully restored power and control back to capital. This restoration has been enabled, in part, by changes within the labour market including a structural shift towards uncertainty, instability and insecurity. Today's workers are told to be flexible, adaptable and mobile; only those willing to imbue this logic will have a chance to succeed. As the traditional means for identity formation has declined, more and more people embrace consumer culture's surrogate world and its transient hedonistic pleasures to fill the void left by industrial collapse. Despite offering an appearance of material wealth and prosperity, much of this is fuelled by an unprecedented amount of private debt. Nevertheless, consumerism fails to assuage the nagging sense that something has gone wrong or is missing; more and more people are depressed, anxious and insecure.

The changes New Labour wrought to the Labour Party yielded electoral success at three general elections. These shifts included revisions to Clause IV and the abandonment of full employment as a governmental policy goal. Of course, they also continued with Thatcher's antitrade union laws, disconnecting around five million traditional working-class voters from the party, particularly in industrially ruinated localities like Steel Town. Such political discontent was intensified with the consensual response to the 2008 global financial crisis. Whilst an opportunity emerged for politicians to think about a different way of organising society, most agreed that an economic rescue package and austerity were the required medicine. The impact of ten years of punitive austerity measures is now clear, including myriad cuts to important support services, the loss of reasonably well-paid public sector employment, the restructuring of the welfare state and a huge gap between the rich and poor. Such measures have hit places that were already struggling—Steel Town—the hardest, exacerbated by further waves of industrial retrenchment. In essence, the 2015 steelwork's closure spelled the end to Teesside's 150 years of industrial might.

Therefore, the book so far has provided a constitutive context, outlining social, cultural and political changes from the nineteenth and into the twenty-first century. Whilst the core structural changes associated with the shift from post-war capitalism to neoliberalism are vast and include deindustrialisation, the ascent of insecure and uncertain employment, the 2008 financial crisis and unprecedented net migration figures, a large amount of the literature on Brexit and English nationalism has omitted history, contextual conditions and the political economy. Instead, many commentators have opted for potentially more simplistic and reductionist accounts, suggesting cultural prejudices like racism and xenophobia hold more explanatory weight in understanding English nationalism. The following chapter delves into some of this literature, shedding light on analyses that focus on neoliberalism, cultural prejudices, intellectual deficiency and a desire to return to Empire, before outlining this book's methodological approach. This provides the platform for the three data chapters outlined thereafter.

Notes

1. Harvey, D (2005).
2. Mitchell, W & Fazi, T (2017).
3. Slobodian, Q (2018), p. 13.
4. Slobodian, Q (2018).
5. Hall, S (2012).
6. Stiglitz, J (2010).
7. Hall, S (2012).
8. Sandel, M (2012) *What Money Can't Buy: The Moral Limits of Markets*. London: Allen Lane.
9. Piketty, T (2014).
10. Badiou, A (2012a) *The Rebirth of History: Times of Riots and Uprisings*. London: Verso, p. 13.
11. Mitchell, W & Fazi, T (2017).

12. Atkinson, R (2020) *Alpha City*. London: Verso.
13. Telford, L & Lloyd, A (2020).
14. Harvey, D (2005).
15. Telford, L & Lloyd, A (2020).
16. Bloodworth, J (2019) *Hired: Undercover in low-wage Britain*. London: Atlantic Books.
17. Hall, S, Winlow, S & Ancrum, C (2008).
18. Burgum, S (2018) *Occupying London: Post-Crash Resistance and the Limits of Possibility*. London: Routledge.
19. Kotzé, J (2019); Winlow, S (2001).
20. Tcherneva, P (2020) *The Case for a Job Guarantee*. Cambridge: Polity Press.
21. Briggs, D, Ellis, A, Lloyd, A & Telford, L (2020) New Hope or old futures in disguise? Neoliberalism, the Covid-19 pandemic and the possibility for social change. *International Journal of Sociology and Social Policy*. 40(9/10): 831–848; Briggs, D, Ellis, A, Lloyd, A & Telford, L (2021).
22. Mitchell, W & Fazi, T (2017).
23. MacDonald, R, Shildrick, T & Furlong, A (2020) 'Cycles of disadvantage' revisited: Young people, families and poverty across generations. *Journal of Youth Studies*. 23(1): 12–27.
24. Garthwaite, K (2016) *Hunger Pains: Life Inside Foodbank Britain*. Bristol: Policy Press.
25. Winlow, S & Hall, S (2013).
26. Streeck, WG (2016); Tcherneva, P (2020).
27. Fisher, M (2018).
28. Fraser, N (2016) Progressive neoliberalism versus reactionary populism: A choice that feminists should refuse. *Nordic Journal of Feminist and Gender Research*. 24(4): 281–284.
29. MacDonald, R, Shildrick, T & Furlong, A (2020).
30. Heath, J & Potter, A (2004).
31. Kotze, J (2019); Lloyd, A (2013) (2018a); Telford, L & Lloyd, A (2020); Warren, J (2018).
32. Horsley, M & Lloyd, A (2020).
33. Horsley, M (2015).
34. Horsley, M (2015).
35. Lasch, C (1979) *The Culture of Narcissism: American Life in an Age of Diminishing Expectations*. New York: W.W. Norton & Company.
36. Treadwell, J, Briggs, D, Winlow, S & Hall, S (2013) Shopocalypse now: Consumer culture and the English riots of 2011. *British Journal of Criminology*. 53(1): 1–17.
37. Hall, A (2019) Lifestyle drugs and late capitalism: A topography of harm. In Smith, O & Raymen, T (eds.), *Deviant Leisure: Contemporary Perspectives on Leisure and Harm*. London: Palgrave Macmillan, pp. 161–186.
38. Lloyd, A (2018a), p. 157.
39. Kotzé, J & Antonopoulos, G (2019) Boosting bodily capital: Maintaining masculinity, aesthetic pleasure and instrumental utility through the consumption of steroids. *Journal of Consumer Culture*: 1–18. Also see: Gibbs, N, Salinas, M & Turnock, L (2022) Post-industrial masculinities and gym culture: Graft, craft, and fraternity. *British Journal of Sociology*. 73(1): 220–236.
40. Fisher, M (2009) (2018).
41. Fisher, M (2009), p. 21.
42. Wilkinson, R & Pickett, R (2009) *The Spirit Level: Why Equality is Better for Everyone*. Westminster: Penguin.
43. Fisher, M & Dean, J (2014) We can't afford to be realists. In Shonkwiler, A & Berge, L (eds.), *Reading Capitalist Realism*. Iowa: University of Iowa Press, p. 29.
44. Goodall, L (2018) *Left for Dead? The Strange Death and Rebirth of the Labour Party*. London: William Collins.
45. Winlow, S, Hall, S, Briggs, D & Treadwell, J (2015) *Riots and Political Protest: Notes from the Post-Political Present*. Abingdon: Routledge.

46. Embery, P (2020).
47. Lever, J & Milbourne, P (2017) The structural invisibility of outsiders: The role of migrant labour in the meat-processing industry. *Sociology*. 51(2): 306–322.
48. Lloyd, A, Devanney, C, Wattis, L & Bell, V (2021) 'Just tensions left, right and centre': Assessing the social impact of international migration on a deindustrialised locale. *Ethnic and Racial Studies*. 44(15): 2794–2815.
49. Lemos, S & Portes, J (2008) *New Labour? The Impact of Migration from Central and Eastern European Countries on the UK Labour Market*. Germany: The Institute for the Study of Labour.
50. Fitzgerald, I & Smoczynski, R (2015) Anti-polish migrant moral panic in the UK: Rethinking employment insecurities and moral regulation. *Czech Sociological Review*. 51(3): 339–361.
51. Murray, D (2017) *The Strange Death of Europe: Immigration, Identity, Islam*. London: Bloomsbury Publishing.
52. Lemos, S & Portes, J (2008), p. 2.
53. Fitzgerald, I & Smoczynski, R (2017) Central and Eastern European accession: Changing perspectives on migrant workers. *Social Policy and Society*. 16(4): 659–668. Bushell, M (2021) *Probing the Urban Night: A harm-based study of migrant workers in the North East Night-time economy*. Unpublished PhD thesis.
54. Anderson, B (2010) Migration, immigration controls and the fashioning of precarious workers. *Work, Employment and Society*. 24(2): 300–317; Anderson, B (2014) Nations, migration and domestic labor: The case of the United Kingdom. *Women's Studies International Forum*. 46: 5–12; Davies, J (2019) From severe to routine labour exploitation: The case of migrant workers in the UK food industry. *Criminology & Criminal Justice*. 19(3): 294–310.
55. Lever, J & Milbourne, P (2017).
56. Tuck, R (2020) *The Left Case for Brexit*. Cambridge: Polity Press.
57. Winlow, S, Hall, S, Briggs, D & Treadwell, J (2015).
58. Jenkins, S (2007) *Thatcher & Sons: A Revolution in Three Acts*. London: Penguin.
59. Telford, L & Wistow, J (2020).
60. Winlow, S, Hall, S, Briggs, D & Treadwell, J (2015), p. 69.
61. Levitas, R (2005) *The Inclusive Society? Social Exclusion and New Labour*. 2nd edition. Basingstoke: Palgrave Macmillan.
62. Driver, S & Martell, L (1998).
63. Levitas, R (2005), p. 114.
64. Mitchell, W & Fazi, T (2017).
65. Embery, P (2020), p. 26.
66. Dean, J (2012) *The Communist Horizon*. London: Verso, p. 15.
67. Fotopoulos, T (2016) *The New World Order in Action: Globalization, the Brexit Revolution and the 'Left'*. San Diego: Progressive Press; Traverso, E (2019) *The New Faces of Fascism: Populism and the Far Right*. London: Verso.
68. Lapavitsas, C (2019) *The Left Case Against the EU*. Cambridge: Polity Press.
69. Horsley, M (2015).
70. Garland, J & Treadwell, J (2012) The new politics of hate? An assessment of the appeal of the English defence league amongst disadvantaged white working-class communities in England. *Journal of Hate Studies*. 10(1): 123–141.
71. Burgum, S (2018).
72. Burgum, S (2018).
73. Horsley, M (2015).
74. Blyth, M (2015).
75. Etherington, D (2020) *Austerity, Welfare and Work: Exploring Politics, Geographies and Inequalities*. Bristol: Policy Press; Winlow, S, Hall, S, Briggs, D & Treadwell, J (2015).

76. Blyth, M (2015); Etherington, D & Jones, M (2018) Re-stating the post-political: Depoliticization, social inequalities, and city-region growth. *Environment and Planning A: Economy and Space.* 50(1): 51–72.
77. O'Hara, M (2015) *Austerity Bites: A Journey to the Sharp End of Cuts in the UK.* Bristol: Policy Press.
78. Mendoza, K (2015) *The Demolition of the Welfare State and the Rise of the Zombie Economy.* Oxford: New Internalisation Publications Ltd.
79. Howker, E & Malik, S (2013) *Jilted Generation: How Britain Bankrupted its Youth.* London: Icon Books Ltd.
80. Garthwaite, K (2016).
81. Beatty, C & Fothergill, S (2016) 'Jobs, welfare and austerity', working paper, Sheffield University, Centre for Regional Economic and Social Research, p. 2.
82. Haddow, K (2021) 'Lasses are much easier to get on with': The gendered labour of a female ethnographer in an all-male group. *Qualitative Research:* 1–15.
83. Garthwaite, K (2016).
84. Ruddy, A (2017) The new 'spectral army': Biography and youth poverty on Teesside's deprived estates. In Blackman, S & Rogers, R (eds.), *Youth Marginality in Britain: Contemporary Studies of Austerity.* Bristol: Policy Press.
85. Kotze, J (2019); Wakeman, S (2015) The moral economy of heroin in 'Austerity Britain'. *Critical Criminology.* 24(3): 363–377.
86. Gooch, K & Treadwell, J (2020) Prisoner society in an era of psychoactive substances, organized crime, new drug markets and austerity. *British Journal of Criminology.* 60: 1260–1281; O'Hara, M (2015).
87. MacDonald, R, Shildrick, T & Furlong, A (2020).
88. Etherington, D (2020); Mendoza, K (2015).
89. Temple, D (2018) Harm and transforming rehabilitation. In Boulki, A & Kotze, J (eds.), *Zemiology: Reconnecting Crime and Social Harm.* Basingstoke: Palgrave Macmillan, pp. 265–282.
90. Galbraithe, JK (1994) *The World Economy Since the Wars: A Personal View.* London: Reed Consumer Books Ltd, p. 86.
91. Etherington, D (2020); Mendoza, K (2015); O'Hara, M (2015).
92. *Nomis* (2020) Labour Market Profile—Redcar and Cleveland.
93. McGuiness, D, Greenhalgh, P, Davidson, G, Robinson, F & Braidford, P (2012) Swimming against the tide: A study of a neighbourhood trying to rediscover its 'reason for being'—the case of South Bank, Redcar and Cleveland. *The Journal of the Local Economy Policy Unit.* 27(3): 251–264, p. 254.
94. Telford, L & Lloyd, A (2020).
95. Warren, J (2018).
96. Telford, L & Wistow, J (2020).
97. Lloyd, A, Devanney, C, Wattis, L & Bell, V (2021).
98. Bates, D (2017) The 'red door' controversy—Middlesbrough's asylum seekers and the discursive politics of racism. *Journal of Community & Applied Social Psychology.* 27(2): 126–136, p. 127.
99. Hart, H (2018) '*Keeping Busy with Purpose': Virtuous Occupations as a Means of Expressing Worth During Asylum.* Unpublished PhD thesis.

Chapter 3

The quest to understand nationalism

As neoliberalism's crises continue to accumulate, many people have returned to the political scene to voice their discontent with a system that fails to provide socio-economic security and stability. In essence, the dawn of a new political age has emerged, with more and more people, particularly in post-industrial areas, returning to politics to demand that something is done to protect their dwindling lifestyles. Borrowing from Antonio Gramsci, some have therefore claimed the interregnum now envelops society and politics, that is, where the current world order is decaying, but there currently exists no unified political body that can move us towards a different form of political economy.[1] A decrepit system is thus likely to engender decaying symptoms, expressed through the rise of nationalism—UKIP, Brexit and the eventual fall of the Red Wall—a phenomenon that has also been conceptualised as populism,[2] national populism,[3] nationalist right[4] and the new nationalism.[5]

How have academics attempted to understand what has been referred to as an era of unprecedented political change[6]? This chapter delves into some of this literature, primarily on Brexit, including the focus on the rise of cultural prejudices like racism, a desire to return to Empire, and neoliberalism's debilitating impact upon society through deindustrialisation, poorly paid work, austerity and how this has intensified a palpable sense of voter disillusionment. It demonstrates the primacy to quantitative research methods and how they often focus on symptoms rather than aetiology, potentially failing to shed light on biography, history and contextual conditions. Therefore, the chapter closes with a brief discussion of this research project's qualitative methodology. This provides the final building block for the empirical data outlined thereafter.

Brexit

The debate over European membership had been simmering beneath the surface for some time after the 2008 financial crash. In 2011, around 100,000 members of the public signed a petition demanding a say on

DOI: 10.4324/9781003198666-4

membership of the EU. A large rump of Conservative MPs are also Euro-sceptics, signing a letter in 2012 that demanded a referendum be held in the next Parliament.[7] However, the issue intensified with the staggering rise—and fall—of the United Kingdom Independence Party (UKIP). Although UKIP's vote collapsed in the immediate years following Brexit, the party's influence on British politics has been profound. Heralding its arrival onto the political scene with its success at the 2014 European elections, the party's modus operandi was to ensure Britain's withdrawal from the EU. Although many Euro-sceptic Conservative voters lent their support to the party, the bulk of its support came from white working-class people in Northern localities. UKIP acquired over 3.8 million votes nationwide at the 2015 general election, and as mentioned, it finished third in Steel Town. Robert Ford and Matthew Goodwin believed UKIP posed a significant electoral threat to the Conservatives and Labour,[8] though they failed to transform widespread support into elected representatives due to Britain's first past the post-electoral system. Nevertheless, the party principally appealed to older white working-class men because these voters felt disempowered, believing Labour nor the Conservatives offered little means to voice their dissatisfaction in the years of austerity measures.[9] Their support also potentially symbolised wider value divides in society, not least working-class peoples' unease with the decline of tradition, as well as the importance of both national identity and the need to restrict immigration.

Marco Steenbergen and Tomasz Siczek have pointed to the importance of Nigel Farage, particularly his charismatic leadership style in the face of years of political spin and deceitfulness.[10] Farage presented himself as authentic and different to Westminster's political elite, often posing for the media with a pint in his hand and a cigarette in his mouth. UKIP's stance on immigration and its desire to leave the EU also appealed to many, essentially offering what Harold Clarke and colleagues believe to be a simplistic solution to complex structural problems in the neoliberal era.[11] Nevertheless, UKIP harnessed an anti-establishment narrative, attracting support under debilitating social conditions outlined in the previous chapter—namely, austerity and widespread concerns about the National Health Service.

This sense of an anti-establishment backlash in Britain erupted in 2016, as Britain voted to Leave the EU by 52%–48%. Branded as an anti-establishment revolt and spearheaded by Nigel Farage and the now Conservative Party leader Boris Johnson, most commentators across the political spectrum, the media and academics failed to foresee the result.[12] The desire to vote Leave differed geographically, with England and Wales voting to Leave whilst Scotland and Northern Ireland voted to Remain, leading some to suggest that it was driven by a specific sense of Englishness—an attachment to place and national pride.

Nevertheless, the Leave vote harnessed proportionally the most support in England's deindustrialised zones of the north. Symbolising this was its overwhelming support in the North East of England, where heavy industry and shipbuilding previously dominated the regional economy. All of Teesside's core areas voted to Leave, often by a significant margin. Whilst Middlesbrough voted to Leave by 65%–35%, Stockton elected to Leave by 62%–38%; Steel Town's Leave vote stood at nearly two-thirds to one, a locale eight miles away harnessed the proportionally highest Leave vote in Britain.[13] As some have tried to problematise the idea that the working class drove the Brexit vote,[14] others have claimed it is the most class correlated vote in the modern era.

The sociological and political forces behind Brexit have been the subject of academic investigation for five years. Some have placed emphasis on the degradation of working conditions in the neoliberal era, with Bob Jessop[15] stating the current labour market is a race to the bottom; social insecurity and economic uncertainty prevail. Along with Colin Hay and Wolfgang Streeck,[16] Jessop posits Brexit in the context of the restructuring of the nation state in capital's interests and thus the privatisation of public utilities, as well as increases in net migration figures, which served to disempower the working class. These structural changes occurred alongside a political consensus that there is no alternative to neoliberalism; therefore, Brexit offered an alternative channel for peoples' dissatisfaction with society and politics.

Others, however, have suggested Brexit is about a desire to return to empire and perceived racial purity. Gurminder Bhambra[17] focuses on the language of the Leave campaign and the somewhat crude idea of take our country back, which generated hostile divisions about who belongs in England and who does not. Whilst the referendum campaigns are widely believed to be hostile, the idea also in part refers to corrupt and undemocratic politicians. Lending support to Bhambra, though, are Suman Gupta and Satnam Virdee,[18] claiming the Englishness that underpinned Brexit was driven by a desire for the imperial project. Whilst these scholars have not spoken to any Brexit voters, they suggest they are racists because they lent their support to a political project that heightened notions of racial purity and the power of the British state, who has a troubling past regarding Empire. Others, however, dismiss the idea that Brexit embodied a desire for Empire because throughout the Longue durée of Empire, most working-class people believed it served capital's interests rather than theirs.[19] Moreover, Bhambra, Gupta and Virdee fail to convincingly explain why a third of the black, Asian and ethnic minority community voted to Leave the EU.

Ben Pitcher, Duncan Bell and Srdjan Vucetic have supported the claims that racism is rooted in Brexit,[20] particularly Bell and Vucetic who claim that Brexiteers' proposed trade deal (CANZUK) is a neo-imperial project, demonstrating how the age of Empire lives on in the present.[21] Indeed, whilst it is fair to say that some racist people voted to Leave, these scholars tend to omit an explanation of why such voters express racist sentiments. Simon Winlow, Steve Hall and James Treadwell have therefore dug underneath surface accounts to identify the root causes of today's racism.[22] They suggest that racism has changed; it is no longer about imagined superiority that was prevalent in the age of Empire but brought by neoliberalism's structural reconfigurations. This includes deindustrialisation, the ascent of transient and precarious work, the decline of a sense of community and mechanisms like trade unions which gave some working-class people a voice in society. Deprived of these material realities, many working-class people grew tired with their living standards and voiced their discontent through Brexit.

David Bailey, Hay and Jessop[23] also shed light on the importance of neoliberalism's constitutive context in understanding today's political discontent, not least the decimation of remunerative industrial and public sector jobs alongside low investment in infrastructure in deindustrialised areas. They also explicate the 2008 financial crises impact upon society, including how austerity measures intensified the social conditions of those that have been 'left behind', particularly degrading working conditions and the state of public services. Over time, these changes combined to create myriad discontent expressed through Brexit.

Some research evidence potentially supports the aforementioned theoretical analyses. For example, Harry Bromley-Davenport and colleagues[24] interviewed Brexit voters in Sunderland, a deindustrialised and relatively deprived area like Steel Town in Teesside. Like myself & Jonathan Wistow, they emphasise the importance of deindustrialisation, non-unionised and lowly paid employment, and New Labour's desertion of its post-war commitments as important contributory factors to today's nationalism. Although the scholars expose potentially important historical changes, they suggest Brexit voters' concerns with immigration embody 'the power of political discourse in creating a moral panic'.[25] Whilst this theoretical framework has advanced intellectualism, some note that it neglects the working class and their material realities such as mass migration's impact upon poverty-stricken communities and the potential loosening of communal cohesion.[26] Moreover, it also depends upon a belief in both politicians and what the media say. However, as we will see, growing evidence perhaps exposes flaws in this assertion, since people are cynical, sceptical and fatalistic, often not believing in what politicians or the media espouse. Perhaps, the moral panic theory is therefore problematic, rehashing once important conceptual tools in a fundamentally transformed social world.

Other researchers like Ron Johnston and colleagues utilised secondary survey data, conducting regression analysis and statistical inference. They suggest that Brexit exposed two core antagonisms in society—educational attainment and age—with those older aged voters with few qualifications more likely to vote Leave.[27] However, Roger Eatwell and Matthew Goodwin suggest this political chasm is more nuanced; half of those aged between 35 and 44 voted for Brexit. Johnston and colleagues tendency to utilise statistical data to cluster rather than explicate the interaction between social, economic, political and cultural factors is representative of what Charles Wright Mills termed abstracted empiricism. Such analyses tend to offer a view of the world where 'structure fades out of sight, history is banished from thought',[28] suggesting that Brexit was driven by older individuals suffering from a dearth of knowledge and who float above neo-liberalism's material realities. However, others note that older voters, who lived through the aftermath of the Second World War, contend that living in democratic societies is important, whilst only a fraction of younger people do.[29] Perhaps, this could thus be a core reason why older voters tended to support Brexit, as the EU is widely regarded as insulated from democratic contestation.

Others have used quantitative data and statistical modelling, claiming those who hold anti-immigrant attitudes and are hostile to a 'politically correct' society were more likely to vote for Brexit.[30] Although this claim may hold empirical weight, their methodological approach tends to focus on symptoms rather than structural causes. Hall and Winlow[31] thus note that quantitative research tends to omit aetiology and misidentify root causes. Streeck[32] draws attention to the role of macro-political economic issues including the 2008 global financial crisis and an unprecedented gap between the rich and the poor, whilst Winlow and colleagues[33] note how multiculturalism involves a balancing act between tolerating cultural difference and preserving traditional cultures, potentially engendering animosity towards immigration. However, Panu Poutvaara and Max Steinhardt[34] utilise quantitative data to conduct regression analysis and inference. Their modelling indicates that there is a causal link between 'bitterness'—characterised as 'not achieving what one deserves'—and concerns over immigration. Although recent research points to the importance of immigration concerns in explaining today's nationalism, Poutvaara and Steinhardt tend to present Brexit in individualised rather than structural terms. Such methodologies therefore potentially depend on a problematic philosophical basis to study the complexity of nationalism.

Utilising data from a national annual household survey to conduct statistical analysis, Tak Chan, Morag Henderson, Maria Sironi and Juta Kawalerowicz[35] argue that Brexit was partially driven by divides over cultural values; those who were more likely to take pride in the nation were more likely to vote Leave. Whilst this offers an empirical basis for further investigation, some scholars stress that quantitative methods offer '*symptomology* rather than *true aetiology*'[36] as the depth of both history and the present and how they shape today's nationalism are often not considered. Relatedly, Stefanie Walter analysed 19,367 news columns to investigate how EU citizens were portrayed by the mainstream media.[37] Essentially, EU citizens were cast in a negative manner by regional newspapers, potentially intensifying the polarity of Brexit and fuelling dissatisfaction.

Recent work by Paul Embery explores the role of New Labour and their abandonment of commitments to full employment, nationalisation of public utilities, a cradle to the grave welfare state, trade unionisation and protecting the interests of the working class.[38] Therefore, New Labour generated feelings of betrayal in deindustrialised locales which manifested in Brexit. Others have focused on virtual reality rather than broader contextual conditions.[39] Marco Bastos claims that fake online social media accounts were active during the Leave campaigns, which generated shaky knowledge about various political issues like immigration, impacting negatively on the Remain campaign. Whilst the use of botnets and fake accounts may have increased during the referendum, this potentially promulgates the idea that Brexit voters are dupes who cannot think critically about society and politics.

However, Joanie Willett and colleagues interviewed 24 Brexit voters in a relatively deprived part of Cornwall, in Southwest England.[40] Like recent research,[41] the participants were aware of racist accusations and reserved about discussing their views on immigration. However, they were not too concerned about immigration; instead, their discontent was rooted in austerity measure's impact upon their local community and the slow-motion decline of local industries. On the other hand, many academics emphasise the hegemony of immigration concerns, particularly since the 1990s when immigration to the United Kingdom intensified.[42] Utilising YouGov survey data, they claim cultural values possess more explanatory weight for the rise in nationalistic sentiments than the economy.

A lack of educational attainment has often been associated with Eurosceptic sentiments, though some have drawn on data from the European Social Survey and suggested that this is overstated.[43] Nevertheless, Noah Carl claims that Brexit was driven by England's deep-seated Euroscepticism. Essentially, England has always been one of the most Eurosceptic nations, partially because it is separated from the European continent and thus lacks a common identity with its European neighbours. However, Gordon MacLeod and Martin Jones, as well as Emma Dowling, argued that Brexit represents a symptom of the crisis of neoliberalism, not least the system's inability to absorb most of the population in its master narrative of social prosperity and economic stability.[44] Relatedly, many political economists like Costas Lapavitsas point to how the EU represents neoliberal values, embodied in the freedom of movement for capital, labour, services and commodities,[45] which will be further explicated in Chapter 5. Compelling countries to embed this ideal in their polity has aided the deindustrialisation of many areas across the Western world including Steel Town, since capital has shifted to low-wage economies where they can exploit the workforce more and thus maximise profitability.

Like Johnston and colleagues and Eatwell & Goodwin, Jennie Bristow has pointed to how Brexit exposed today's generational divides, suggesting the 'Baby Boomers' have been blamed for vote Leave.[46] She analysed how the mainstream media portrayed the older generation in the wake of Brexit, claiming many broadsheet outlets condemned older Leave voters for further damaging young peoples' life chances, not least their prospects of acquiring remunerative employment and home ownership. Relatedly, Lorenza Antonucci and Simone Varriale outline how leaving the EU will intensify lowly skilled EU migrants' precarious socio-economic position, as higher skilled employees are likely to be favoured in the future.[47] Therefore, they suggest non-United Kingdom, higher-skilled EU citizens possess a slight advantage in climbing the social structure.

Nonetheless, Aihua Zhang conducted statistical analysis and claimed Brexit was driven by a lack of higher education degrees amongst the working class.[48] Therefore, Zhang notes that a fractional increase in voter turnout amongst degree holding adults would have resulted in victory for the Remain campaign. This philosophical underpinning, that is, positivism's confusion of statistical correlation with a complex set of processes, feelings, sentiments and experiences, means that Zhang glosses over neoliberalism and potentially more explanatory structural factors. Some argue that these methodologies misdiagnose what science is, confusing statistical manipulation with scientific rigor.[49] Contrarily, Nikolay Mintchev recently explored how racism is embedded in the Brexit vote, not least through the 'exclusionary rhetoric perpetrated by Leavers'.[50] Perhaps, these opinions played an important part in Brexit; however, the analysis tends to omit potentially important macro-conditions, not least capitalism's mutation from its postwar anomalist phase to neoliberalism and the impact on working-class life in areas like Steel Town.

Offering a theoretical commentary, similarly to Gupta and Virdee, Matthew Creighton and Amaney Jamal suggest that racism has manifested in both overt and discreet ways before and after the referendum on European membership.[51] In particular, Brexit emboldened racists in England because it normalised prejudice and intolerance. However, others claim prejudice is sometimes generated by structural changes like deindustrialisation and a palpable sense of loss; those that feel disempowered in society are more likely to identify other social groups as responsible for their plight. Similarly, Slavoj Zizek[52] notes that intolerance is not merely an individual characteristic but is engendered under certain socio-structural conditions, not least inequality, and exploitation. Maya Goodfellow, though, suggests prejudices directed towards immigrants are not new; in the early twentieth century, immigrants were cast as responsible by the mainstream media and some politicians for further eroding both working conditions and tradition.

Qualitative research by Lisa McKenzie focused on the context that potentially generates anti-migrant sentiments.[53] She found that non-voters and Leave voters rooted their dissatisfaction in deindustrialisation, the ascent of low-paid work, poor housing stock, disillusionment with mainstream politicians and a sense of loss. This structural backdrop meant the EU referendum provided a unique chance to inform politicians about their unease with the state of society and politics. Drawing upon quantitative data from the 2014–2019 British Election Study, others note that many economically abandoned areas were more likely to vote for Brexit as local people felt they had more to gain from voting Leave; they could either continue with neoliberalism or try and ignite structural change to their benefit.

Similar to Goodfellow, Tina Patel and Laura Connelly refute the idea that England is a post-racial country; instead, they claim that racism is expressed discreetly.[54] They utilise 13 qualitative interviews with Leave voters, demonstrating how their respondents were aware of racist accusations who stressed that they are not racist. But for Patel and Connelly, this was merely a defensive rhetorical tool utilised by the participants to disconnect themselves from their own prejudices. The respondents also tended to cast themselves as victimised rather than privileged by their skin colour. This argument is similar to other scholars who claim that Brexit has unleashed waves of 'post-racial xeno racism' in England towards migrants who are often cast as the other—undeserving and thus relegated to the margins of society.[55] However, several other academics like David Goodhart problematise the notion that Brexit signifies the intensification of racism in English society.[56] Goodhart claims a great liberalisation of social relations has occurred under neoliberalism, whereby the overt cultural prejudices that prevailed in post-war society have declined. Whilst some scholars may view this as an attempt to normalise pedestrian/casual forms of racism, he believes that:

> By describing as racist everything from ethnic cleansing to national citizen preference and the greater comfort people (of all backgrounds) often feel in settled communities amongst people they are familiar with, the term loses precision and force and ends up calling into question what most people regard as normal human feelings.

Going further, Goodhart suggests that the core political divide is between the 'somewheres' and the 'anywheres'. Whilst the latter were more likely to vote Remain and are cosmopolitan and thus not afraid to move to other cities or countries, the former are more rooted to place, community, family and are unhappy with significant cultural change. However, Adrian Pabst believes that binarising Brexit is too crude since it needs to consider historical, social, economic, cultural and political forces.[57]

The need to take stock of a broad range of factors is elucidated by ethnographic work in deindustrialised Ashington in the North East of England,[58] an area with a similar socio-economic and political history to Steel Town in Teesside. Along with Embery, McKenzie and Winlow and colleagues' research, Andrew Dawson places emphasis upon the importance of the deindustrialisation process, the increasing insecurity and uncertainty of employment and the Labour Party's abandonment of the traditional working class. He suggests sentiments towards migrants in deindustrialised areas are complex; some people are tolerant whilst others are hostile. Whilst nostalgia for the post-war period's stable communities is often present in these Brexit voting locales,[59] others suggest that Remainers are nostalgic too.[60] Utilising quantitative data from 3,000 survey respondents in the United Kingdom, who were asked various questions about nostalgia including 'do you think Britain was a better place to live 50 years ago?', they claim that both Leave and Remain voters express nostalgic sentiments. But the core difference is a sense of traditional nostalgia symbolises Brexit voters, whereas an egalitarian nostalgia that is concerned with wealth being shared more fairly characterises some Remainers.

As mentioned, Brexit harnessed support from around three million people who abstain in general elections, often in deindustrialised areas. Nonetheless, it is important to mention that neoliberalism has borne witness to a sizable decline in voter turnout at general elections, particularly amongst those in deindustrialised places who work in poor jobs and feel as though they have no stake in society.[61] Whilst there is a lack of qualitative research on non-voters, recent research that incorporated electoral abstainers found feelings of political betrayal and nihilism.[62] This was tethered to the Labour Party and their collusion with the Conservatives, manifesting in the well-trodden notion that 'all politicians are the same'. Whilst the rise of Jeremy Corbyn as Labour Party leader raised some optimism about reconnecting the party with the working class, he oversaw the defeat of the Red Wall at the December 2019 general election, whereby some post-industrial areas that had never elected/had not elected a Conservative MP in 50 years—Steel Town—voted for the Conservatives often by a significant margin. As we will encounter, the historical connection between the traditional working class and Labour Party in areas like Steel Town has now reached an unprecedented low.

Other qualitative research by Valerie Walkerdine with Brexit voters in a former steel-making region in Wales ascertained discontent with the loss of industrial jobs, cuts to the welfare state and the loss of community.[63] Like Dawson's research, the discontent towards immigration was nuanced with some concerned, and others possessing more pressing worries around work and community. Contrarily, Rob Calvert-Jump and Jo Michell[64] utilise local authority data and bivariate choropleth maps which displays the statistical prevalence of various social, economic and cultural characteristics in certain regions through colouring/shading. Like other academics,[65] they argue that possessing less than five GCSEs is correlated with voting for Brexit and therefore educational background is a crucial factor in shaping voting preference in the EU referendum.

Whilst a handful of academics have conducted qualitative research with Brexit voters in some of England's most economically abandoned locales, suggesting the vote is rooted in history and political economy,[66] Sivamo-han Valluvan and Virinder Kalra claim Brexit was principally about hostil-ity towards immigration and ethnic change.[67] This was primarily expressed through overt and racist anti-immigrant sentiments; the political refusal to adequately intervene in the refugee crisis; the desire for border controls and 'go home' vans. Whilst this might be true, such an analysis tends to frame racism as an individualised characteristic that erupts at different periods rather than brought by certain historical conditions like social inequality and widespread feelings of disempowerment.

Of course, there are a 'plurality of possible drivers of Brexit'[68] and schol-arly quests to identify one cause are likely to be futile. Therefore, this chap-ter so far has outlined the core analyses on Brexit. Whilst there is a rump of qualitative research that sheds light on history and political economy, much of the academic analyses has been dominated by accusations of rac-ism, bigotry and intellectual deficiency. These accounts have often been generated by potentially impoverished quantitative methods, providing symptoms rather than aetiology. The explanations outlined here also sug-gest that voters' concerns have often been pathologised and individual-ised. Theoretical concepts that might aid our understanding of English nationalism are also largely absent. Whilst most academics failed to fore-see Brexit and the fall of the Red Wall, partially because 'little could be gleaned any more about the condition of the destabilized crisis societies of the present from opinion surveys',[69] the literature that has emerged in the ensuing years potentially demonstrates that many scholars have failed to adopt their methodological approach to cultivate more complex analyses. Therefore, some have suggested that researchers need to engage in a funda-mental methodological stock take,[70] to move beyond the three core issues that clutter the literature:

1. The hegemony of quantitative based accounts that encounter diffi-culty in situating sentiments within a broader structural context;
2. The dearth of in-depth qualitative research that seeks to understand why people express nationalistic sentiments;
3. The paucity of theoretical concepts that might aid our understanding of nationalism.

This chapter now briefly turns to the methodological approach deployed in this book, that is, intensive face to face interviews (N = 24) and ethno-graphic vignettes in post-industrial Steel Town.

Methodological note

Face-to-face interviews and ethnographic descriptions of Steel Town's core features like the decaying town centre and impoverished neighbourhoods were considered the best means to understand nationalism. Although there is a lack of qualitative research on Leave voters in post-industrial areas, there is a dearth on individuals who abstain. Whilst Brexit and the eventual fall of the Red Wall have been tethered to the idea of the left behind or return of the silent majority, not much is said about the 13 million people who abstained in the EU referendum.[71] Therefore, focusing on both Brexit and non-voters generated an understanding of their similarities and differences, as well as the implications for society, politics and the future.

Like other qualitative researchers,[72] my biography is an inescapable part of this research, since it previously aided access to Brexit voters,[73] not least through my previous job as a barman for over six years at a working men's social club. Therefore, I often witnessed hostility towards the political class and immigrants, meaning I was potentially better prepared to listen to remarks that other academics from more middle-class backgrounds may have found difficult to listen to.[74] Indeed, the use of several gatekeepers secured access to 14 Leave voters, nine 'non-voters' and one Remain voter for this research (N = 24). The interviews were conducted across 2018–2019. Seven of the 'non-voters' have never voted; one has sometimes voted for the Labour Party at general elections but has not voted for over a decade; and the remaining non-voter always votes Labour but was out of the country at the time of the Brexit vote. None of these nine individuals voted in the EU referendum, though many expressed a desire to Leave. I also interviewed one Remain voter, and they are included in the book's research sample as they substantiate the political discontent, though their views cannot be generalised to other Remain voters.

The face-to-face interviews were semi-structured, mostly lasting around 50 minutes. Most of the interviews were carried out in the respondents' private residence, cafes and pubs in Steel Town. My understanding of Steel Town and the way participants spoke about its social and economic decline engendered a need to ethnographically observe the locale. Therefore, I spent many hours immersed in Steel Town's high street, deprived neighbourhoods and pubs like Wetherspoons. I listened to what went on and observed interactions, making notes upon leaving the field. As ethnographers document,[75] observational data provides further context to peoples' lives, though my observations were sporadic rather than a lengthy ethnographic immersion because of the difficulty in conducting ethnography with an atomised social group.

Twenty-one respondents live in Steel Town, and the remaining three live in the surrounding locales. Most of the sample is aged between 40 and 50, five are retired and four are aged between 18 and 20. Twelve are male and 12 are female. They all possessed some connection to Teesside's industrial history. Many respondents were previously employed by the steelworks and petrochemicals industries, others possessed a significant other who did like a partner—mainly a husband—or relative. Their current job roles included part-time work in the night-time economy, retail, children's centre workers, postal workers, supermarket assistant, a clothes shop owner, self-employed joiner, fencer, window cleaner and four primary school teaching assistants. All respondents are white, representative of local demographics; local authority data outlines how the local authority Steel Town is situated in possesses the highest proportion of white British individuals in England and Wales at 97.6%.[76] Nevertheless, as previously encountered, surrounding localities like Middlesbrough are much more ethnically diverse including migrants from Eastern Europe, Africa and the Middle East. As this is a small sample size, it does not offer universal applicability but analytical generalisability.[77] This is where the empirical findings can be confirmed or problematised by other qualitative research on nationalism in areas that possess similar social conditions.

Conclusion

The rise of English nationalism expressed through UKIP, Brexit and the eventual collapse of the Red Wall have all been political events that shocked most mainstream media commentators, politicians and academics. Literature reviewed in this chapter outlines the various perspectives on these trends, including narratives of the 'left behind'; economically and culturally marginalised working-class people in areas like Steel Town who have lost out under neoliberalism. Relatedly, some have placed nationalism within a broader macro-context—namely, neoliberalism and its erosion of working conditions through deindustrialisation and the ascent of low-paid service work, as well as the imposition of austerity measures which negatively impacted upon those groups more likely to voice nationalistic sentiments. Others, though, have suggested today's nationalism is rooted in historical processes that continue to shape the present, particularly the age of Empire.

In this way, many analyses have focused on the prejudices of Leave voters, including racism, bigotry and xenophobic distaste towards immigration. Whilst these analyses may hold some empirical weight, the dependency upon quantitative methods—mostly survey research—does not elicit nuance by placing nationalism within historical processes, structural changes, biography and place. Moreover, it often fails to offer theoretical concepts that might aid our understanding of English nationalism. Utilising an ethnographically informed account might enable us to push beyond these problems, generating a more complex analysis of nationalism in Steel Town. The next three chapters provide original qualitative data to the contextual skeleton outlined so far, before discussing the societal impact of the COVID-19 pandemic and speculating on the future. As we will now see, nationalism in post-industrial Steel Town is rooted in history and the political economy.

Notes

1. Fraser, N (2019) *The Old Is Dying and the New Cannot Be Born: From Progressive Neo-liberalism to Trump and Beyond*. London: Verso.
2. Moffitt, B (2020) *Populism*. Cambridge: Polity Press.
3. Eatwell, R & Goodwin, M (2018).
4. Hall, S & Winlow, S (2020).
5. Halikiopoulou, D & Vlandas, T (2019) What is new and what is nationalist about Europe's new nationalism? Explaining the rise of the far right in Europe. *Nations and Nationalism*. 25(2): 409–434.
6. Eatwell, R & Goodwin, M (2018).
7. Shipman, T (2017) *All Out War: The Full Story of Brexit*. London: William Collins.
8. Ford, R & Goodwin, M (2014) Understanding UKIP: Identity, social change and the left behind. *The Political Quarterly*. 85(3): 277–284.
9. Ford, R & Goodwin, M (2014).
10. Steenbergen, M & Siczek, T (2017) Better the devil you know? Risk-taking, globalization and populism in Great Britain. *European Union Politics*. 18(1): 119–136.
11. Clarke, H, Whiteley, P, Borges, W, Sanders, D & Stewart, M (2016) Modelling the dynamics of support for a right-wing populist party: The case of UKIP. *Journal of Elections, Public Opinion and Parties*. 26(2): 135–154.
12. Salter, B (2018).
13. Telford, L & Wistow, J (2020).
14. Bhambra, G (2017) Brexit, Trump and 'methodological whiteness': On the misrecognition of race and class. *British Journal of Sociology*. 68(1): 214–232.
15. Jessop, B (2018a) Neoliberalization, uneven development, and Brexit: Further reflections on the organic crisis of the British state and society. *European Planning Studies*. 26(9): 1728–1746.
16. Hay, C (2020) Brexistential angst and the paradoxes of populism: On the contingency, predictability and intelligibility of seismic shifts. *Political Studies*. 68(1): 187–206; Streeck, WG (2020) *Critical Encounters: Capitalism, Democracy, Ideas*. London: Verso.
17. Bhambra, G (2017).
18. Gupta, S & Virdee, S (2020) *Race and Crisis*. Abingdon: Routledge.
19. Tuck, R (2020).
20. Pitcher, B (2019) Racism and Brexit: Notes towards an antiracist populism. *Ethnic and Racial Studies*. 42(14): 2490–2509.
21. Bell, D & Vucetic, S (2019) Brexit, CANZUK, and the legacy of empire. *The British Journal of Politics and International Relations*. 21(2): 367–382.
22. Winlow, S, Hall, S & Treadwell, J (2017); Winlow, S, Hall, S & Treadwell, J (2019) Why the left must change: Right-wing populism in context. In DeKeseredy, W & Currie, E (eds.), *Progressive Justice in an Age of Repression*. Abingdon: Routledge, pp. 26–41.
23. Bailey, D (2019) Neither Brexit nor remain: Disruptive solidarity initiatives in a time of false promises and anti-democracy. *Contemporary Social Science*. 14(2): 256–275; Hay, C (2020); Jessop, B (2018b) Bonapartism in the United Kingdom: From Thatcher via Blair to Brexit. In Beck, M & Stutzle, I (eds.), *The New Bonapartisms: Understanding the Rise of Trump & Co with Marx*. Berlin: Dietz Verlag, pp. 95–117.
24. Davenport, H, MacLeavy, J & Manley, D (2018) Brexit in Sunderland: The production of difference and division in the UK referendum on European Union Membership. *Environment and Planning C: Politics and Space*. 37(5): 1–18.
25. Davenport, H, MacLeavy, J & Manley, D (2018), p. 8.
26. Horsley, M (2017) Forget 'moral panics'. *Journal of Theoretical and Philosophical Criminology*. 9(2): 84–98.
27. Johnston, R, Manley, D, Pattie, C & Jones, K (2018) Geographies of Brexit and its aftermath: Voting in England at the 2016 referendum and the 2017 general election. *Space and Polity*. 22(2): 162–187.

28. Young, J (2012) *The Criminological Imagination*. Cambridge: Polity Press, p. 6.
29. Tuck, R (2020).
30. Bowman, J & West, K (2021) Brexit: The influence of motivation to respond without prejudice, willingness to disagree, and attitudes to immigration. *British Journal of Social Psychology*. 60: 222–247.
31. Hall, S & Winlow, S (2015) *Revitalizing Criminological Theory: Towards a New Ultra-Realism*. New York: Routledge.
32. Streeck, WG (2016).
33. Winlow, S, Hall, S & Treadwell, J (2017).
34. Poutvaara, P & Steinhardt, M (2018) Bitterness in life and attitudes towards immigration. *European Journal of Political Economy*. 55: 471–490.
35. Chan, T, Henderson, M, Sironi, M & Kawaleowicz, J (2020) Understanding the social and cultural bases of Brexit. *British Journal of Sociology*. 71: 830–851.
36. Hall, S & Winlow, S (2015), p. 99.
37. Walter, S (2019) Better off without You? How the British media portrayed EU citizens in Brexit news. *The International Journal of Press/Politics*. 24(2): 210–232.
38. Embery, P (2020).
39. Bastos, M (2021) This account doesn't exist: Tweet decay and the politics of deletion in the Brexit debate. *American Behavioral Scientist*. 65(5): 757–773.
40. Willett, J, Tidy, R, Tregidga, G & Passmore, P (2019) Why did Cornwall vote for Brexit? Assessing the implications for EU structural funding programmes. *Environment and Planning C: Politics and Space*. 37(8): 1343–1360.
41. Telford, L & Wistow, J (2020).
42. Leeper, T, Hix, S & Kaufmann, E (2020) Pricing immigration. *Journal of Experimental Political Science*. 8(1): 63–74.
43. Kunst, S, Kuhn, T & Werfhorst, H (2020) Does education decrease Euroscepticism? A regression discontinuity design using compulsory schooling reforms in four European countries. *European Union Politics*. 21(1): 24–42.
44. Dowling, E (2021) The social structure of Brexit and the crisis of globalisation: Towards an analysis of the disjuncture. *Austria Z Sociology*. 46: 257–277; MacLeod, G & Jones, M (2018) Explaining 'Brexit capital': uneven development and the austerity state. *Space and Polity*. 22(2): 111–136.
45. Lapavitsas, C (2019); Mitchell, W & Fazi, T (2017).
46. Bristow, J (2020) Post-Brexit boomer blaming: The contradictions of generational grievance. *The Sociological Review*. 1–16.
47. Antonucci, L & Varriale, S (2020) Unequal Europe, unequal Brexit: How intra-European inequalities shape the unfolding and framing of Brexit. *Current Sociology*. 68(1): 41–59.
48. Zhang, A (2018) New findings on key factors influencing the UK's referendum on leaving the EU. *World Development*. 102: 304–314.
49. Kotze, J (2019); Streeck, WG (2016); Telford, L & Wistow, J (2020); Young, J (2012).
50. Mintchev, N (2021) The cultural politics of racism in the Brexit conjuncture. *International Journal of Cultural Studies*. 24(1): 123–140, p. 138.
51. Creighton, M & Jamal, A (2020) An overstated welcome: Brexit and intentionally masked anti-immigrant sentiment in the United Kingdom. *Journal of Ethnic and Migration Studies*. 1–22.
52. Zizek, S (2018) *Like a Thief in Broad Daylight*. London: Penguin.
53. McKenzie, L (2017a) It's not ideal: Reconsidering 'anger' and 'apathy' in the Brexit Vote among an invisible working class. *Competition and Change*. 21(3): 199–210; McKenzie, L (2017b) The class politics of prejudice: Brexit and the land of no-hope and glory. *The British Journal of Sociology*. 68(S1): 265–280.
54. Patel, T & Connelly, L (2019) 'Post-race' racisms in the narratives of Brexit voters. *The Sociological Review*. 67(5): 968–984.

55. Abranches, M, Theuarkauf, U, Scott, C & White, C (2020) Cultural violence in the aftermath of the Brexit referendum: Manifestations of post-racial xeno racism. *Ethnic and Racial Studies*. 1–19: 16.
56. Babones, S (2018) *The New Authoritarianism*. Cambridge: Polity Press; Goodhart, D (2017); Lind, M (2020) *The New Class War*. New York: Atlantic Books; Pabst, A (2018) *The Demons of Liberal Democracy*. Cambridge: Polity Press; Winlow, S, Hall, S & Treadwell, J (2019).
57. Pabst, A (2019).
58. Dawson, A (2018) Hating immigration and loving immigrants: Nationalism, electoral politics, and the post-industrial white working class in Britain. *Anthropological Notebooks*. 24(1): 5–21.
59. Walkerdine, V (2020) 'No-one listens to us': Post-truth, affect and Brexit. *Qualitative Research in Psychology*. 17(1): 143–158.
60. Richards, L, Heath, A & Elgenius, G (2020) Remainers are nostalgic too: An exploration of attitudes towards the past and Brexit preferences. *The British Journal of Sociology*. 71(1): 74–80.
61. Telford, L & Wistow, J (2020).
62. Winlow, S, Hall, S & Treadwell, J (2019).
63. Walkerdine, V (2020).
64. Jump, C & Mitchell, J (2020) Educational attainment and the Brexit vote. *Environment and Planning A: Economy and Space*. 52(5): 826–832.
65. Johnson Manlie Pattie & Jones (2018).
66. Mahoney, I & Kearon, T (2018) Social quality and Brexit in Stoke-on-Trent, England. *International Journal of Social Quality*. 8(1): 1–20; Winlow, S, Hall, S & Treadwell, J (2017) (2019).
67. Valluvan, S & Kaira, V (2019) Racial nationalisms: Brexit, borders and Little Englander contradictions. *Ethnic and Racial Studies*. 42(14): 2393–2412.
68. Jump, C & Michell, J (2020), p. 827.
69. Streeck, WG (2017) The return of the repressed. *New Left Review*. 104: 5–18, p. 13.
70. Winlow, S, Hall, S & Treadwell, J (2019).
71. Shipman, T (2017).
72. Ellis, A (2016); Haddow, K (2021); Lloyd, A (2018a); Williams, K & Treadwell, J (2008) Similarity and difference: The ethnographer, the subject, and objectivity. *Methodological Innovations Online*. 3(1): 56–68; Winlow, S (2001).
73. Telford, L & Wistow, J (2020); Telford, L & Lloyd, A (2020).
74. Also see Ellis, A (2016); Winlow, S (2001).
75. Briggs, D (2017); Gooch, K & Treadwell, J (2020); Lloyd, A (2013); Raymen, T (2018); Winlow, S (2001).
76. ONS (2012) *Ethnicity and National Data in England and Wales: 2011*. London: Office for National Statistics.
77. Kotze, J (2019).

Chapter 4

The industrial age

The previous chapters have provided the book's contextual skeleton, consulting the historical record on capitalism's development from the mid-nineteenth century, documenting its implications for Steel Town and the broader Teesside region. Whilst the book has theoretically outlined these developments, the next three chapters shed empirical light on those caught up in these structural trends. Given the ubiquity of quantitative methods in explaining the rise of nationalistic sentiments in England's post-industrial locales, exploring the respondents' biographies is of fundamental importance, documenting their previous attachment to the industrial age and its associated culture of coherency, longevity, socio-economic improvement, optimism and community. It also enables us to see what has been lost throughout neoliberalism's longue durée, not least socio-economic stability and security. Much of the literature outlined in the previous chapter merely described political change, but by using qualitative methods and considering the capitalist totality in Steel Town, we can perhaps develop a more complex structural understanding of the area's recent shift to nationalism.

This is the first of three data chapters to add to the contextual underpinning documented so far. The chapter's point of departure is the Second World War. Whilst several of the older participants mentioned this event, as mentioned, it offers explanatory potency for capitalism's development from the mid-twentieth century. As the data highlights, this epoch continues to shape partially idealised memories of the past, whereby ICI and the steelworks offered a lucid biography, economic security and a feeling of social accomplishment. Shifting to neoliberalism, though, signalled the end of these working conditions, particularly through the deindustrialisation of the local economy including the 2015 steelworks closure. This generated widespread joblessness, mental ill health and palpable worries about the future. Firstly, the chapter returns to post-war capitalism's stable and secure lifeworlds in Steel Town in Teesside.

DOI: 10.4324/9781003198666-5

Stability and security

I park up on a council house estate in Steel Town. A small library sits in the middle of the road—it used to open six days a week but only opens on a Tuesday and Wednesday due to austerity measures. Outside is a small bookcase stating: 'books 10p'. Despite possessing numerous security alarms, the library was broken into during the early hours of the morning several weeks ago. A public meeting was also recently held at the neighbourhood's pub to discuss criminal activity, particularly burglaries and criminal damage.

Several of the gardens and small cobbled yards next to Jimmy's house are dishevelled with large weeds growing in the pavement's crevices. I hop over the gate, as it only partially opens, and a small man opens the door. He has grey hair with a longish fringe that is neatly combed to the right. He has a pair of black shoes on and a well-worn blue chequered shirt. I have not met Jimmy before, but he looks happy to meet me.

The bungalow is small, with the living room situated in between a single bedroom and the kitchen. One of the first things I notice is the household's darkness. The off white blinds are partially closed and the internal décor appears as though it has not been modified for decades. The wallpaper is purple and has various orange and black stains on, and in some areas, it is hanging off the wall. The carpet is dark green with chequered patterns and there is an old gas-fire erected on the wall. I sit down and sink into the sofa because the springs have lost their life. To the right is an old, grey armchair, it possesses numerous tears and has obviously seen better days. The living room is somewhat untidy with shelves and bookcases surrounding the room, holding CDs and DVDs which are gathering dust. A lavender deodoriser sprays behind me, purifying the room. Despite the obvious economic struggles, Jimmy was friendly, welcoming, and made sure I was comfortable in his home by offering me a warm welcome and a drink.

These notes were taken from my first meeting with Jimmy. He is 75 and grew up in a local mining village, though he has lived in Steel Town for over 30 years. Hung above his living room door lies a black and white landscape photo of the old village. Like Jimmy, his grandad worked down the pit excavating ironstone. The abundance of industrial work in the local economy meant that, when the site closed in the 1960s, he was able to accrue employment at the local steelworks. Jimmy recalls these times fondly, suggesting people knew and cared for one another in the local community. He says:

> I was born in 1945. I don't remember much of the war, but it was hard—my grandad had a ration book and we got hand me down clothes. I remember as a kid, my grandad would give his brown pay packet to my gran. He wouldn't even open it. She would give him

money for his Woodbines [cigarettes]. I remember these times crystal clear—no mobile phones, computers, but you were happier.

Although Jimmy's memories of the immediate aftermath of the Second World War have somewhat dwindled, he recalls the epoch's debilitating structural conditions, as poverty, socio-economic deprivation and poor housing were the norm for many working-class people.[1] Whilst structural conditions were difficult, the hardships encountered during the Second World War generated feelings of communal obligation and commitment to one another, with worn clothes passed onto those who were economically destitute. Sacrifice, commitment and a sense of duty potentially defined Jimmy's grandparent's fixed and rigid gender roles.[2] Anna, 87, offered a similar story. Much of her life was spent looking after her three children, whilst her husband laboured at the steelworks. Nonetheless, this is a role she enjoyed, taking pride in her children's upbringing. Anna recalls how:

> When it [Teesside] was bombed during the war, they tried to target the industry, but it didn't do much damage. We were under the dining table, terrified, but the war pulled everyone together.

Steel Town and the broader Teesside region were essential to the domestic war effort, building tanks, ammunition, bridges, aircraft and chemicals to fuel explosives and attacks overseas. Foreign attacks on Teesside's industry were thus purposeful, serving to weaken the nation's defence efforts and generate fear and panic amongst local people. However, observe how Anna suggests people were united by a structural sense of common duty. What mattered was protecting and looking out for each other in a period of profound social distress and turbulence. Of course, the structural combination of a myriad gap between the rich and poor, economic inequality, the Great Depression and the Second World War meant the legitimacy of laissez-faire capitalism was called into question. As alternative ideological frameworks garnered traction including Soviet Union style communism, which was cast as capitalism's ideological opponent, the potential of a working-class revolt intensified as discontent was widespread. The destruction wrought, in particular, by the Second World War meant many people were traumatised and homeless; many towns had been completely destroyed as 'everyone lost something and many lost everything'.[3] Returning home to live with squalor, disease and poverty would have been unpalatable for war heroes and their loved ones. Western capitalism was therefore restructured, putting social security and economic stability at the core of its post-war modus operandi. Whilst stable industrial work was a core component of Teesside's local economy from the mid-nineteenth century, it was also at the centre of the capitalist system's post-war era. However, industrial workers witnessed sizable advances in their living standards due to increased wages and more unionisation, brought in part by a historical compromise between capital and labour.[4] Jimmy outlines how:

> At 16 when I went onto the big mills, you did shift work 2–10, 6–2, but you got your weekends off. It was quite hard work. It was something everybody did—when the mines were open you either went down the pits to work or went in the steelworks. Jobs were plentiful then. ICI had also just started.

Jimmy's working life was mapped out before he left school, since he was safe in the knowledge that industrial work existed in abundance in the local economy. Although he accrued stability and security, capital glossed over health and safety concerns by being uninterested in Jimmy's young age. Whilst Jimmy could have also become a miner, harnessing a deep-seated commitment and duty to one another, working conditions were physical and dangerous with deaths a frequent occurrence; mothers and wives would sometimes live in fear not knowing if their sons and husbands would return home from work.[5] As Jimmy notes, ICI expanded upon its industrial bases and was cast by many of the research participants as an outstanding company to work for. Alice, 60, grew up in a nearby town. She can potentially be identified as the antithesis of Jimmy's relative impoverishment, living in relatively comfortable conditions. Alice spoke of how:

> When I worked there [ICI] and my husband, the elderly people were looked after not just financially with pensions, but socially, housing. If you had a job for ICI, it was for life, and some people did. It was perfect. They provided care throughout employment and after. When I was young, I just really wanted to work for ICI, I don't know why but I did. When I went for an interview in telecommunications when I was about 18 or 19, I didn't get the job, but the lady said we will keep your interview on file. I thought well, okay, thanks, but that is the end of it, and I was really disappointed. But a year later they came back to me and offered me the job. That would not happen anywhere today, but that's what it was like. You weren't forgotten, you were respected and looked after.

Alice offers a narrative whereby there is a palpable feeling that stability and security were woven into Teesside's local economy. This was a time where many working-class people were not treated poorly at work; rather, they laboured safe in the knowledge that employers were interested in and needed their services. Although ICI employed around 30,000 people at Wilton and Billingham in Teesside—in addition to those employed in the local supply chain,[6] she emphasises a family centred ethos whereby they were looked after both in employment and retirement. This meant Alice obtained satisfaction from her job role. As ICI offered adequate remuneration and sizable pensions, Alice did not have to worry about paying the bills and could plan for her retirement. This was a reality for many working-class people in Teesside's industrial economy, as Pete, a retired ex-shipbuilder, outlines: 'My classmates did [work at ICI or the steelworks], schoolfriends, hundreds of them went there, did apprenticeships. It was all they knew'. Laissez-faire capitalism's debilitating structural conditions including joblessness, hopelessness and economic hardship had faded into the background; relatively well-paid industrial work was now at the centre of working-class life in places like Steel Town.

Jimmy further demonstrated the sense of accomplishment and pride attached to industrial work: 'Some of the steel made here is on the Sydney Harbour Bridge in Australia, our steel went all over the world'. These conditions meant that there was a widespread perception that even if you obtained few qualifications upon leaving school, you would still be able to ascertain relatively decent work, since many working-class people could 'finish a job at dinner-time and go and get another one in the afternoon'.[7] Matty is 54 and he worked at ICI before ascertaining a job at the steelworks, though he now works as a postman. He has always lived in Steel Town and he describes the post-war era's lucid biographies:

> I left school at sixteen and went into an apprenticeship as a mechanic, then went straight onto British Steel. I was at ICI after—I trained people to drive forklifts. It was a brilliant job, great pay, forklift trucks, dumper trucks, ten-ton trucks. It was good craic. I would say it was my best job.

Evidently, Matty developed various skills during his apprenticeship, which he knew was subsequently required in the local economy. This meant he was able to utilise his skills for local employers, working towards something that was both achievable and needed. In this way, many respondents claimed working at British Steel and ICI generated economic stability and a subjective sense of self-worth, pride and usefulness. As Matty equipped junior employees with the skills and knowledge to contribute productively to the area's industrial prowess, he also outlines how there was a sense of camaraderie at ICI since employees often got on well with one another.[8] Mary, 54, an ex-ICI-worker noted that she 'Loved it'.

Of course, the working conditions described here including adequate remuneration and longevity were an anomaly in capitalism's history, engendered by the combination of unique socio-structural conditions in the first half of the twentieth century. This was a temporary sacrifice from capital, accruing *exploitative stability* to the industrial working class[9] to ensure its long-term survival.[10] It could be argued that these working conditions were therefore not brought by morals and ethics from capital; instead, the profit motive had to be transiently restrained and thus the working class awarded socio-economic betterment to stabilise capitalism after a tumultuous period. Governmental commitments to full employment were a core part of this, serving to nullify working-class dissatisfaction and obtain their commitment to the capitalist system. This awarded many industrial workers a yardstick to use against exploitative employees who attempted to discipline or dismiss them, since as Katie, 42, claimed: 'You would be able to say oh, fuck you mate, I'm off' and find an alternative job. Substantiating their relative bargaining power at work was mass trade unionisation. Archie is retired and spent 30 years working as a postman, though his father was a steelworker. He said:

> When I was younger, you had to be in a union. If you weren't—it was a closed shop. The only thing that annoys me about that is that if we went on strike, fought hard picketing, tried to get us extra money, we would come in and people would get the benefits for doing nothing. I won't name names. When I first started, you were called a *scab*. I have always been Labour and a member of the union. But the unions in the past called strikes for hardly anything at all.

Note how Archie outlines how trade unions were once central to working-class life and held sizable bargaining power in some labour markets, as only union members could be employed. Although it awarded some employees an internal defence tool against their employers, Archie recalls how it occasionally generated workforce divides. Even during an epoch of unprecedented working-class bargaining power, including historical advances in material conditions, many working-class people were content with capitalism so long as it awarded them social security; they were not politically radical and had little interest in pushing beyond capitalism.[11] Nonetheless, post-war capitalism's values of duty and reciprocity engendered a sense of togetherness on the shop floor of industrial work; observe how Archie describes a sense of shame towards those who did not engage in strike action. Whilst trade unions awarded workers like Archie a defence mechanism, he suggests they held too much power. As previously outlined, this was a contributing factor to the demise of capitalism's post-war era and will be explored shortly.

Whilst trade unionisation and industrial work's sense of social satisfaction and economic stability were recalled fondly by the research sample, many also spoke about industrialism's dirtiness and smelliness, impacting detrimentally on the local population's health and well-being. Although Pete lives in a nearby locale, he previously lived in Steel Town for several years. He is an ex-shipbuilder and steelworker, and had this to say:

> I remember one of the big fires there (ICI). I went down to film it, trying to get through different gates there. All of the houses around

it were covered in dust and debris, so were the cars and the people. It was like a soot, all over floors, carpets. They had to pay out thousands in compensation.

Similarly, Archie stressed that:

At times, it was a very smelly place. You could smell the works. But it was good employment, and it was all some people knew. I had a lot of friends who worked there.

The processes required to synthesise chemicals at ICI were hazardous, containing various risks. Whilst workers had to take health and safety protocols seriously, the wider area became defined by smog and thus poor air quality, which is where Teesside's residents contemporary nickname—smoggies—originates from.[12] At the height of the petrochemicals industry's production and thus pollution, a rump of Teesside's residents voiced their dissatisfaction and protested. As Pete remarks, rather than ICI responding to negative externalities by constructing more adequate health and safety mechanisms, local people received economic inducements to pacify their dissatisfaction. Notice how Pete and Archie's sentiments also demonstrate how industrial labour 'ordered the political and social fabric'[13] of Teesside's towns. Matty also exposed industrialism's deficiencies:

It [steelworks] was very dirty, cleaning out massive tunnels or going down them chiselling. Black as hell, lots of water in it to keep it cool. I worked long hours—I did days, went home and did a night shift. It wasn't stopped back then. Some lads would help you out on your night shift and you would just sleep somewhere for a little bit. If I did two days like that in a row, I would be fucked.

Matty draws attention to the 'harshness and the physical toils of day-to-day working life under industrial capitalism'[14] in Teesside. Employment conditions were not clean or easy; employees had to display myriad strength and were engulfed with dirt which had detrimental effects on their physical health and well-being. Other empirical work also ascertained that industrial employees often worked night shifts, dwindling the amount of time spent with their partner and children,[15] meaning they were sometimes *absent fathers*. Notwithstanding, capitalism's post-war phase generated a sense of commonality and bonds amongst co-workers, evidenced by how Matty's colleagues helped him rest to mitigate his tiredness. Whilst steelworkers were awarded relatively good pay, many health and safety protocols were poor demonstrating how capital did not really care for the industrial workforce's health and well-being; rather, industrial employees accrued anomalist conditions at work due to a transient compromise between labour and capital.

The backbreaking work often involved with toiling at ICI and the steel-works and the thick clouds of pollution, evidenced by Pete, Archie, Matty and others, perhaps problematises the idea of a golden age. The recent terms offered by Anthony Lloyd[16]—*somewhat mythical*—better illuminate the reality of working-class life under post-war capitalism, highlighting how they obtained socio-economic betterment whilst capital still received most of the surplus. Capital in the mid-twentieth century harnessed working-class identities that were intimately attached to their local area; industrial workers and their loved ones were not primarily concerned with social mobility, since they were able to comfortably pay the bills and mort-gage and have disposable income for leisurely practices. They looked to the future safe in the knowledge that they would be comfortable in retirement, whilst they were confident that their children and grandchildren would also live a life characterised by social stability and economic security. As the industrial age required labourers in large numbers to ensure the system's reproduction, it generated the presence of stability which enhanced their livelihoods to an extent that had never been witnessed before.

However, whilst many respondents spoke about the ability to easily obtain work in Teesside, a sizable amount were confined to the locale's industry. In the 1960s, for example, 56% of Teesside's employees worked in the manufacturing sector, whilst this had fell to 43% by 1975.[17] Not-withstanding, industrial work generated various employment roles and, therefore, they were not merely confined to dirty and dangerous jobs. Alice, who we met earlier, laboured in admin, whilst three female par-ticipants organised business travel. Relatedly, Julia, 50, a primary school teacher, highlighted how her husband 'ran the IT system' at the steelworks. As a result, most people in Teesside under capitalism's post-war phase pos-sessed some relation to the area's industrial base.

Whilst Steel Town's industrial background generated coherency, the town's cultural conditions were also recalled fondly. Many spoke nostal-gically about what they regarded as the 'good old days', whereby stable industrial work existed in tandem with a sense of community and com-monality. Anna spoke of how in Steel Town 'During the summer, there was loads of swings, roundabouts—this was in the 60s. It was very busy. There was loads of shops in the high-street too'. Steel Town's cultural aes-thetics were described in positive terms; many people visited the area from the surrounding locales and other towns to utilise its cultural amenities including the sea and beach. Archie illuminated how:

> When I was a young lad, Steel Town was a booming place. You had the seafront, on a summer's day it would be heaving. Lots of stalls on the beach, trampolines, slides, roundabouts, there was everything. People went for days out and they would enjoy themselves. There was fun palaces and stalls, ice cream kiosks, the high street was booming

as well. Lots of shoppers, the racecourse too. I can remember there was loads of buses to take people home from the races. It was a big, booming place.

Chloe is 55. Her son worked at the steelworks and she continued the story:

> When I was young, I used to always come down here to the amusements and seafront. My mam would tell you, we had bus trips coming here, from Leeds, Bradford, different areas. The beaches and amusements used to be full—it was like a proper day out. My mam and dad would take us down here for ice-cream, fish and chips.

Although the sentiments outlined above are somewhat idealistic since this epoch still contained a sizable gap between the rich and poor, embedded racism, sexism and homophobia amongst parts of the working class,[18] whilst industrial labour in Teesside lacked autonomy, it is substantiated by a sense of social, economic and cultural expansion. Steel Town provided various cultural pleasures for both locals and tourists, engendering more job opportunities for residents. Whilst people would travel many miles to visit Steel Town, local people often utilised the area for family day trips. This was elucidated by Julia: 'When I was little, it used to be quite a lively summertime holiday destination. People would stay or at least come for days out. The beach was busy, the town was busy'. Relatedly, Dave, 52, said: 'When I was younger, I used to look out of the window at my dad's [a former steelworker] and watch people come in their droves on the train, coming to Steel Town'. Such structural conditions cemented a sense of togetherness and community, which as Pete outlines, generated a lively arena for leisure and pleasure:

> I have plenty of photos from the 60s and 70s showing the club outings: York races, Bridlington or Steel Town for the day, club trips. The core thing I made my trade in was as an entertainer in pubs and social clubs. In them days, you could work seven nights a week and three afternoons. It was busy, there was loads of work. I remember living in Steel Town, we would do a bingo at Ashington at 10am, pack away, do another venue at 2, pack away and do another club at the night-time.

In the post-war period, social clubs were a fundamental component of working-class life, reaching their peak in the 1960s and 1970s.[19] Social clubs provided working-class people with leisurely activities such as bingo, pool, snooker, dominoes, darts, football clubs, cheap alcohol and a space to discuss the issues that mattered in their local area. As the living standards of the working class increased in a way that had no historical precedent, many people across the North had disposable income to spend in their locality which benefitted Pete. Whilst working men's social clubs were originally forged in the nineteenth century to provide a leisure arena to the working class to pacify their discontent about industrialism's hardships,[20] they also contained gendered inequalities as only men could use the bar area whilst women were mainly confined to playing bingo in the function room. However, social clubs further enriched working-class life, providing a valuable source of community spirit.

From Pete's viewpoint above, people were tethered to the locale they lived in, both working in the local area and enjoying their leisure time there too. There was seemingly little desire to move out of the town and move up the social structure; they were generally content with the industrial epoch.[21] Mary spoke about how this aided a sense of community:

> When I moved to Potters Road [pseudonymised], on the first day I had about nine people on the road scraping wallpaper off. After a while, it was really nice, if you needed an onion you would go knock on somebody's door. So, it was really nice, everybody looked out for one another.

Offering similar sentiments is Alice:

> In terms of community, it was better. More women were able to stay at home, we had less than people have now as a result, but it did make for a better community. We knew all of our neighbours. When my kids were growing up, they would run in and out of the neighbours' houses, like surrogate grandchildren.

Alice draws attention to gendered inequalities in the industrial age; women were generally subservient to their husband's needs as they were cast as the breadwinner. Staying largely at home also meant that women's leisure opportunities were restricted. However, none of the respondents recalled this negatively; rather, it provided further stability, security and coherency to working-class life, since people knew their place in the socio-economic hierarchy. Perhaps this demonstrates how working-class culture has always contained a small C conservatism, possessing pride in family, law, order, place and national identity.[22] This is contrary to neoliberalism's nomadic worldview, which now dominates society's core institutions and politics.

In some of the respondent's views, fixed gendered roles under post-war capitalism awarded working-class life further clarity. After a prolonged period of hell on earth brought by the Great Depression and the Second World War, social democratic political economy and ideology fostered a working-class culture that revolved around community, class and locality. The horrors of war, which brought everybody together, meant there was widespread recognition that collectivism and thus community spirit were important. Nevertheless, some argue that the constitution of the working class always serves capital's interests[23]; the stable and secure lifeworlds of the industrial age were tolerated by capital since it did not threaten capitalism. Indeed, it aided its stabilisation and ensured its survival after a historically unprecedented unstable period.

As Chapter 1 outlined, there was a perception in both politics and in working-class culture that the industrial age would continue indefinitely; stability, community and longevity at work were mere doxa. Observing Teesside's industrial epoch in the 1970s, North[24] remarked how 'the coming decades should see new changes and developments which will do much to enhance its industrial greatness'. Remember how Archie, though, identified how many trade unions were rather militant and disrupted peoples' working lives, business owners and politics. Structural crises emerged again in the 1970s, particularly stagflation, the intensification of an embittered relationship between industrial workers and their employers which engendered more strike action, as well as the 1978 winter of discontent.[25] This brought an end to post-war capitalism's relatively short period of socio-economic security and stability; a new phase of capitalism was generated which was based upon competitive individualism, marketisation and freedom for capital to maximise profitability.[26] Whilst the loss of industrial jobs occurred steadily throughout the post-war era in Teesside, the shift to neoliberalism in the 1980s accelerated the transformation of the local economy. It is to this that the book now turns.

Industrial retrenchment

I drive six miles south to Steel Town. The cafe I'm meeting Katie at is on the seafront, and as I head towards it, I can see the closed steelworks, peaking above the various households that sit along the left-hand side of the road. A symbolic piece of history that lies dormant, yet it continually haunts the present, demanding to be remembered for what it represented and offered Steel Town throughout a sizable part of the twentieth century.

As I park on the right-hand side of the road, two old people sat on a bench opposite observe my struggle to parallel park. I get out of the car and head towards the café. The North Sea's cold air permeates my body and knocks me off balance. The two long stretches of grass that lie either side of the café have turned yellow in the heat of the last few weeks. An old, tattooed and overweight man sits and tucks into some food on a rusty table outside. Signs advertising 'all day breakfast' and 'ice cream' are etched into the café. The building is small and it's decaying white paint suggests it needs some investment into its aesthetics.

Before I arrived, Katie informed me that she was perched in the corner reading a newspaper and as I entered, she immediately recognises me from the description I gave her. 'Nice to meet you Katie', I remark. She claims this cafe is the cheapest in Steel Town—a cup of tea costs me a £1.

Katie is 42 and looks tired and stressed. Today is her day off after working three 12-hour shifts as a nurse for an agency. Her dark hair is tied up loosely in a bobble and she has a few wrinkles across her forehead and under her eyes.

It is not long before our conversation shifted to Steel Town's and the broader Teesside region's industrial retrenchment. Deindustrialisation is recalled with sadness, resignation and fatalism, particularly as it is intimately connected to her biography. Whilst many of her friends and neighbours worked at the steelworks or ICI, her husband was employed at the steelworks. Although a severe bout of deindustrialisation hit Teesside in the 1980s, compelling many steelworks and shipyards to close, ICI managed to weather the storm until the mid-1990s when it gradually downsized its workforce and was marketised. Katie noted how:

> I know friends of mine who would leave school and walk into apprenticeships at ICI, I know the chemical plants are still there, but it's not like it was, the same. A lot of them did the apprenticeships and went onto great things. Or like British Steel, it was a given that you would go in and do an apprenticeship then you would have a job for the rest of your life. *There is nothing like that now.*

Offering a similar story is Roger who is in his early 50s. Steel Town has been his home since birth, and he has laboured in various employment roles like a sales assistant for a car firm and a bus driver. He claimed:

> ICI has been sold off bit by bit. My brother worked for ICI, it was good money. People still call it ICI, but I don't think it is now, is it? It is different companies on that complex, but it is not advertised as ICI.

As documented, ICI dwindled in the 1990s as competition from abroad intensified. As capitalism entered its neoliberal phase, its core values began to erode the post-war era's compromise between capital and labour, meaning ICI responded by deindustrialising their Teesside sites and making workers redundant. What remained of ICI was sold off to other companies, leading Alice to suggest:

> It [ICI] is unrecognisable now. From what I know, there isn't really any ICI left, the works are there, but they have been taken over by other companies—Hunstman, BASF, lots of other companies. I don't think there is any ICI left at all in the North East. A lot of European countries operating there, it certainly doesn't exist the way it did. It just disappeared.

The post-war era's stability and security in Teesside, shaped in part by ICI's demands for a large labour force, quickly disappeared from the area with the shift to neoliberalism. Operating since 1926 in Teesside, ICI provided thousands of working-class people with good remuneration and lucrative pensions, meaning its workforce was branded as the aristocrats of the working class.[27] When it closed its doors, many ICI workers were able to secure employment 'offshore', where many still work today. This refers to the well-paid jobs at the oilrigs in Aberdeen, where around 3,000 people from Teesside work.[28] Although some former ICI workers are employed at what remains of Teesside's petrochemicals sites, it is a mere fraction of the 35,000 employees that were employed at Wilton and Billingham in the mid-1970s. Whilst ICI's employees were imbued with a sense of infinite socio-economic betterment, capital is malleable and able to dispense with areas once profit margins start to dwindle. In effect, it traverses the world and partially reconfigures localised social relations, pursuing its own expansion and survival despite the inevitable social distress in locales like Steel Town.

A *structural feeling of loss* has characterised much of working-class life in Steel Town throughout neoliberalism. ICI was completely sold off in 2007, meaning its famous name was lost from the Teesside region. Other respondents also highlighted that they were 'saddened' to witness the privatisation of Northern Dairies in the 2000s, since it used to deliver milk to sizable companies including both ICI and the steelworks. Some also pointed to the closure of Teesside's PowerStation in 2011 which was based at Wilton; it possessed the largest generating capacity in Europe but ceased operating after the chemical sites diminished. However, all respondents spoke about the relatively recent closure of the steelworks in 2015 as symbolising the area's socio-economic decline. As Chapter 2 outlined, whilst SSI took over the site in 2011 it was a short- rather than long-term fix since the plant contained outdated production facilities. Its closure was cast in debilitating and fatalistic terms, with Mary claiming it was: 'Terrible, absolutely dreadful'. As rumours started to circulate about its closure, a 'save our steel' banner was held high at Middlesbrough football matches 'but nothing happened' regarding the site's survival. Several respondents and their families also mentioned that they took part in protests in Steel Town. Several thousand people attended the protests, including the area's former Labour MPs. Emma is nearly 50 and has lived in Steel Town for a decade. Her husband was employed at the steelworks for 20 years and she said:

> There was loads of rallies about it all, we did all of them. Of course, it happened again [threat of closure], so we did more rallies, but nothing happened.

Although many participants suggested they intended to protest, they did not; rather, they voiced their discontent from the comforts of their own home. Perhaps this symbolises Robert Pfaller's notion of interpassivity,[29] whereby the respondents accrued the political act of protesting to other people to allow them to participate on their behalf. This made them feel as if they were involved and doing something useful, though they did not really do anything at all. These interpassive individuals failed to protest, in part, because they believed protesting would not solve anything. As we will encounter, this sense of powerlessness is a contributing factor to the shift to nationalistic sentiments in recent years as:

> Commitment to collective fatalism endures as meaningful change is branded impossible and the masses to be mobilised instead defer decision-making and action to others, or other 'things', in the hope that they will act on their behalf.[30]

Such conditions are contrary to capitalism's post-war epoch's relative collectiveness, mass trade unionism and class language offered by Archie like scabbing. Perhaps protests today form 'a kind of carnivalesque background noise'[31] to neoliberalism. Protests generate a cultural background of political vibrancy and engagement, providing a democratic means for people to voice their dissatisfaction with the inequalities of neoliberalism. However, nothing really changes. Neoliberalism continues as life's core background force and therefore working-class life continues to degenerate. Protests fail to significantly damage neoliberalism, particularly its core logic that people are subservient to the needs of the market. Such a context meant that the steelworks closed; thousands of people lost their jobs. Emma outlines how:

> If it didn't shut, he [Emma's husband] would still be there. It affected him badly, but he knew it was coming. He went to work one morning, then basically was told to just go home. So, we knew it was coming but it was just brutal the way they did it. They would think they would have given them time, but he went in and they said sorry—just go home. He was really proactive, he went to the job centre and into manic overdrive trying to get a job. Every day he spent hours and hours trying to get something. We were one of the *lucky ones*; we have a low mortgage and no debts. It brought a lot of stress.

Whilst Emma's husband wanted to remain at the place he had worked for 20 years, they no longer required his services and thus made him redundant. The stability brought by the industrial age had disintegrated and with that the area's final labour market that offered a perceived 'job for life'. The closure engendered significant mental ill health, compelling him to search for employment in a labour market where remunerative work is difficult to obtain. Although he provided his services for a relatively lengthy period, observe how SSI let him go quickly and did not forewarn him of its closure; the company was concerned with profitability and not the workforce's health and well-being. Emma's husband and the working class more broadly have historically obtained a sense of purpose and pride from work, but the steelwork's closure meant he witnessed a subjective shift from a satisfied steelworker to a dispirited job seeker. This meant he had to be in a prolonged state of readiness, eagerly waiting to apply for any form of work, no matter how degrading and poorly paid. Katie offered a similar story about her husband who also lost his job:

> There were lots of rumours, then a day before you were due in you got an email saying we can't pay you—we have gone under. That was strange. Three weeks before that they made him [husband] sign another contract for another company. So, there was obviously an idea that this was going to happen as they passed it onto another company and got half of the workforce off their load. He didn't get paid—full months wage gone. At the time, I was working down here at the nursing home, I was only bringing in £1200/£1300 a month. There is five of us in the family, and with tax credits they went on what you earned before, well we obviously earned a good wage then, so I got nothing. I think we got £5 a week, so we had to survive off £1200 a month when my rent was £600. That was for nearly a year, he was going for job after job, went on a couple of courses with that money the government put in for training, he did his offshore survival, but at the end of the day there was nothing for him to go into. He was applying every week and just getting knocked back, that was demoralising for him because I was the main wage earner, and he was used to working. He got *depressed, miserable*. It was pretty shit really.

Such sentiments elucidate how capital no longer possesses a degree of commitment to the workforce, demonstrating how this merely formed a *transient ideological mask* in the post-war era to ensure its survival.[32] With capital seeking to mitigate its economic losses from the steelworks, it passed employees onto numerous contractors. In effect, it failed to shoulder the responsibility for their livelihoods, since its raison d'être is the maximisation of profitability; it does not genuinely care about workers. Notwithstanding, historical studies have suggested that whilst industrial workers obtained a sense of social accomplishment, work was still viewed instrumentally, that is, to obtain a pay-packet, pay the bills and provide for one's family.[33] Perhaps, Katie's views provide further evidence of this, displaying how the loss of the steelworks meant they struggled to pay the bills and provide for their family. The individualisation of social relations under neoliberalism, embodied by the abandonment of full employment as a policy goal and the relatively recent erosion of welfare support, meant Emma's husband was engulfed in a subjective state of *frenzied inertia*—jobless for nearly 12 months. Mary outlines how the steelworks closure impacted on Steel Town:

> One of the blokes my husband has recently decorated for—he did alright cause he got a good pay out. But some people didn't, and obviously it is hard. If your grandad has worked there, and your grandad's grandad, *that tradition*.

Micky is 18 and works part time at a local social club. He had this to say:

> My uncle, my dad and my grandad all worked there. My grandad was quite high up, he helped my uncle and dad get a job there. They all grafted their arses off for how many years and then it just closed down, all them people lost their jobs. They earned a lot of money and then suddenly nothing, it is ridiculous really. They should have been able to help them more. It made my grandad very depressed as well, he had been there a lot of years. He is in a state of depression I don't think he'll ever come out of.

Corresponding biographies were once a core part of the industrial age and working-class life, with principally sons following in their father's and grandfather's footsteps and accruing industrial employment.[34] This meant working-class people could rely upon their social networks and local community to help find them work, which was thus sometimes obtained through a family member or friend vouching for them.[35] With the industrial ruination of Steel Town, Micky's ability to continue a tradition that started in Teesside with the discovery of iron ore in the 1850s has ceased to exist. This structural change engendered mental health problems, with Micky's grandad enduring a prolonged state of depression. Other people could not deal with this, though. Claire is 40 and has worked in a series of dead-end jobs like a barmaid, as well as several years on welfare. She claims:

> It's very bad for the area, a lot of people lost their jobs. A lass I went to school with, her husband killed himself over it. It was really bad, really sad. It was just before Christmas as well.

The nuanced sentiments evidenced earlier demonstrate how the diminished identity and associated sense of self-worth brought a 'loss of the feeling of existing'[36] amongst many ex-steelworkers. The link between an absence of social stability and mental ill health has also been documented by other scholars,[37] outlining how it is intimately connected to neoliberal political economy and ideology. However, many scholars have omitted this from their analysis of the steelworks closure and the resultant increase in mental health problems. Recent research,[38] for instance, documented how football could be utilised to improve some of the ex-steelworker's mental ill health; a central aim was to make them more 'resilient'. Resilience is a term that has recently seeped into social science from psychology and bacteriology, essentially attempting to prepare people to be psychologically robust enough to 'withstand the onslaught of neoliberalism'.[39] Therefore, it is no longer about the industrial age's collective resistance but individual adaptation. By focusing on the individual, rather than structural conditions, it could be argued that this depoliticises the steelworks closure, failing to transform individual discontent into politicised dissatisfaction.[40] In effect, resilience encourages ex-steelworkers to focus on themselves rather than pursue structural change; the core issue is your attitude and ability to cope, not neoliberalism. Perhaps this psychologises the deindustrialisation process and the associated social distress, offering what some identify as 'magical thinking' to solve structural problems.[41]

Whilst the Conservative government offered a £50 million package to remedy the social turmoil of the steelworks closure, consisting of various courses for retraining and skills enhancement, most participants viewed it as rather ineffective. Many respondents spoke about the difficulties involved in retraining, particularly given working at the steelworks involved a niche set of skills. The older ex-steelworkers appeared to find it the most difficult to retrain and find employment, as many had been jobless for over two/three years. Indeed, many had been proud steelworkers for many years and were compelled to visit the job centre to ascertain work, something everybody spoke of as degrading and humiliating. Emma suggested:

> They [ex-steelworkers] got all this retraining, but it wasn't great. We would go to job fairs and put your name down, but they would say 'oh we don't have any jobs at the moment'. It was weird. You would get a piece of paper saying you had done a course, but it didn't mean anything. Some lads went on course after course, like computers for beginners or intermediates, but then what? There was money for starting a business, but everybody was doing it. My husband felt like it was pointless.

Focusing on the former steelworkers' skills perhaps serves an ideological function, directing attention away from structural changes like industrial collapse, the ascent of low-paid and non-unionised employment and the emergence of a reserve army of labour. The core logic is for the jobless to adapt, compete and develop their curriculum vitae. However, remunerative work in Steel Town and the Teesside region is difficult to acquire, and the volume of the area's employment roles is not enough for its labour supply.[42] Many skilled graduates cannot find work in Teesside, meaning courses for beginners or intermediates are unlikely to possess much value in competitive, neoliberal labour markets.

Many of the respondents, particularly Emma and her husband, knew about this, but they engaged in the psychosocial act of fetishistic disavowal.

They possessed the knowledge that jobs were difficult to obtain and that IT courses for beginners held little value, but they suppressed this uncomfortable knowledge from the conscious to the unconscious, enabling Emma's husband to continue to try and find work and sustain a meaningless exchange with those at the job fairs. Such pointless form filling ensured that the former industrial employees were kept in an individualised state, perhaps diminishing their ability to come together to voice their discontent with industrial collapse. Others highlight how this form filling has increased under neoliberalism, particularly for the unemployed, which 'seems to have no function other than to fill the time that might otherwise be devoted to reflecting on the sources of the problem',[43] not least neoliberalism and its drive to accumulate profit no matter what the costs are in places like Steel Town. Moreover, form filling in the face of a dearth of remunerative jobs is bereft of social substance; all those involved realise that it is pointless and, therefore, not real. Jean Baudrillard outlined how life under neoliberalism is an imitation, deprived of meaning and purpose.[44] Job fairs benefited companies as they were able to promote their business and receive the contact details of despondent job seekers, enhancing their reserve army of labour to draw upon when required. Essentially, it served their economic interests rather than the interests of the former steelworkers. Therefore, it was a superficial exchange relation, engendered by neoliberalism and its values of competition, individualism and self-enhancement.

Observe how Emma also claimed many former steelworkers started their own company. Whilst this can generate a good wage and livelihood, it is principally emblematic of the structural changes in the labour market away from social security and various benefits towards no benefits and uncertainty.[45] How much work self-employed people possess fluctuates, eroding stability and security. Many respondents like Pete claimed it gives workers more freedom as they 'decide when they go to work'. Perhaps, this is partially true, though it also depends upon disposable income in Steel Town and the surrounding area. As the region has witnessed deep industrial retrenchment, many self-employed people encounter competition in overcrowded marketplaces. Many respondents, for instance, spoke of how they knew people that had started a dog walking company after losing their job at the steelworks. Ellie is 40 and has lived in Steel Town for most of her life. She said:

> My uncle had been there [steelworks] for years and lost his job. He was gutted. He has set up his own dog walking company, he looks after peoples' dogs and walks them. It gets him outdoors, but he was sad.

Working outdoors is perhaps a cleaner and safer working environment to industrialism's dangerousness and dirtiness, though he now works alone and has lost the steelwork's collectiveness and banter. The structural reconfigurations brought by neoliberalism means Steel Town's and Teesside's historical identity—formed around the industrial age—has now withered.

The diminishment of industrialism's lucid biographical trajectory engenders various problems, as Julia outlined:

> It was a really hard time. My husband worked there for twenty years, we thought it would never happen. Luckily, he found a job and often works at home, but when he travels he goes to Birmingham, Manchester, sometimes even Wales. I know families who lost their main wage earner. Some of them have eventually got decent jobs, but they are working away. One of them is now working for a local chemist delivering prescriptions. *Nothing good is on the doorstep anymore.*

As Chapter 1 outlined, Steel Town's steelworks possessed various structural problems and was threatened with closure in 2010, leading to its temporary mothballing. Despite this prolonged period of uncertainty and instability, most respondents suggested that they did not believe that it would close. Our current structural conditions are based upon an increasing uncertain and insecure future, though people often live with the belief that everything will stay the same. In essence, as the industrial age's relative security has subsided, people fetishistically disavow the future's debilitating structural conditions to cope with the present. The knowledge of an increasingly insecure labour market, the potential for the mass automation of the workforce and the impact of global warming are, indeed, too difficult to subjectively face.

As a reserve army of workers, competitive individualism and socio-economic precarity were normalised, many respondents expressed reflexive impotence.[46] They knew that the area had lost thousands of remunerative jobs. They knew that work in the locale was difficult to obtain. They knew that their children and grandchildren face difficulties obtaining what many of the older generation took for granted, not least stable work and a mortgage. But they felt as though they could not do anything about it; all they could do was cynically and individualistically adapt within a crumbling culture. Many former ex-steelworkers therefore moved elsewhere in the United Kingdom to find better work; others moved abroad. Although this might enhance one's chances of obtaining a better income, the fragmentation of the workforce dwindles time available to solidify relationships with loved ones and friends.[47]

Whilst the closure of the steelworks generated significant social distress in Steel Town and the surrounding area through joblessness, mental health problems and a subjective loss of self-worth, some people who were able to find work believed they were *lucky* to do so. Other former steelworkers were able to retire, having worked for several decades and thus possessing a sizable pension. However, many were not able to do this, as Matty explains:

> My brother [Little Dave] was in British Steel from when he was 16, so 32 years and he walked away with a thousand pound. He didn't get his

redundancy or owt, a thousand pound! That's all he knew from when he was a kid. He's a caretaker at a school now, he has just been given a bungalow. He is finding it alright, plodding away, nowhere near the money. He was a foreman and on over fifty grand a year, but you see a lot of people like that, the *devastation*.

Despite giving his services to the steelworks for over three decades, serving the requirements of capitalism's core logic—profit maximisation, capital accumulation and market expansion—the company did not shoulder the responsibility for his unexpected redundancy. Rather, they gave him a low fee that would struggle to pay his monthly bills. Observe how this is contrary to the sentiments expressed about the post-war epoch where there was a sense that ICI looked after their employees both at work and in retirement. Many companies in the neoliberal epoch often attempt to find ways to avoid taking any liability—financial or otherwise—to workers.[48] Such structural change demonstrates how capital has accumulated more and more power under neoliberalism, ensuring that the stability and longevity previously awarded to Steel Town's workers is now often absent.

Little Dave's working life has primarily been spent as a proud steelworker, but his employment is now defined by the absence of social purpose and fulfilment. It performs no function other than to pay the bills and survive. Tom, self-employed and in his 50s, outlines this background condition of structural uncertainty:

> Directly the closure didn't affect me, but indirectly through my work— window cleaning and other bits, it did badly. From my point of view work-wise, it hit me a lot financially. I was probably a spinoff of the five thousand people who were affected. I know about 20 families around here who used to be my customers, who aren't now. Equally, people who had lost their jobs and moved away. . . . I am not saying we are as bad as the villages of the mining era, where we will never get over it, but it was bad.

Evidently, industrial ruination under neoliberalism continues to have a detrimental impact upon Steel Town long after sites have closed.[49] The slow-motion deindustrialisation of Teesside, a process that was largely initiated by capital to restore its dwindling returns on investments, has generated significant social distress, impacting detrimentally on those caught up in the process. This historical restructuring has left a sizable wound in Teesside, illuminated by Sophie: 'It is like whenever you have been away, and you get onto the parkway and you saw all of the steelworks or ICI, *you knew you were home*'. Whilst the industrial age and its associated cultures have all but gone from post-industrial Teesside, many people continue to recall this era as it generates fond recollections of a perceived brighter epoch, characterised by socio-economic betterment, community spirit and opti-mism about the future. Therefore, it might be argued that:

> The deindustrialised zones of the north have a rather ghostly aspect. The postmodern political silence is punctuated by the faint echoes of a forgotten history; memories of cultures, codes, hopes and dreams that seek to intrude upon the present, demanding to be remembered, reawakened and manifested as politics. But with every passing year the ghosts of history fade and their resurrection becomes less likely.[50]

At the time of writing, Steel Town's steelworks continues to physically intrude upon the present since it has not yet been completely knocked down. Many participants suggested that I should look on Google Earth to see how huge the site is, whilst others believed it is 'disgraceful' that ex-steelworkers and their families have to witness it 'left to rot'. Micky encapsulated the site's uncertainty:

> Apparently, there might a be a job going taking it all down. They said they aren't looking for experience, they will train you up. So, I think it was bad that it closed. I would have liked to work there, but with it closing I might be able to get a job, demolish it and get rid of it. Appar-ently, it is getting totally demolished. I would take up the opportunity.

Beginning in the late 1970s, Micky's grandfather started a generational tradition and began working at the steelworks, aiding Teesside's industrial prowess as post-war capitalism ran into various structural crises. Both his uncle and dad continued this heritage into the 2000s.

However, the opportunity to continue this has diminished, with Micky now struggling to acquire work in an industrially emaciated local econ-omy, though the potential opportunity to demolish the steelworks may mean he has some role to play yet, potentially ending a process that began over 151 years ago.

Conclusion

Capitalism's structural shocks in the early twentieth century, not least the Great Depression and the Second World War, meant society was trans-formed and therefore living standards improved in a way that possessed no historical precedent. The industrial age awarded many industrial workers like Matty, Alice, Pete, Jimmy, Katie's and Emma's husbands and others, a stable and secure foothold in society. Evidence outlined here suggests industrial work was dirty and occasionally dangerous, though it was laced with feelings of coherency, pride, togetherness and community. Dur-ing capitalism's anomalist phase, Steel Town boomed in popularity with

Teesside's residents and day trippers. Industrial work existed in tandem with the coastline and the town's various cultural amenities. Although many believed the presence of stability and security were permanent features of life in Steel Town, capitalism's structural shocks in the mid-1970s meant it shifted into its neoliberal phase.

Industrial retrenchment across the Western world has been a central component of this shift, enabling capital to move their industrial plants overseas to maximise profitability. Whilst ICI dwindled throughout the 1990s, the relatively recent steelworks closure was recalled with a palpable feeling of loss and sadness. Many witnessed a rapid subjective transformation from a proud steelworker to frenzied inertia, frantically searching for employment in a labour market that had been transformed. Whilst some moved away, others who obtained work containing much poorer working conditions believed they were fortunate to do so. Some were unable to cope with this new reality, encountering various mental health problems. A future of permanent socio-economic stability never manifested in reality; it was a *psychic projection* partially engendered by capitalism's industrial age.

As the data revealed, deindustrialisation does not only impact upon those directly caught up in the process, but it also impacts upon the wider community, in part as the availability of remunerative jobs to the next generation is now at a premium. As Chapter 3 demonstrated, many scholars have pointed to the importance of employment conditions, particularly in post-industrial and left behind areas, as holding explanatory value in the recent shift to nationalism. As such, the next chapter explores the labour market's current configuration in Steel Town, particularly the absence of stability and security. The neoliberal restoration has increased the use of mechanisms in the workplace that maximise profitability, not least targets and mandatory overworking. Such conditions tend to generate fatalistic views of the future. These issues are outlined in the next chapter, providing further context for the dissatisfaction expressed about politicians, the European Union, immigrants and refugees.

Notes

1. Judt, T (2010).
2. Hoggart, R (1958).
3. Judt, T (2010), p. 41.
4. Raymen, T (2018); Raymen, T & Smith, O (2019).
5. Wilkinson, E (1939).
6. Telford, L & Lloyd, A (2020); Warren, J (2018).
7. Blackwell, T & Seabrook, J (1985), p. 121.
8. Telford, L & Lloyd, A (2020).
9. Winlow, S & Hall, S (2006) (2013).
10. Hall, S (2012); Horsley, M (2015).
11. Hall, S, Winlow, S & Ancrum, C (2008).
12. Warren, J (2018).

13. Beynon, H (1991), p. 68.
14. Ellis, A (2016), p. 26.
15. Goldthorpe, J, Lockwood, D, Bechhofer, F & Platt, J (1969).
16. Lloyd, A (2018a).
17. North, G (1975); Warren, J (2018).
18. Winlow, S, Hall, S & Treadwell, J (2017) (2019).
19. Tremlett, G (1987) *Clubmen: History of the Working-Men's Clubs and Institute Union.* London: Secker & Warburg.
20. Tremlett, G (1987).
21. Hoggart, R (1958).
22. Embery, P (2020).
23. Winlow, S & Hall, S (2006).
24. North, G (1975), p. 141.
25. Mitchell, W & Fazi, T (2017); Streeck, WG (2016) (2020).
26. Harvey, D (2005); Slobodian, Q (2018).
27. Shildrick, T, Macdonald, R, Webster, C & Garthwaite, K (2012).
28. Warren, J (2018).
29. Pfaller, R (2017) *Interpassivity: The Aesthetics of Delegated Enjoyment.* Edinburgh: Edinburgh University Press.
30. Kotze, J (2020) The commodification of abstinence. In Hall, S, Kuldova, T & Horsley, M (eds.), *Crime, Harm and Consumerism.* Abingdon: Routledge, pp. 54–69, p. 61.
31. Fisher, M (2009), p. 14.
32. Hall, S (2012); Lloyd, A (2013) (2018).
33. Goldthorpe, J, Lockwood, D, Bechhofer, F & Platt, J (1969).
34. Winlow, S (2001).
35. Willis, P (1978).
36. Stiegler, B (2019), p. 8.
37. Winlow, S & Hall, S (2006); Kotze, J (2019) (2020); Lloyd, A (2018a); Raymen, T (2018); Winlow, S, Hall, S & Treadwell, J (2017) (2019).
38. Dixon, K, Belshaw, D, Johnson, P & Flynn, D (2019) Using football cultures as a vehicle to improve mental health in men: The case of the Redcar and Cleveland boot room. *Sport in Society.* 22(7): 1258–1274.
39. Streeck, WG (2016), p. 40.
40. Fisher, M (2018).
41. Ehrenreich, B (2005) *Bait and Switch.* New York: Henry Holt & Company, p. 226.
42. Telford, L & Lloyd, A (2020).
43. Ehrenreich, B (2005), p. 219.
44. Baudrillard, J (1994) *Simulacra & Simulation.* Ann Arbor, MI: The University of Michigan.
45. Cederstrom, C & Fleming, P (2012) *Dead Man Working.* Winchester: Zero Books; Fisher, M (2018).
46. Fisher, M (2009), p. 21.
47. Winlow, S & Hall, S (2012).
48. Bloodworth, J (2019); Streeck, WG (2016).
49. Telford, L & Lloyd, A (2020).
50. Winlow, S, Hall, S & Treadwell, J (2019), p. 33.

Chapter 5

Absent futures

The chapters so far have outlined a constitutive context, documenting industrialism's stability, security and associated sense of social accomplishment. As the data revealed, post-war capitalism harnessed working-class identities that were tethered to social class, place and community. Shifting to neoliberalism, though, has fundamentally restructured the life worlds of working-class people in places like Steel Town. Over four decades of neoliberalism have transformed the local labour market, often making economic uncertainty, transience and insecurity default working conditions. The perceived job for life and longevity of industrial employment, evidenced in the previous chapter, now form ghosts from a previous history. Such a structural transformation has adhered to the economic requirements of the neoliberal restoration—namely, awarding capital more and more control over the workforce to ensure that they possess the power to adequately dismiss and discipline employees. As we will see, the abandonment of governmental commitments to full employment thus serves a function, enabling capital to maximise profitability despite the inevitable human costs.

Whilst the last chapter explored industrialism's working conditions and coherent life worlds, this chapter's purpose is to explicate current working conditions in Steel Town and the surrounding area. Neoliberalism has generated the absence of stability, security and longevity at work; people often regard their employment as a mere steppingstone to something better. However, alternative opportunities are often circumscribed in the area, meaning people are left to individualistically dwell on their working conditions, which often involve a precarious joblessness to insecure work cycle. As the regulatory straitjacket of post-war capitalism has been eroded, capital now possesses more control over the workforce, evidenced by the rise of the use of targets and an expectancy to overwork/engage in paid overtime. Such conditions generate mental health problems and fatalistic outlooks, engendering a sense that the future is absent.

Such a constitutive context provides further insight into the experiential realities of those that express nationalistic views in post-industrial Steel

DOI: 10.4324/9781003198666-6

Town. It is within this totalising experience that political sentiments are formed and grow. Therefore, this chapter's emphasis on absent futures lays the foundations for the discussion of nationalistic sentiments.

Absence of fixed biographies

I arrive at a deprived neighbourhood on the outskirts of Steel Town. The rain pours. In front of me lies a row of shops: bookmakers, pizza takeaway and a working men's social club. A sign stating 'function room to hire' is hanging off the wall. It looks like they need the business as not many people are around, though a few locals enter the bookies, and a police van has just driven up the road. It is 12:30 pm. This locale owes its existence to the now closed steelworks.

After waiting in my car for five minutes, a young lad with a perm haircut comes running around the corner. He is about five foot four, pale and has bags under his eyes. He recognises the description of my car and comes over, says, 'Hello', and asks if I can wait. He has been to the job centre and they need some identification documents to secure an interview for a one-year joinery apprenticeship. He tells me he is 'buzzing' and can't believe they have sorted it out so quickly, since usually it takes several weeks. I reply, 'Of course, no problem'.

Whilst I wait, a grey-haired man exits the social club. He has a small oxygen tank on his back and two cables running up to his nose—a possible indicator of heavy smoking and subsequent lung problems. A couple of local workers in dirty, high-viz clothing arrive and enter the local shop, presumably on their dinner break. Outside, the public bin is overflowing with litter. All around me lies social decay—closed steelworks, dilapidated buildings and a job centre that imposes individualised solutions to structural issues.

After waiting twenty minutes, Micky arrives, looking elated. He takes me to his flat. Micky informs me that the interview is arranged for next week, and he is relieved to finally have a chance at employment. He takes me into the kitchen, pulls out a small table, places his yellow lighter in the middle and we begin our conversation.

Micky had an unstable time at school and moved to different ones in Steel Town. Although he went to college, he hated it and left to undertake a two-year mechanic apprenticeship. The local firm, however, told him he was on constant trial and tried to extract free work from him. They prematurely dismissed Micky, weeks before Christmas, citing a lack of affordability. He was gutted but he said there was no point fighting it. In fact, he thinks he was lucky because he had a part-time job at a social club which meant he still had some income. He works there today, but his hours have been reduced to around ten a week.

This ethnographic description reveals deindustrialisation's debilitating social impact under neoliberalism, including Micky's inability to ascertain employment. Observe how his previous employers reproduced the core ideals of neoliberalism including the absence of duty, morals and ethics towards employees, casting Micky as a commodity to extract value from until they no longer required his services. Trials at work, often involving a period whereby the individual does not get paid, functions to generate anxiety, stress and worry; an ideological tool to individualise workers and thus stymie collective action.[1] Whilst he was treated poorly at work, Micky expressed no urge to join with other economically insecure young people and do something about these working conditions; rather, he displays feelings of fatalism and resignation.

Olly is 20 and works in a local store. His dad worked at the steelworks for a decade, but these opportunities have disintegrated for Olly, who now struggles to find a foothold in Steel Town's local economy:

> I don't think there are many opportunities here. They only have retail shops, McDonalds, no big companies anymore, you are limited. I did a bit of window cleaning before, but they wouldn't work around my college timetable, so I left. I work at a newsagent now a few days a week. I just want to get on, I might go back to window-cleaning as it is more money and better experience. In the shop, I am just behind a till. I suppose it is a job and gives me a bit of money.

Whilst neoliberal ideology emphasises freedom, opportunity and that hard work will eventually equate to success, there is a discrepancy between ideology and reality in places like Steel Town.[2] The *cold reality* is the absence of stability, fixity and an inability to forge a decent livelihood from employment. In this way, Olly's employment fails to offer industrialism's social satisfaction; rather, it is merely something he engages in to survive. Teesside's local economy is now characterised by lowly paid jobs that no longer contain industrial work's camaraderie or togetherness, whilst they often also fail to provide the apparent benefits of neoliberal ideology like freedom and flexibility.[3] Note how Olly suggests he desires socially secure employment, though he is swept up by broader forces like industrial retrenchment in the neoliberal era, shaping his experience of ascertaining work. More and more young people in these locales are struggling to find employment, as Micky outlines:

> You try and try. Your family push you to try and then you try and put all your effort in and get nothing back. It is hard. It is also hard because your family don't think you are doing anything, but they don't see the graft you are putting in. It is all online now, but I prefer to go and hand a CV in. You can't see anybody through a computer, can you? With me not having a full-time job, I am literally in this house all the time. I try and try to *fill up* my day, painting and decorating, when I can't fill up my day I feel really down.

Although Micky constantly tries to find work, his pursuits so far have been unsuccessful, engendering feelings of inadequacy and a lack of self-worth.

Whilst his family encourage him to apply for jobs, they cynically disbelieve Micky's efforts to find work and intensify his feelings of lack. Mary also highlights problems with Steel Town's local labour market:

> Before, there were more opportunities for people, even when my son left school, 22 years ago—not that long ago, there was still some good chances. But it isn't the same now. I would not want to be growing up now, there is so much pressure on kids.

Matty outlines similar sentiments:

> It is hard these days. They [young people] don't even get replies when they go for jobs. We used to get a letter saying 'sorry' if we haven't got the job, now they [employers] don't even get back in touch.

Shifting to neoliberalism has meant successive governments have maintained Thatcher's policy change of ditching with commitments to full employment. Some have argued that this restructuring was purposeful, with Alan Budd, Thatcher's former economic advisor, admitting that the emergence of a reserve army of labour could help capital regain control over the workforce after their power was somewhat constrained in the post-war era.[4] Harvey suggests that governments in the United States and United Kingdom, particularly the Thatcherites, were inspired by the Powell (1971) memorandum, which argued that the balance of power had shifted too far towards industrial workers and that abandoning full employment would divide employees and lessen their ability to undermine capital's disciplinary mechanisms. What this has also eroded is the post-war epoch's 'ethico-cultural strait-jacket',[5] with capital now possessing the ability to pick and choose its workers. Before the COVID-19 pandemic hit the United Kingdom, many politicians celebrated record low unemployment rates. However, over a million people without jobs in the United Kingdom is considered normal and generally accepted by the political class under neoliberalism.

Throughout capitalism's longue durée, the recognition of the workforce has been important to ensuring compliance at work, particularly in the post-war period, since capital required a large labour force to fuel capital accumulation and profit maximisation. This meant many workers at ICI and the steelworks like Matty felt valued, appreciated and cared for. However, the system no longer requires a workforce in the numbers it once did to function; it is far more dependent upon exploiting workers in the Global South. Therefore, whilst many employees can now be exploited with impunity, those that do not have jobs are often faced with the absence of recognition; observe how Matty notes that some employers do not respond to job seekers. This structural change is felt most acutely in locales constructed in the industrial age, as Katie notes:

> My son hates it [Steel Town], he wants to get out. He said it's awful. There is *no future*, there's nothing. He is very money orientated, he wants to have a nice house and a nice car, and he thinks staying here won't get him that, so he has to go elsewhere. He hates it—sometimes he sits there and says why do we have to live here? There is absolutely nothing here for them [young people], nothing at all. You would either go to the steelworks or ICI and that has gone now. There is nothing. When you can't get a job, it filters down to your children, they don't have nothing to look forward to.

The industrial age's social stability and economic security, evidenced in the previous chapter, is now absent from Steel Town's local labour market. Whilst many jobless individuals in the post-war era may have joined together to protest against localised unemployment, neoliberalism encourages people to pursue individualised solutions to structural problems, to move elsewhere and pursue the 'good life' beyond the stultifying constraints of contemporary working-class culture.[6] Forget togetherness; all that matters is individual adaptation. As a result, Katie's son desires to move elsewhere and obtain the consumer symbols associated with the 'good life'. Evidently, there has been a subjective change when compared to the sentiments in Chapter 4, there is a lack of attachment to one's localised class position, community and collective action; instead, neoliberalism's individuals tend to view reciprocal relations, obligation and togetherness as a barrier to self-enhancement.[7] However, there is a discrepancy between ideology and reality, since moving elsewhere occasionally requires disposable income, accommodation and employment in advance, particularly for those in economically uncertain situations like Katie's son. Katie therefore describes how many people encounter a structural feeling of inertia:

> There is nothing like it [industrial work] now. You can go work in a pizza shop on a weekend or in retail, there is nothing. Even the apprenticeships aren't great. There is nothing, hairdressing—crap. Joinery there is some of that, but there is nothing industrialised anymore, things like that.

Sentiments outlined demonstrate the debilitating impact of the shift from an industrialised to service economy, often comprised of low-paid jobs in retail and call centres.[8] This historical change has not benefited people like Katie's son, who struggle to ascertain work and forge a stable livelihood. Many of the apprenticeships in these post-industrial locales are short term, and the chances of being offered a permanent post at the end of one's initial training and skills enhancement are slim. Again, the structural opportunities provided to some of the older respondents in the previous chapter, such as five-year apprenticeships at ICI which included extensive training and a job guarantee,[9] are now absent in Steel Town.

Whilst half of school leavers acquired an apprenticeship in the 1990s, structural changes have dwindled this once valuable employment trajectory. The massification of further and higher education has been a core component of neoliberalism, particularly from 1997 onwards with New Labour, whereby Tony Blair admitted that one of their core areas of focus was 'education, education, education'.[10] However, many participants spoke about the pressures placed upon young people now and the requirement to obtain relatively good educational qualifications, particularly in comparison to the post-war age. Ellie, for example, said: 'If you haven't got six A-levels and four degrees, you aren't worthy'. Jess is 40 and has lived in Steel Town for over two decades. She worked in admin at ICI but is now a teaching assistant. She claimed:

> Our son doesn't know what he wants to do, he has just turned 16 after leaving school. He is at college studying music, but he said even after I get out of college with this qualification I don't know what I want to do because the music industry is so hard to get into, so competitive, what am I going to do with it? The upside is it's easier to go back to college and retrain for something—at least you can pretty much get on a college course.

Micky agrees:

> I feel as though there isn't much around. They drill your head that you need to get an education, decide what you want to do, but you come out of college and there is no work for you to be able to put them skills into trades. It is difficult really. There seems to be apprenticeships advertised, but they never get back to you. I must have applied for thousands of jobs and apprenticeships, and I hardly get a response back. People are pushing young people to get jobs earlier on in life, but there isn't anything for us to go onto. I don't think education really matters; it is about how hard you work rather than how smart you are.

Such sentiments shed light on core characteristics of Steel Town's labour market: the absence of stability, security and certainty. Unlike the previous chapter, where many of the older participants claimed it was once relatively easy to ascertain work, the ability to accrue remunerative employment after leaving school is rather difficult, meaning young people often drift onto college courses. This has led some theorists to suggest that today's youth are the 'blank generation'.[11] Whilst they often find it difficult to acquire meaningful employment, they have also been cut adrift from history's core anchoring points like social class and community, whilst many feel hopeless and thereby embrace consumerism to mitigate their sense of lack.[12]

Although Micky has completed a college course, been dismissed from a mechanical apprenticeship and endured a reduction in his part-time hours at the social club, he espouses neoliberal values of opportunity and hard work by suggesting one's work ethic is the key to shaping lives. As some scholars remark, the logic of this notion is to not attempt to collectively resist unequal social conditions; rather, be positive and focus on the self.[13] Essentially, this awards neoliberalism the structural space required to secure its hegemon,[14] free from stringent critique and the working class's previous collective demands for the redistribution of wealth.

Returning to education, the futility of completing some higher education courses in terms of attaining remunerative work was also highlighted by many participants. Kev is nearly 50 and has always lived in Steel Town. His brother was made redundant at the steelworks, whilst Kev owns an independent clothes store but is 'six or seven grand in debt'. He said:

> I know plenty of kids who have gone to uni [university] and done like a media studies degree and there is nowt for them when they get out. So, they end up doing the job they could have done when they left school. It might not be the job you want but at least it is some money in your pocket you know what I mean? That's what life revolves around, cash in ya pocket.

Whilst neoliberalism tends to celebrate education's expansion as a new freedom that was only available to a minority in the post-war era, it potentially masks what would otherwise be mass unemployment.[15] Emphasising the importance of education also covers up economic uncertainty, social insecurity and the absence of stability in post-industrial Steel Town. As the supply of graduate jobs does not meet the demand, employers are able to demand qualifications that were previously not required. Remember the sentiments in Chapter 4, industrial employees did not require a good educational portfolio to attain a relatively well-paid job at ICI or the steelworks. At the same time, Kev also elucidates how many graduates, despite being nearly £40,000 in debt, are expected to be satisfied with acquiring work that does not utilise the skills developed during their university degree.

Perhaps, there is a tension here between neoliberalism's emphasis on meritocracy, self-enhancement and immediate gratification, often fuelled by credit cards and loans,[16] and what Mark Fisher branded as 'a deflation of expectations'.[17] Living in an era defined by deindustrialisation, intense competition in the labour market and the extension of transitions into employment and owning a home,[18] most young people will live a life that is relatively socio-economically poorer than their grandparents and parents. However, they are expected to be okay with these conditions. Olly elucidated the *deflation of expectations*: 'I think there is loads of voluntary work, that is a good thing because you can learn how to talk to people and get experience'. Whilst volunteering is sometimes important to university graduate's prospects of obtaining work, it is free labour masked as a chance to enhance the self and gain an advantage over other precarious young people.

What the sentiments above embody is an extrapolation of the science fiction movie trilogy The Hunger Games.[19] Whilst most young people are not trying to kill each other to survive—although lethal knife crime involving young people in some post-industrial areas has increased in recent years[20]—the movie contains similarities to life under neoliberalism. Essentially, many young people are demoralised and forced to individualistically adapt to unjust structural conditions. Young people tend to view one another as an enemy to eclipse rather than somebody to join with and pursue structural change. Whilst those in the Hunger Games have an opportunity to escape their social class and attain wealth, people occupying post-industrial zones like Steel Town often encounter an unemployment to insecure employment cycle, intensifying the locale's decline. As Chapter 3 documented, today's working conditions particularly in post-industrial areas have been identified as a contributory factor towards English nationalism. It is to this that we now turn.

Insecure work to joblessness

The absence of socio-economic stability, certainty and an identity from employment in post-industrial areas has been outlined by many researchers.[21] Many of these employment pathways are now defined by instability and uncertainty, with workers staying at a company for a relatively short period of time before moving elsewhere. Both employers and employees under neoliberalism appear to possess little obligation or commitment to one another. For those at the lower ends of the social structure, working life appears to be defined by periods of insecure work and joblessness. Mia is 20 and has lived in Steel Town since birth. She previously worked part-time at a café, dropped out of a criminology degree at the local university and now works at Sure Start. Whilst her dad also works there, he was temporarily made unemployed during an internal restructuring phase, though he managed to secure a different role. She outlines how this was:

> Awful, it was awful. His confidence was gone, he was depressed I think. Crying all the time, but he had to come to work and keep going. That was for about three weeks, he lost his job when the interviews were starting, thankfully, it was a shock. It was through matrix,

done on the scales, he had been there for 14 years, so he didn't think he would lose it.

Chapter 4 outlined how many ex-steelworkers struggled to cope with unemployment, and Mia's father also struggled to adapt. This amounted to what Stiegler referred to as the 'the loss of the feeling of existing',[22] whereby depressed people's social world is deprived of purpose and meaning. Indeed, the absence of the post-war epoch's labour protections meant that he was easily dispensed with. Alice highlights this absence of security:

> When I was younger, it was so rare that somebody was made redundant, it was noteworthy or a topic of conversation—oh my god have they been made redundant, what are they going to do? It was a massive thing, but now it is like alright, again? It is every day.

Alice identifies the prevalence of unemployment in Steel Town and the surrounding locales under neoliberalism; it no longer surprises her and has therefore become naturalised. Such a negative cultural backdrop meant many of the respondents were *passive observers*, unable to avert the accumulation of social debris. Whilst structural conditions continued to worsen, reflexive impotence engenders a subjective non-belief in the possibility of positive change; all they can do is adapt. Indeed, Ellie was a teaching assistant on a temporary contract, and she was released of her duties thereafter. Whilst she was jobless for several months, she eventually found another temporary (three years) position working with special educational needs children. She further outlines the absence of stability:

> My sister works in Tesco. She has just been told her job is on the line, she has been there ages, and works in stock control. Tesco have brought in this technology so people who work in that area are no longer needed. She has young children, doesn't drive, her partner works on shifts, so she can only do 5am-10am or 5am-11am. Because she isn't flexible they won't keep her on or move her elsewhere. What they want is people who are available 5am-11pm. If you can't do them hours, they don't want you. Because of computers and stuff, they have taken over the jobs they do, there is no need for her anymore. It is not a definite, but that is how it is looking. I think that is the scary thing about life now, *you never know when your job is at risk*.

Advancements in technology throughout capitalism have been utilised to downsize the labour force, degrade working conditions and maximise profitability.[23] The speed of technological change over the last two decades, though, is historically unprecedented, with many jobs being *technologically displaced*.[24] Whilst the agricultural industry has shed many jobs, employment in both banking and IT have also been heavily hit. In the near future, driverless cars and the mass automation of fast-food and call centres are a possibility; some customer service functions are entirely automated already through a combination of telephonic menus and voice recognition software. By 2035, 35% of jobs in the United Kingdom may be technologically displaced.[25] However, this possesses the potential to undermine the capitalist system, not least through mass unemployment and the intensification of widespread political dissatisfaction. As the previous chapters have documented, throughout its history capitalism has used its structural crises to shift to another epoch of growth and expansion. A state funded job guarantee could be an important governmental tool in the future, and as Chapter 7 will document, it can provide a sense of social accomplishment and satisfaction that is sorely needed in places like Steel Town.

It is important to note that the broader shift towards intensified exploitation and insecurity in workplaces is not a new phenomenon. Instead, it is a return to capitalism's constitution in the Victorian age and embodies its dehumanised drive to maximise profitability despite the inevitable human costs in places like Steel Town.[26] As capitalism's regulatory constraints are removed, such as the labour protections that formed part of the class compromise in the post-war era, it *rebounds* to its fundamental essence. Thomas Piketty's point holds weight here, that is, without a regulatory straitjacket that restricts capitalism and the profit motive's tendency to generate social and economic inequalities, social distress tends to intensify.[27]

Nevertheless, as many of neoliberalism's workers often encounter bouts of insecure jobs to joblessness, they often view employment in instrumental terms; a steppingstone to something better in the near future. Roger, who we met in Chapter 4, claims:

> My daughter had a job in a café. The café had 16 different young people employed, they all kept leaving. The woman wasn't a very nice person to work for—other people said it was awful. But it was another experience for her ya know, like to sell herself.

Rob is 18. He is studying art at college and works part-time at McDonalds. He said:

> When I first looked for a part time job at 16, it was hard. I put a lot of CVs out, but it is the saying 'who you know' that worked for me because my mum's friend worked there and put a good word in. That's how I got the job. I clean the bins, mop the floors, it is hard labour. It is hard. We have to mop the toilets. But it is only part-time, gets money in my pocket and looks good on my CV.

Todd McGowan argued that capitalism's power partially hinges upon how it infiltrates the citizenry's psyche, hopes and dreams with *the promise*.[28] Capitalist ideology suggests that if the employed and jobless continue to work hard and strive for socio-economic betterment, then the dynamism and innovation of capitalism will deliver structural improvement in the future. Essentially, then, people are energised by their inability to obtain their objects of desire; for Roger's Daughter and Rob, this includes stable and secure employment. Neoliberal capitalist ideology encourages them to be determined and work hard, even if that involves enduring low-paid and degrading work, to achieve success in the future. Whilst this jolts them into action, industrial retrenchment and the increasing precarity of work means *the promise* eludes many in Steel Town. This is made worse by other conditions at work including targets and overwork. As some scholars have highlighted, it is 'critical to investigate the contextual factors that lead citizens to adopt anti-immigration and Eurosceptic attitudes',[29] amongst other contributory issues. It is in this spirit that we now turn to other working conditions.

Targets and overwork

As neoliberal ideology including marketisation, individualism, competition and maximising profit has further seeped into the social structure, the use of performance measurements like targets has intensified.[30] This is particularly the case since the 2008 global financial crash and the advent of the austerity age, whereby the solution to problems generated by capitalist markets was to impose more market instruments. As displayed, neoliberalism's restorative component has been further enhanced by austerity, since many public assets have been privatised. This includes many agencies within the criminal justice system, national health service and education. In effect, these organisations have been restructured around neoliberal values including productivity, efficiency and performance management.[31] Sophie is 45 and works part time as a primary school teacher, living in one of the most comfortable socio-economic conditions out of the research sample. Whilst she obtains a reasonable wage, she suggests her job is defined by:

> The recording of the assessments, planning, conversations you have with parents have to be recorded, the paperwork and admin. More *targets* to meet.

Trev is 52. He has lived in Steel Town for over 20 years and works as a postman:

> There is a lot more targets and pressure from managers now. We are always short of staff, but they won't take anybody on. It is bad. About

ten of us are retiring soon, all that experience. If they don't take any young people on, how will they get the knowledge? They need to employ people in Steel Town; jobs here are not many. I've got two lads—one is at college and one who is 12. I worry about what they are going to do, how are they going to get a job?

Targets imposed by managers potentially serve to individualise and fragment the workforce. Under neoliberalism workers become somebody to compete against and outdo, rather than join with in collective unity and voice their dissatisfaction at degrading working conditions. Some have argued that by keeping employees—like Sophie and Trev—in an individualised state of perpetual business, targets generate an absence of stability and security.[32] This intensification of absent certainty at work potentially means targets further stagnate wages, given the logic is employees must meet targets to be awarded an increase in pay. However, meeting targets can sometimes be out of the workforce's control, as Claire, a former retail employee, highlights: 'When I worked there [a jewellery store] it was dead, we didn't hit any targets or out like that. Nobody was coming in'.

The absence of commitment and duty to workers means many are expected to passively accept an increase in their workload. Notice how Trev suggests this drive to maximise profitability impacts detrimentally on employees and those in the local area, since no consideration is awarded to their socio-economic needs. Instead, cold calculations are made about how to maximise profit and thereby satisfy shareholders rather than the workforce. Whilst many older postal workers are due to retire soon, capital's drive to maximise profit and not employ more permanent staff postpones problems, chiefly the lack of transmission of knowledge and skills to future employees. This internal contradiction, though, generates consequences for the workforce. Chloe illuminates how:

> They [managers] just expect you to do more. Like today I was supposed to finish at three, but I didn't finish until half past three because they just push more and more on you. When you say I can't get this done then they say well why not, why not? So, you feel like you have to rush round to get it done, but why should I? Why should I, like? I've got things to do after work. I have got a life; I've got my grandson to see. I don't like the way they just push more and more on you, all the packets, they want every minute out of you basically, and they aren't prepared to give anything back for it. I think most jobs are like that these days, aren't they?

The manager's mindset has been reshaped by neoliberal ideology; the core focus is now on maximising surplus value and not the worker's interests and health and well-being. This generates an organisational expectancy, however, to overwork, as Emma outlines: 'Their [teachers] workload is astronomical—you couldn't get me to be a teacher if you paid me a million pounds'. Whilst some might cast such stress generated by targets and overwork as immoral and unethical, capitalism's internal drive to accumulate profit and thereby magnify labour productivity makes the workforce distress in Steel Town outlined previously an inevitability under neoliberalism.[33]

The negative ideology of capitalist realism has also been internalised by Chloe. Whilst industrial workers possessed sizable bargaining power in the post-war era, often using strike action to hold exploitative employers to account, such collective resistance has declined under neoliberalism.[34] Although Chloe expresses her concern about degrading working conditions that are a source of stress and worry, she also believes she is powerless in doing anything about them; they are just how working conditions are these days. Therefore, for Chloe and others, the only realistic response is to cynically adapt in the workplace to the absence of social and economic stability, in part because collective action is now believed to be idealistic and more of a threat to one's material conditions than the degrading conditions participants like Chloe now work under. As a physical manifestation of capitalist realism, Fisher suggests that managers under neoliberalism operate to solidify workers' non-belief in positive change.[35] Kev believes that:

> Line managers are jumped up little pricks who haven't got a clue what they're talking about, but you have to be passive not aggressive like they are to you. Play them at their own game. They will try to goad a reaction out of you, I can mention a couple of managers who are masters at it, you just have to be clever at it and see what they're doing and play them at their own game. There is nothing more annoying for a manager than somebody who is cleverer than them, they hate it.

Whilst many were compelled to overwork, in part because of neoliberalism's stagnation of wages, many respondents also worked paid overtime to make ends meet. At busy periods like Christmas, the requirement to do overtime is intensified for both the worker who needs the additional money and the employer as demand on their service increases. Indeed, we met Matty in the last chapter. He was previously employed at ICI and then the steelworks, though he now works part time delivering the post on Teesside for around £1,100 a month. He said:

> You're just a number, you're only as good as your last overtime, seriously. I hate to say it, it's awful, but it's true. Just a bum on a seat. I used to do a lot of overtime until last year. I used to bail them out,

the latest I stayed out delivering one time was half ten at night, nine o clock mostly. Most people would say I'm stupid for doing that, but I like helping people, you know what I mean? That's just me, the way I've been brought up. They [managers] take the piss out of us. I like to do the job properly, but last year they put me in the van doing deliveries over Christmas for several weeks on rounds that I didn't know, and it was getting later and later with the dark nights. The manager didn't care so I rang him up and said you can stick this up your arse now because I don't know the walk, take me off this round and put me back onto my normal shift, and I haven't done any overtime since.

Whilst Matty displays elements of the post-war epoch's value system including mutuality and reciprocity, neoliberalism's emphasis on profitability and individualism means the relationship with his manager is negative; the latter knows somebody else will work overtime if Matty refuses. Observe the distinction in the sentiments above and in Chapter 4—as capitalism's regulatory sleeve that constrained profit has been removed it means employing more staff is now illogical and irrational since it would intensify labour costs. Considering the speeding up of the production process, some have suggested that life under neoliberalism is non-stop, 24/7.[36] With capital demanding more and more time from employees, the divide between work and one's private life has now disintegrated. The absence of stability and security means time spent away from work becomes a time where people feel as though they should be working. This is the context in which people are sleeping less and less. Despite laissez-faire capitalism's inequities like widespread unemployment and impoverishment, people slept for around ten hours. But under neoliberalism, it is between six and seven hours. The erosion of sleep and a subjective state of *frenzied inertia* at work leads Mark Fisher to suggest that:

> While 20th-century experimental culture was seized by a recombinatorial delirium, which made it feel as if newness was infinitely available, the 21st century is oppressed by a crushing sense of finitude and exhaustion. It doesn't feel like the future. Or, alternatively, it doesn't feel as if the 21st century has started. We remain trapped.[37]

This sense of entrapment was illuminated by Tom who suggested that: 'A lot of people are too busy with work', meaning they are unable to spend an adequate amount of time engaging in family and friendship activities. At the same time, Ellie claimed her employment is: 'Highly stressful. I had four and a half years where I didn't have a day off. It was only when I had a terrible flu and I couldn't get out of bed that I did'. Although most of the research respondents voiced their concerns with today's working conditions many do not collectively protest but instead occasionally protect the self. Matty notes how:

> I had a big dispute last year. I had plates in my legs and it took me two years to get it recognised as a work's accident cause the previous managers said to me it isn't a work accident—you're responsible for your own actions. I was out delivering until late at night, and I had to fight it and fight it and I won not so long ago. I have two plates now. The union man was really good and helped me. When I went around work to get support for my case, I got five signatures out of fifty staff, that's all, five people that were willing to help and say that they recognise I did what I did—shocking. You see, nobody helps, they couldn't be bothered to write something, they couldn't be arsed to do it, you know what I mean? I had no back up really. . . . Like I said, you're just a number mate, you aren't a human being, they don't have feelings, it is just do this, do that.

Observe how these working conditions and thus relationships amongst colleagues are contrary to the reciprocal and mutual relationships often harnessed at ICI and the steelworks, though being a member of a trade union enabled Matty to emerge victorious from his workplace dispute and obtain recognition for his injuries. Nonetheless, whilst relative collectiveness was forged in industrialised labour markets in places like Steel Town under post-war capitalism, Bernard Stiegler claims that neoliberalism has brought the 'liquidation of the I as well of the we'.[38] Scouring the cultural debris of industrial retrenchment under neoliberalism, Steel Town's workers like Micky, Olly, Matty, Ellie and Chloe, amongst many others, no longer derive a collectivised identity from their employment. In effect, they are left to deal with inequitable workplace conditions on their own.

Conclusion

Capitalism's historical shift from post-war capitalism's industrial era to neoliberalism was not perceived by Olly, Mary, Micky, Katie's and Jess's son and others as heralding the arrival of more freedom and flexibility within the labour market. Instead, most of their employment trajectories were characterised by the absence of stability, security and a positive future. Neoliberalism, though, encouraged individuals to move away from Steel Town and pursue employment elsewhere, rather than collectively resist unjust structural conditions. Lengthy and stable apprenticeships afforded by the industrial age that once awarded many school leavers in Steel Town a route towards something better were absent. Rather, many endured underemployment and joblessness; some went onto university though it often failed to subsequently generate a remunerative job. Industrialism's job for life and thus longevity were ghosts from a distant history; a shadow of social insecurity and economic uncertainty now hovered over Steel Town and its local residents' livelihoods. Conditions at work including targets and a mandatory hard work ethic further degraded their working lives, often generating mental ill health and palpable stress.

The first two data chapters shed empirical light on the 'long and painful history of deindustrialisation'[39] under neoliberalism in Steel Town and Teesside; the relatively well-paid industrial jobs have been replaced by insecure and uncertain employment. This has fundamentally restructured material conditions in Steel Town. Within this context, it is perhaps not surprising that many of Steel Town's residents have begun to voice their discontent with politics, demanding structural change. How do the respondents feel about liberal politicians, the European Union, immigrants and the idea of a second referendum on EU membership when they have witnessed nothing but decline under neoliberalism? And what can the political dissatisfaction that has erupted in recent years in locales across the fallen Red Wall like Steel Town tell us about the future?

Notes

1. Ehrenreich, B (2005) (2009).
2. Telford, L & Lloyd, A (2020).
3. Kotze, J (2019); Lloyd, A (2013) (2018); Warren, J (2018).
4. Harvey, D (2005).
5. Lloyd, A (2018a), p. 158.
6. Raymen, T (2018); Whitehead, P (2018).
7. Horsley, M & Lloyd, A (2020); Winlow, S & Hall, S (2013).
8. Lloyd, A (2018b) Efficiency, productivity and targets: The gap between ideology and reality in the call centre. *Critical Sociology*. 46(1): 83–96; Lloyd, A (2019) Harm at work: Bullying and special liberty in the retail sector. *Critical Criminology*. 28(0): 669–683.
9. Telford, L & Lloyd, A (2020).
10. Levitas, R (2005).
11. Stiegler, B (2019), p. 19.
12. Fisher, M (2009) (2018); Raymen, T (2018).
13. Kotze, J (2019) (2020); Streeck, WG (2016).
14. Hall, S (2012).
15. Standing, G (2011); Streeck WG (2016).
16. Horsley, M (2015); Horsley, M & Lloyd, A (2020).
17. Fisher, M (2014) *Ghosts of My Life: Writings on Depression, Hauntology and Lost Futures*. London: Zero Books.
18. MacDonald, R, Shildrick, T & Furlong, A (2020).
19. Fisher, M (2018).
20. Ellis, A (2019) A de-civilizing reversal or system normal? Rising lethal violence in post-recession austerity United Kingdom. *The British Journal of Criminology*. 59(4): 862–878.
21. Bloodworth, J (2019); Lloyd, A (2013); Southwood, I (2011) *Non-Stop Inertia*. London: Zero Books.
22. Stiegler, B (2019), p. 8.

23. Wood, E (2017).
24. Streeck, WG (2016).
25. Ford, M (2015).
26. Winlow, S & Hall, S (2013).
27. Piketty, T (2020) *Capital and Ideology*. Cambridge: Harvard University Press.
28. McGowan, T (2016) *Capitalism and Desire: The Psychic Cost of Free Markets*. New York: Columbia University Press.
29. Carreras, M, Carreras, Y & Bowler, S (2019) Long-term economic distress, cultural backlash, and support for Brexit. *Comparative Political Studies*. 52(9): 1396–1424, p. 1398.
30. Whitehead, P (2018).
31. Mendoza, K (2015).
32. Southwood, I (2011).
33. Harvey, D (2005); Mitchell, W & Fazi, T (2017).
34. Harvey, D (2005); Lloyd, A (2019).
35. Fisher, M (2018).
36. Crary, J (2015); Bushell, M (2021).
37. Fisher, M (2014), p. 8.
38. Stiegler, B (2019), p. 20.
39. Harvey, D (2014).

Chapter 6

Nationalism

The previous two data chapters addressed the formative context for the nationalistic perspectives outlined in this chapter. To begin with, capitalism's anomalist era in its longue durée was explicated, particularly the industrial age's relative stability and security. As remunerative industrial employment and a busy seaside resort characterised Steel Town, it was perceived to be expanding socially, culturally and economically. A modicum of community spirit pervaded the area, as well as a sense of obligation and reciprocity. Perhaps, this was a deviation in capitalism's history; it was not the embodiment of the system's normal functioning but a transient period to mute support for alternative ideologies that began to grow in the shadow of the early twentieth century. Capitalist crises in the 1970s, though, enabled a system geared around the cold calculations of augmenting profitability to ascend once again, with neoliberal political economy and ideology eventually becoming normalised. Emblematic of this in Steel Town was the closure of the local steelworks, identified as the end of the industrial age's stability and continuity.

Shifting to neoliberalism meant much of Steel Town's labour market was now characterised by uncertainty and instability. Although neoliberal ideology claimed people were now free to be more mobile and climb the social structure, there was a discrepancy between ideology and reality, not least the presence of unemployment, underemployment, a lack of stable apprenticeships and periods of work to joblessness. The proliferation of targets and overwork intensified a sense that employment conditions favoured employers at the expense of workers. As scholars contend, context is of fundamental importance in understanding how people think and feel about the social world.[1] Therefore, the final data chapter explicates the nationalistic sentiments engendered by Steel Town's constitutive context, including dissatisfaction with New Labour, a desire to Leave the EU, discontent with immigration, political correctness and a second referendum, culminating in the collapse of the Red Wall in December 2019. Firstly, it turns to what some respondents regarded as the Labour Party's abandonment of working-class people in places like Steel Town, further elucidating how history continues to shape the present.

DOI: 10.4324/9781003198666-7

The Labour Party and politicians

All participants suggested that politicians were shielded from the working class's everyday realities. Although they claimed politicians promised the world and often espoused a desire to protect their interests, their pledges were dispensed with once they were elected. Symbolising their sentiments of politicians was an absence of belief, faith and trust. Most of the participants had historically voted for the Labour Party. In recent years, though, they had begun to express their disgust towards the Party and its inability to defend their social, cultural and economic interests. Despite Steel Town and the broader Teesside region possessing a Labour MP often since the post-war era, deindustrialisation and the ascent of poor employment continued. No matter who was elected, the area continued to degenerate. For some, this discontent started with New Labour, as Pete highlights:

> I looked to the Liberals once Tony Blair came into power. He was an absolute hypocrite, you could just see through him, absolutely abhorrent. To stand there and take us to war on lies, we have been in more wars than enough due to lies. The lies that still get told about Iraq, Afghanistan, nothing gets done about it.

Emma agrees:

> Blair, I mean, he sided with the American President, Bush. He took us to war. Politicians are just out for themselves, ready for their next career move. Are they really for the working person? I have lost all faith in them. I have now moved to the Conservatives, but I don't think they are any good.

As is well known, hundreds of thousands of people died during the Iraq war, which has left sizable parts of Iraq beholden by ethnic conflict, war, infrastructural destruction and the rise of ISIS. Whilst Tony Blair has been branded as a war criminal by many members of the public, he has generally been protected from the law and public accountability. As mentioned, although Blair was an articulate speaker, he ushered in a new political era characterised by spin, deceit and often baseless rhetoric about not stopping the forces of globalisation. Whilst Pete and Emma identify this disingenuousness as shifting them away from the party, such a shift is not representative of a fidelity to the Liberal Democrat's or Conservative Party's core ideals; rather, it is brought by a sense of political abandonment. Whilst some have suggested that Blair is recalled fondly in post-industrial areas,[2] participants in this study believed he tarnished the party, in part through the Iraq War. Jimmy (retired) claims:

> I didn't like Tony Blair. The Iraq war was illegal, lots of people killed for nothing and it didn't do any good. They are still fighting in the

> Middle East, it is worst now. He changed the party to New Labour. I can remember Harold Wilson and Callaghan, they were proper Labour. Their values were different.

Although James Callaghan solidified the end of the post-war settlement by suggesting it could not go on indefinitely, turning to the IMF for a financial loan, the era of New Labour was regarded as embodying a decisive break with the party's history. Blair shed the party's skin by shifting it away from governmental commitments to full employment, collective action and the public ownership of core services. Blair believed that capitalism's free markets alongside a welfare safety net would ameliorate the worst effects of social inequality, whilst ensuring economic growth in a social world he deemed as too mobile and meritocratic for the post-war era's class antagonisms to matter anymore.[3] He believed that social inequalities should be addressed through policy measures, rather than identifying neoliberal ideology and political economy as the core issues at stake. This allowed the market to operate unhinged from the state; economic inequality intensified, and the post-war period's regulatory straitjacket was further eroded. Archie, a lifelong Labour voter, noted how 'A lot of their policies were Toryish'. Within this context, working-class people's internal defence mechanism at work—trade unions—withered, whilst the left-liberal, cosmopolitan bubble that represented Blair's championing of the free market and competitive individualism thrived. Although support from traditional Labour voters like Emma, Pete and Jimmy declined in areas like Steel Town, Blair's approach appealed to many voters, particularly further up the social structure, as he won three general elections.

The restructuring of the Labour Party under Tony Blair and then Gordon Brown meant that discussion of politicians blended into a general dissatisfaction with the political class. The idea that no matter who you voted for—nothing changed—was prevalent, and, indeed, time and time again, the terms 'they are all the same' came to the fore. This reflects how the Labour Party, in particular, failed to challenge the Conservative Party's commitment to neoliberal polity including the privatisation of state assets, the transfer of wealth from the bottom to the top of society and the weakening of trade union power. Katie has always voted Labour and she offers views of the political class that were representative of the samples:

> The majority of them are arseholes, they start off saying *oh I wanna make things better*, but they get sucked in. Look at the state of Westminster, it is the most archaic place ever. They don't change the bloody rules they have, you read it and think howay, we are living in the 21st century. You think *come on, change with the times*, but they get sucked into this little Westminster bubble and they forget what it is like to live in the real world.

Katie expressed a deep-seated discontent about politicians, suggesting that they do not serve the people and are shielded from the reality of working-class life. Essentially, the melodrama of parliamentary democracy in the neoliberal epoch often compelled politicians to dispense with ideological worldviews and accept the depoliticisation of the economy and social life. Relatedly, Tom highlights what he perceived as the archaic practices of parliamentary politics: 'Ayes to the left, noes to the right, forget having all that shit'. This was regarded as a distractive tool, expunging of what actually matters to people in post-industrial Steel Town including industrial job loss, remunerative jobs, degradation of working conditions, Steel Town's economic decline and, as we will encounter, a desire to restrict immigration and leave the EU. Most respondents suggested that politicians enact a *subjective distance* from people in places like Steel Town, serving to erode their duty to represent the people. Micky, a non-voter, elucidates how:

> All of them [politicians] are tapped, off their rocker. Their heads are in the sky or up their arse—it certainly isn't on Earth. They just want to rise to the top. They don't care about the country; they just want to be top dog. They come across like they want to help us, but really, they don't give a toss. All they want is more money in their pocket and status.

Evidently, the melodramatic world of parliamentary capitalism means little to people like Micky who persistently tries to ascertain remunerative work but is entrapped in a ten hours per week, minimum wage job at the local social club. From Micky's viewpoint, politicians merely view people like him as an obstacle to their own desire for self-enhancement and prestige, suggesting they utilise their privileged position as a steppingstone to the advancement of their own careers. Although capitalo-parliamentarianism[4] emphasises the virtues of democracy, Alain Badiou claims that politicians often do not serve the working-class but themselves and capital. Most participants claimed politicians are more concerned about their own property portfolios and business interests, harnessing connections for their next career move rather than addressing material conditions in places like Steel Town. Matty, another lifelong Labour voter, said:

> I hate them all mate, they are a waste of time. When they come on television I turn it off, it makes me so frustrated and mad. How can they carry on and get paid big sums for it? It's like when they were claiming for daft stuff, fraudulent. If people like me did that, I would be jailed! They were claiming for stuff like soup and that, and some of them would have two apartments and a flat and put it in their kid's name. One rule for them, another one for us.

As the data reveals, politicians were regarded as deceitful, corrupt and unaccountable, with the 2009 expenses scandal continuing to shape these sentiments. Although they receive a sizable salary and extensive expenses, many politicians illegally rented out their second homes, overclaimed for council tax and claimed for trivial items including their breakfast. Six former MPs and peers were given short prison sentences, including former Labour MP Elliot Morley who was found guilty of £32,000 of fraud. A handful also resigned, though most merely apologised. This scandal coincided with the political consensus over the handling of the global financial crisis and the imposition of austerity measures, leading to a historical decline in living standards.

As previously mentioned, in 2010, the Conservative Party joined a coalition government with the Liberal Democrats, imposing austerity which was felt most acutely in post-industrial places like Steel Town. Stringent cuts were inflicted upon the public sector as well as the welfare state, leading to a myriad rise in foodbank usage in deprived areas.[5] Recent empirical work across Teesside illuminated how austerity had further intensified the difficulties in obtaining work, particularly for young people, whilst the welfare state had become more punitive and disciplinary.[6] Whilst poverty and hardship have increased, the Conservative Government and its ideologically aligned right-wing media increased their rhetoric on explaining inequality through an individualised lens. Rather than highlighting deindustrialisation, a lack of jobs and the erosion of the welfare state as core issues, they principally pointed to the apparent feckless cultural behaviours of the nation's poor including drug misuse and their lack of motivation to work; the latter being debunked in numerous studies.[7] The coalition government also further privatised various state assets including some services within the NHS, which many politicians have utilised to enhance their wealth, as Katie shows:

> They [politicians] have conflicts of interest all over the place. When they voted on whether landlords should make sure they have places fit for people living there, the majority of Conservatives are landlords themselves! Many politicians have shares in arms companies or private firms investing in the NHS. How are they allowed to vote on that? The whole system is just corrupt.

Capitalo-parliamentarianism was regarded as providing ideological cover for MPs to enhance their personal fortunes, often by investing in private businesses then voting for laws and regulations that aid their interests. David Harvey offers the idea of the 'state finance' or 'state-corporate'[8] nexus to identify the revolving door between governments and multinational corporations. This door offers politicians opportunities to meet advisors, civil servants and access to legislative power for the financial industry to get a seat around the table when writing legislation that governs their industry. Other commentators, for instance, have highlighted how over 200 MPs, mainly Conservatives, possess connections to private healthcare companies, whilst many Lords also have connections to private health firms.[9] Such collusion demonstrates how neoliberalism has not withdrawn the state; instead, it has co-opted the nation state to facilitate profit maximisation.[10]

Steve Hall's notion of special liberty is also elucidated by Katie.[11] Attached to neoliberalism's values of egotistical, competitive individualism, many politicians were perceived to have awarded themselves special liberty to rise above society's accepted norms and rules to do what is required to enhance the self, regardless of the harms it causes in post-industrial Steel Town. Capitalism's core forces of profit, envy, greed and the systematic stimulation of desire for social prestige combine to sometimes produce an individual willing to ruthlessly pursue their own advancement. Indeed, the respondents' views of politicians formed a negative belief that nothing can change. Sophie highlights how:

> I've voted maybe three times—usually Labour. I don't vote very often. I just think whoever gets in—it will be the same. They used to come door knocking around here, but you don't get that anymore. You just get the odd brochure through. I just don't believe them anyway. Whatever they say and whatever they might do, they don't follow it up. False promises. They just sugar-coat things. I'm not big on politics at all, if it is going to happen, *it is going to happen.*

As mentioned, a core feature of politics under neoliberalism, particularly in post-industrial and left-behind zones, has been a rise in non-voting.[12] This increased in the New Labour era as around 4–5 million working-class voters stopped voting. Whilst this may be regarded by many as political indifference, it is generated by a non-belief; no fundamental political economic restructuring is possible. History has stopped; all that remains is an acceptance of neoliberalism's industrial retrenchment and a decaying political arena that is unable to inspire belief in a better world. Although Sophie has mainly not voted, the few times she has voted means her engagement with politics is temporary and fleeting, often embodying an *interpassive act*—once her vote has been enacted, she need not do anything else other than wait for the elected politicians to act on her behalf; no political campaigning or protesting because she did her part. Such interpassivity, as we will see, potentially forms a useful ideological function for neoliberal capitalism, enabling capital to cement the redistribution of wealth from the bottom to the top of the socio-economic hierarchy whilst Steel Town's residents passively accept the locale's degeneration.

The interpassivity of Sophie also demonstrates how capitalist realism has been soaked into her psyche; the idea that an alternative world can be created has diminished, along with the collapse of industrial work and an ascent of insecure employment and the absence of a political voice are just how things are today. Throughout its history capitalism has displayed a breath-taking ability to change to survive, though today it has entered a historically unique constitution; it has become what Hegel classed as *indeterminate*,[13] whereby a concept becomes so large and omnipresent that it eventually means nothing at all. Observe how Sophie suggests structural change is disconnected from neoliberal ideology and politico economy. The New Labour era was a crucial phase in the development of capitalist realism, since they consolidated the system as life's core background force and thereby adhered to many of Thatcher's ideals, cementing market forces in areas of life that were previously untouched like the health service and education. Such a political environment fosters a widespread attitude of negativity in places like Steel Town. Mark Fisher outlines how capitalist realism operates as a structural feeling that:

> It is easier to imagine the end of the world than the end of capitalism. Other systems might be preferable to capitalism, but capitalism is the only one that is realistic. Or it can be seen as an attitude of resignation and fatalism in the face of this—a sense that all we can do is accommodate ourselves to the dominance of capitalism and limit our hopes to contain its worst excesses.[14]

This generates a sense that there is no point in engaging with politics because no matter what politicians are elected the same debilitating trends continue. Ellie elucidates how:

> I have never voted, and I don't intend to—unless something really sways me. My nanna would slaughter me for it, she used to say women fought for your rights, and that was obviously good. I don't take any of it in, when they [politicians] come on TV I don't listen. They promise this, promise that, then they get the votes and elected and totally change. *Nothing ever happens.* So, I just think—what am I actually voting for?

Whilst Ellie is relatively disengaged from politics, it is important to note that her discontent is not fixed but pliable and thus can be harnessed under a new political project. Aspects of social democracy's value system are also present, that is, the emphasis placed upon political engagement after laissez-faire capitalism's social inequalities and the battle for female suffrage. Also note the psychic distance Ellie adopts towards politicians on TV; there is little point engaging in the political spectacle under a world governed by the narrow confines of capitalist realism. In many ways, the election of Jeremy Corbyn in 2015 as the Labour Party leader was heralded as an opportunity to reconnect with the working class in areas like Steel

Town. Whilst Corbyn committed the party to nationalising key industries, increasing the minimum wage and abolishing tuition fees, Corbyn stayed liberal on the cultural field and emphasised the positive aspects of immigration, open borders and appeared to find it difficult to praise the monarchy and the British army. Indeed, only four participants suggested they were a fan of Corbyn, the others disliked him or were reserved. Whilst Julia noted how 'To be honest the way I feel about them all now, if there was a general election, I just don't think I would bother voting. I am just so sick of them', whilst Alice said:

> Jeremy Corbyn [laughs]. One of the first things he did that meant I haven't had any interest since was refusing to acknowledge the monarchy. That was it for me. You cannot represent this country and the people if you cannot show respect, it is essential. He is weak, completely weak. I wouldn't trust him with anything. Honestly, I think he is so inadequate he just has to court younger people. It's pathetic. The problem is all of them [politicians]. Nobody listens to us and we have nobody to trust.

Alice's sentiments embody the cultural divide between what David Goodhart casts as the somewhere and the anywhere.[15] Whilst the participants were rooted to place, valued tradition and took pride in the country's flag, since it symbolised their biography including the place they grew up, went to school and ascertained work, generating fond memories of Steel Town's industrial past, Corbyn was regarded as an anywhere—cosmopolitan, globalist and liberal who views the nation's flag as regressive. These culturally liberal tendencies were regarded as viewing the working class's small conservatism and pride in England's industrial history, civil ties, tradition and the English flag as regressive.[16] Alice's opinion that Corbyn did not possess the leadership characteristics to be effective and lead the country under challenging circumstances was prevalent. Many believed he is a political activist and backbench MP, rather than possessing the potential to be the leader of the country's core opposition party. Interestingly, Corbyn's focus on young people, particularly through abolishing tuition fees, was cast as the embodiment of today's politicians, using the citizenry to advance their own interests. Such a failure to relinquish their non-belief was thus tied to political fatalism and scepticism; only more broken promises would await if Corbyn was elected as prime minister. Perhaps, therefore, it was tethered to the Labour Party's consolidation of neoliberal capitalism, as Jimmy outlines:

> I used to vote Labour, but the area has just got worse. The council doesn't do much, so I vote Conservative. Not because I have money, I don't. I don't dislike Corbyn. It's just, I feel *betrayed*.

As the data reveals, the Labour Party were perceived to have failed the working class in places like Steel Town. Although the locale and broader Teesside region had mainly elected a Labour MP since the mid-twentieth century, structural trends like industrial retrenchment, the absence of stability and security, bouts of joblessness to insecure employment and degrading working conditions continued regardless of who held political power. The evidence documented in the data chapters so far meant neoliberal ideology's core tropes of opportunity, meritocracy and individual success had entered a process regarded as 'deaptation',[17] whereby a once functional and coherent ideology is applied in structural conditions where it is no longer operative; neoliberalism was no longer able to absorb the participants into its master narrative. This meant many respondents began to search for an alternative—something to disrupt the status quo, which manifested in the 2016 Brexit vote.

Brexit

Debates on the European Union (EU) and calls for a referendum intensified with the rise and popularity of Nigel Farage and his former party UKIP's victory in the 2014 European Parliament election.[18] Although many participants dismissed UKIP, suggesting they possessed some 'bizarre' candidates who often espoused overt racist sentiments, most admired Farage, praising what they regarded as his honesty and straight-talking political style. In their view, he was not afraid to tell established politicians and the citizenry what he believed, particularly on immigration and the EU, and this was something that they welcomed. UKIP's emphasis upon curtailing immigration, regaining political control over domestic affairs and thus leaving the EU was popular with many participants who supported them, with the party finishing third in Steel Town at the 2015 general election. As mentioned, the town also overwhelmingly voted to Leave the EU in 2016 as the Leave campaign's central message of 'take back control' resonated with many working-class people who felt politically powerless and abandoned. Whilst it failed to inspire some respondents like Chloe who 'Didn't give it a second thought', 14 participants elected to Leave. Many rooted this decision in a desire for an alternative politico economy to neoliberal capitalism such as Roger, 52:

> I've always voted between Labour and the Conservatives, but I aren't happy with them and I voted for Brexit. Before the EU came about, the country was quite good. When we went into the EU we seem to have gone downhill; losing the steel; the good shops. People are fed up.

Such sentiments elucidate how the Labour Party's consensus with the Conservatives since the 2000s, that is, neoliberalism is the only viable form of political economy, enabled Brexit to harness support in post-industrial Steel

Town. With politics therefore reduced to what Adrian Pabst brands as the 'tyranny of small choices'[19] under neoliberalism, observe how leaving the EU was regarded as puncturing the established orthodoxy and averting the area's socio-economic decline. Some scholars have suggested this embodies a desire to return to the imperial project and the racial dominance of whites,[20] though this was absent from the respondent's narratives, it was principally about resurrecting Steel Town's industrial might and popularity as a seaside resort in the post-war age. With the United Kingdom's membership of the EU coinciding with the breakdown of the post-war industrial age and neoliberalism's ascent, it was regarded by many as a contributing factor to Steel Town's slow-motion decline. Kev, a lifelong Labour voter, was the most articulate of the respondents on this question. He said:

> Brexit will be looked back upon as the biggest shock across the world, the day people stood up and said we've had enough. They thought they could force the narrative through the media, but something happened in 2016. 2016 was a pivotal year for humanity, we were the opening gambit on the changing of the world order. We just said no fucking more, no status quo, something different. I was sick of the status quo, constantly at war, constantly in austerity. This is what people forget pre-Brexit, they think it was all amazing, sweet and light. People don't realise how important Brexit is, it was us saying fuck the establishment.

For Kev, Emma and others, accusations that Brexit was all about racism are 'Totally wrong'. Whilst some Brexit voters including some in this study espouse racist sentiments and do not shy away from that, slandering all Leave voters as mere racists is reductionist and forms a discursive mechanism to stymie debate on important and complex issues.[21] Such a narrative fails to explore the impact of neoliberalism's total assault upon post-industrial places like Steel Town; instead, it individualises a structural issue and ensures that the system continues as life's core background force. Covering up the absence of stability and security in Steel Town, it fails to reveal the nuanced driving forces behind Brexit in this research study. Nonetheless, observe how Kev suggests his vote to Leave embodied a rejection of the status quo—deindustrialisation, insecure and uncertain employment, war and austerity measures, which he believes has been neglected by many liberal commentators.

Discussions surrounding Brexit also explored the EU. As England has been identified as one of the most Eurosceptic nations,[22] somewhat inevitably, not one respondent had anything positive to say about the EU; instead, it was regarded as undemocratic and unaccountable. Pete voted to Leave. He claims:

> At least in this country, we vote for a party and we can turn around and say well it hasn't gone well—I voted for them. When we have

unelected officials, who put these people in power? I didn't. The EU is a hierarchy of their own, who are they to tell us what we can and can't do? If we don't like them, we can get onto them. If MPs don't toe the line, we should sack them. This lot in Europe, no, get the cunts out. It is like handing the keys over for your house.

Being a member of the EU was perceived to hollow out the nation's democratic process, shifting further power and control away from Steel Town's residents and awarding it to an undemocratic elite in Brussels. From Pete's viewpoint, capitalo-parliamentarianism is supposed to be a vehicle that channels peoples' dissatisfaction, but the EU insulates itself from democratic debate and the will of its member state's populaces. Intensifying the respondents' feelings of political powerlessness under neoliberalism, the EU further eroded the ability of politics to yield positive change and protect Steel Town from market forces. Essentially, EU membership exacerbated the sense that they had been politically abandoned under neoliberalism.[23]

Considering this, the idea that the EU is a progressive institution was often met with bewilderment, intensifying the disconnect between the political class and people in places like Steel Town. Emma voted to Leave. She believes membership of the EU is:

> Just crackers. We don't vote on European laws—how can it be a democracy? These people in power should be voted for, they can't just be given jobs unaccountably. I am sick of hearing about it [Brexit].

Some scholars believe the EU is undemocratic and, in part, has secured its hegemon through shielding itself from the demands of its member states.[24] For example, the EU's most powerful bodies which shape its policy agenda like the European Commission, International Monetary Fund (IMF) and European Central Bank (ECB) are not elected. Therefore, they are not accountable to anybody; cannot be unseated in democratic elections and possess the power to influence the domestic policies of its 27-member states, especially the 19 members that have adopted the Euro. Changing the policies of the EU requires the approval of the European Council and agreement of over half of its member states, a process Richard Tuck has outlined:

> The European Council has to agree to put any proposed amendment to a special convention 'composed of representatives of national Parliaments, of the Heads of State or Government of the Member States, of the European Parliament and of the Commission', which has to 'adopt by consensus a recommendation to a conference of representatives of the governments of the Member States', each of which has then separately to ratify the proposed amendment before it can come into force. If there are any hold-outs, 'the matter shall be referred to the European Council'.[25]

Perhaps, therefore, the EU's institutional arrangements protect it from demands for structural change and erode the EU's member states policy freedom. Slavoj Zizek believes this 'democratic deficit' was a necessary, inbuilt part of the structure'[26] to consolidate capital's economic interests like the freedom of movement across borders to be able to exploit multiple nation's labour force. As such, it could be argued that the stay and reform argument that was espoused by many commentators and Labour Party politicians before and after the referendum covers up how it was constructed to protect itself from citizenry's demands.[27] Whilst the prominent academic and Greek ex-Minister of Finance Yanis Varoufakis and activist Paul Mason persistently emphasised this idea, they never offered a coherent strategy on how to put it into action. Relatedly, Katie suggests:

> The EU is an unelected group of bullies. What they did to Greece where they blackmailed them, that for me was the final straw. If you've got a group of people who can do that to a country who are on the bones of their arses, then I don't want anything to do with them.

Indeed, the EU is not politically neutral but operates to enforce capital's interests. Embodied in the European Single Market is the four freedoms: freedom of movement for labour, capital, services and commodities. Although capital is free to move across the EU's member states, labour cannot move so freely but rather inhabits the hollowed-out husks of locales like Steel Town. Such an arrangement adheres to capital's interests, as controls over capital's movements cannot be enforced domestically, Steel Town's longue durée of industrial work can be eroded as industrial plants are moved abroad, whilst labour market conditions can be degraded to maximise profitability. Also observe how Katie mentions that the EU sided with capital over employees in relation to the Greek crisis which started during the 2008 global financial crash. After lengthy debates between Greece and the EU, culminating in the extraordinary rise and fall of SYRIZA, the Greek government agreed to several conditional financial loans. Greece would be awarded the loans on the condition that it implemented more marketisation, austerity measures, privatisation of state utilities and the erosion of working conditions. This has intensified joblessness, impoverishment and homelessness, as well as poor economic growth.[28] The EU therefore depoliticised a crisis generated by neoliberalism and imposed more neoliberal mechanisms to maximise profit for capital. Illuminating the sense that the EU is undemocratic and that Brexit is partially a vote for sovereignty, is Alice:

> We are ruled by Europe. We want our autonomy and sovereignty back. To call our own shots and do what we want. The establishment assume we are ill-educated and aren't worried about the future. It's like a lot of young people at the moment, saying when we get to 65, we

shouldn't vote, unbelievable. Older people have *life experience*. I don't vote for myself; I vote for the future—for my kids and grandkids. We need to be strong on our own.

Expressing a desire to give primacy to Steel Town's and England's interests, Alice elucidates how Brexit is attached to Teesside's industrial decline. As the region has endured industrial retrenchment, and the current labour market contains an absence of social stability and economic security, Brexit is regarded as generating more domestic policy freedom to pursue an alternative politico economy. Perhaps, such feelings are also linked to the EU's depoliticisation of the economy, whereby it is protected from democratic demands and imposes neoliberal ideology.[29] In consequence, Brexit is cast by Alice and others as a unique opportunity to renew the democratic process and for the nation state to protect working-class people against the market's tendency to generate social distress.

Importantly, Alice also displays awareness of how Leave voters have been dismissed by many commentators and politicians as intellectually deficient and unaware of their economic interests. However, the nuanced sentiments above demonstrate how this is reductionist, covering up the reality of life in places like Steel Town. As mentioned, neoliberalism had eroded the ability to plan for and imagine the future; the respondents felt a sense of entrapment, unable to psychically project something different. Therefore, it could be argued that the respondents' Brexit vote was generated by an urge to imagine a more positive future, partially driven by feelings of *what once existed*. The older respondents and Alice had witnessed a different world—ICI, the steelworks, parallel and stable biographies, a degree of commonality and community. The Brexit vote was thus an attempt to preserve what little of value remained and hope that elements of the past could be resurrected.

Alice also draws attention to the 'illiberal core'[30] of liberal leftists today. Whilst it is surely necessary for individuals to understand the profound political changes brought about in recent years with the shift to nationalism, many liberals have suggested that nationalist voters' democratic participation should be nullified. It should be noted that the liberal left here primarily refers to the political Left who, as many scholars note,[31] have become liberalised in recent decades. Whilst the liberalisation process has a long history,[32] it was amplified across the New Labour era as they became committed to reproducing neoliberal ideals, whilst critiques of the capitalist system faded from view. These liberal leftists are one wing of the bourgeoisie; the other wing primarily embodied in the Conservative Party. These Brexit voters therefore were not 'against the establishment' per se, but one that favoured one wing of the bourgeoise over the other. The traditional Left was concerned with transformative change and placed emphasis on social class, owning the means of production and economic redistribution to the English working classes, but today's liberal leftists are capitalist realists par excellence; they largely omit social class as an optic to understand the world and mainly focus upon the field of culture rather than political economy. In other words, they are generally content with the system as it stands. As Steve Hall and Simon Winlow suggest,[33] this has involved:

> Pinning the left down to a liberal discourse and preventing it from developing itself as the true voice of all working, underemployed and unemployed people, the unswerving critic of the political and economic elite, and the incubator in which economically feasible alternative systems could be formulated and proposed to the public.

The liberal's emphasis upon cultural issues as the core cause of English nationalism and the dismissal of the underlying economic drivers cover up how there are potential parallels between young people and older individuals' views on society and politics in deindustrialised locales. Rob, 18, notes how:

> I would have voted Leave. We were too tied up in lots of stuff, it would be better if we were independent. It is a working-class area here, there isn't that much money around. It is working class people, living on a budget. Voting Leave would hopefully make us an individual country who don't have to funnel money out of the country and focus on ourselves to make us better.

Whilst Micky was not old enough to vote in the EU referendum, he claims:

> We need more jobs, make our country better. I don't know what it is now [the country]. If we could stay in and have enough money to give people for jobs and apprenticeships, I wouldn't vote to Leave. But because of the financial state of the country, I think we should.

Views above outline how the desire for sovereignty and democratic renewal is engendered by capitalo-parliamentarianism's inability to protect Steel Town's residents and their desire to retain remunerative employment. Both Rob and Micky cannot accrue secure employment; they thus hope Brexit will engender more localised opportunities to forge a stable livelihood. Evidently, both the older and younger participants cast Brexit in similar terms, desiring that the state give primacy to their interests particularly through improving the local economy in Steel Town.

It could be argued that there is a contradiction in the sentiments above, since many participants grounded their Brexit vote in a discontent with the liberal establishment including the Conservative Party, yet they outlined a revitalised feeling of trust in some Conservative politicians to generate significant political economic change, even though they had presided over several years of austerity measures which had brought further socio-economic insecurity and uncertainty to disadvantaged areas. In effect, people in places like Steel Town suffered for economic problems generated by neoliberal polity; Mark Fisher regarded this as 'the most astonishing bait and switch in parliamentary history'.[34] Moreover, some commentators have pointed out that many neoliberal political think tanks suggested that England would be home to a social and economic dystopia post-Brexit.[35] Many economists and institutions like the G20, for instance, persistently warned about the potential consequences of leaving the EU. This narrative was prevalent throughout the referendum campaigns, with most of the political establishment claiming Brexit would have an adverse impact upon the nation's economy. Evidence outlined in this book demonstrates how such an idea fell on deaf ears in post-industrial locales like Steel Town because the dystopia did not await on the horizon; rather, for some, they had been living through it for many years. Steel Town was once home to relatively remunerative and secure industrial work. This awarded many people like Alice, Matty, Mary, Jimmy and others feelings of social accomplishment and pride, with the older aged respondents believing that their children would follow in their footsteps and obtain a reasonably decent standard of living. A functioning community was harnessed, with many respondents recalling an epoch where people knew and spent time with their neighbours.

Shifting to neoliberalism, though, meant that these valued aspects of Steel Town's civic life were dismantled. The relatively recent closure of the steelworks heralded the end of Teesside's industrial might. Many people now worked under hyper-exploitative working conditions, containing an absence of stability and security. The sense of positivity previously attached to some of their working identities was absent, whilst the youngest individuals like Micky, Olly and Rob felt cut adrift from the social, unable to acquire remunerative employment and construct a coherent livelihood. Within this context, the future was absent. When your loved one has lost a remunerative job at the local steelworks, when you do not earn more than the minimum wage, or when you see no future for your children or grandchildren, how can it possibly get much worse? Emma illuminates this with regard to the absence of industrial labour's job for life:

> Definitely not, not anymore. Way back, yeah. My dad used to work at ICI, my husband's dad worked at British Steel, in their day it was and they retired comfortably. But certainly not anymore, not anywhere now. It is a shame, but that is just the way of the world, yet they keep going on about Brexit being bad for the economic climate and all this.

Such a dystopic narrative, therefore, did not resonate in post-industrial zones like Steel Town because those in economically precarious situations had more to gain from voting for Brexit; at least a chance to avert the slow-motion socio-economic decline of the neoliberal era. Indeed, it is worth highlighting that, as Joanie Willett and colleagues note,[36] many areas that received funds from the EU voted to Leave, including Steel Town and most other locales across Teesside. The European Structural and Investment Funds were allocated primarily to poor localities to help reduce regional inequalities across the EU. Teesside was the second principal beneficiary of this in England behind only Cornwall and therefore ahead of other post-industrial locales like Stoke-on-Trent.[37] Teesside received £35 per head annually from the EU and around £160 million was scheduled to be allocated to the region between 2014 and 2020.[38] This was primarily aimed at addressing youth joblessness, increasing skills and promoting social inclusion, with plans to create up to 2,500 new employment opportunities. However, as research with Brexit voters in Cornwall also indicated, the reality of Brexit voters' lives and experiences left them with the belief that they got nothing from the UK's EU membership.[39] The next section turns to the intimate connection between Steel Town's economic decline and cultural issues.

Immigration

Discontent with net migration figures has been a core component of the rise of English nationalism. As mentioned, immigration became a core political issue particularly after the 2008 global financial crisis embodied in part through the rise of UKIP who called for myriad restrictions on immigration.[40] This accelerated debate and divisions on the EU within the Conservative Party, with the former Conservative Prime Minister David Cameron promising to reduce net migration. Specifically, in 2015, he proposed punitive measures including a ban on migrants claiming child benefit for dependents living outside the United Kingdom, as well as removing migrants who had not ascertained employment after six months.[41] This also fuelled debates on the EU's freedom of movement, with Conservative MP Theresa May making unsubstantiated claims that many migrants moved to England to merely utilise the welfare state; a sentiment that led one MP to suggest May was 'Enoch Powell in a dress'.[42] This formed part of the punitive demonisation and scapegoating of migrants that has been a staple feature of the right-wing media and within the Brexit campaign, whereby right-wing politicians like Nigel Farage suggested migrants were the core cause of England's social problems and cultural fragmentation.[43]

Although most respondents were reserved about immigration and wanted to somewhat curtail it, it was a nuanced dissatisfaction that was tethered to Steel Town's death under neoliberalism. Discontent with immigration was often conflated with asylum seekers and refugees. Most expressed little sympathy towards all these groups whereby there was a recurring sentiment that immigrants were favoured by the state over Steel Town's economic needs. At the same time, immigrants were cast as an economic competitor for jobs and housing in an era of already intense competition. Micky outlines how:

> We are human, we should treat everyone fairly, but I don't agree with loads of people coming over here. Okay, they are trying to provide for their family, but we can't even give enough money to British people. So, in that sense because we don't have enough money, we shouldn't be giving it to people from different countries. They aren't 'stealing our jobs' as such, but it doesn't help with money and housing. We have enough problems in this country. If the financial state was different, then I would like to think we could let more in—but how is it right to help them when we can't help ourselves?

Micky expresses minimal sympathy with immigrants, he is not happy with net migration figures, believing they intensify competition in the labour market. Despite adhering to neoliberalism's *sacred promise* that hard work will eventually equate to success by enduring college, an unfair dismissal from a mechanical apprenticeship and a reduction in his hours at the social club, he has not attained social stability and economic security. Whilst he problematises the somewhat crude notion that migrants 'steal jobs', he believes they amplify competition for economically insecure employment at the bottom of the labour market. With migrants tending to work at the lower ends of the labour force,[44] the core political narrative from the liberal left that migrants are an overwhelming positive for society and the economy fails to resonate with Micky's own economic position. Although it is difficult to analyse the impact of immigration on both wages and working conditions, in part because of the different factors that need to be considered like the skills of migrants and current employees, some evidence indicates that in some poorly paid labour markets, wages are constrained by employers taking advantage of poorly paid migrants from Eastern European countries.[45] We met Tom in the previous chapter. He voted Leave and believed that:

> If we didn't have any homeless British people, who are using foodbanks, if we were economically really, really good, then we can take more people. At Christmas, I walked through Steel Town's high-street and even the people selling Big Issue are Eastern Europeans. I'm not being racist, it is almost like our homeless people aren't good enough to sell Big Issue. To me, it just speaks volumes about what is going on—our own people aren't good enough.

Whilst the working class were once at the forefront of the industrial age, helping to build significant global landmarks and acquiring feelings of social usefulness and value, most respondents believed that they were now regarded as obsolete and confined to the historical dustbin. Simultaneously, though, they suggested migrants were favoured, championed by politicians, and even given the low-paid jobs over the native working class. However, as Ruth Milkman notes, the dissatisfaction towards migrants in deindustrialised areas is misplaced; it needs to be directed towards capital.[46] Immigrants are not to blame for Steel Town's historical restructuring from a productive economy to services, though people like Tom search for somebody to blame in the absence of a universal political narrative that could locate the true cause of the area's plight. In many ways, Tom's livelihood is shaped by the same structural forces as immigrants, not least the need to sell his labour power, though neoliberalism's primacy to individualism and social status means he negates identifying migrants as a group that could form a collective struggle against capital. Instead, they are a competitor and thus somebody to outdo under intensely competitive social conditions.

As scholars have outlined, working-class people who express rather racist remarks and suggest migrants are a fundamental problem and cause of a post-industrial locale's degeneration is also partially attached to the Labour Party's failure to challenge neoliberalism and its futility in directing the working class towards the core enemy—capital.[47] As mentioned, the New Labour era consolidated neoliberalism, failing to challenge marketisation, privatisation and myriad inequality. The post-war industrial age's structural tools that enabled working-class people to ground their problems within structural conditions, not least trade unions, working men's social clubs, the shopfloor camaraderie of industrial work and a sense of community are now absent. The disappearance of these mechanisms perhaps forms a 'process of consciousness-deflation',[48] whereby some working-class people misidentify the cause of deindustrialised locales decline. Such a dynamic is intensified by the reactionary right-wing media who largely endorse the Conservative Party's core political ideals, whilst identifying various cultural groups like immigrants as responsible for society's malaise, effectively helping to divide and conquer the working classes. Perhaps, Tom's views are thus a misdirected economic antagonism expressed in a cultural guise, working to conceal the role of neoliberal political economy and ideology—in shaping English nationalism.

Like the other respondents, Tom also acknowledges how many working-class people who espouse nationalistic views have been dismissed as idiots and racists. Whilst some of the participants do espouse racist views, the sentiments evidenced are tied to neoliberalism's structural reconfiguration of Steel Town and Teesside, meaning the liberal left's emphasis on pathologising English nationalism essentially transforms class issues of economic inequality into cultural intolerance, prejudice and bigotry.[49] These hollowed out platitudes resonate little with those that occupy the deindustrialised zones, since they fail to illuminate the reality of life in these areas. The liberal left also fails to acknowledge the nuance surrounding working-class views on immigration, with many expressing racist views that were not simply prejudice but partially borne out of a desire to protect the area. Leave voter Jess outlines:

> We've just had a family arrive at our school, Iraqis, they are lovely, but they can't speak English. Straight away, the eldest boy has got support from an assistant, one to one, been given a house—fair enough. But looking at our school and cuts to education money, schools are struggling. So, we have to find that money as a school for that child who has come over here. I just think you've been accepted in the country, you have a safe place now, which is really good, but why should our school then have to pay for that when we are losing teachers and teaching assistants? I think it's great they have a safe haven, and the upheaval of moving here must be terrible—I'm not disputing that. But they are given that support straight away. If it was your child who is struggling, you wouldn't be given that support. We have a little boy with brain damage, he isn't bad enough to go to special school, but the government only gives us two hours of support a day.

In Jess's view, refugees' inability to speak English intensifies her discontent. Evidently, she and others are not anti-migration per se, but Jess believes refugees/immigrants' needs are prioritised over native citizens. Whilst she is sympathetic towards their plight, she believes that the needs of the native English working class should be given primacy. Placed in this context, the idea that immigration does not exacerbate competition for resources in relatively deprived areas falls on deaf ears, since more migrants at local schools magnifies the dearth of educational facilities and time available to address Steel Town's disadvantaged children's needs. Whilst Archie was out of the country during the 2016 referendum, he would have voted to Leave. He expressed similar views to Jess:

> I think this country lets far too many migrants in. Some of them have had terrible lives mind. My mate used to deliver in Middlesbrough, where the houses have just been rebuilt, people used to smash their windows and write slogans on the walls. He said some of them people haven't done anything wrong. They were working like slaves, doing jobs our young'uns wouldn't get out of bed for. But there should be a cap. *Look around*—we have food banks, we can't feed and look after our own, never mind letting more people in.

Observe how Archie suggests this discontent recently erupted in nearby Middlesbrough, a locale of permanent recession defined by industrial retrenchment, the absence of security and cultural outlooks of despondency and nihilism. Sometimes this can erupt in blind rage, whereby inarticulate anger is directed towards vulnerable social groups who are not responsible for the area's decline. Inarticulate discontent appears to emerge in the absence of a universal political narrative that locates the true cause of working-class people's plight—capital.[50]

Archie also highlights the EU's freedom of movement for labour. Many claim this enables employers to carefully choose their employees, serving to diminish solidarity amongst workforces.[51] Others claim it depopulates some Eastern European nations; for example, Bulgaria has lost a third of its doctors to Western EU states whereby wages and working conditions are better.[52] Whilst Archie claims many young people will not undertake degrading employment, it tends to mask the structural exploitation many of them endure such as Micky, Olly, Rob and Emma's son who all continue to work hard despite working in poorly paid jobs. Although there was a widespread sense that migrants intensified competition for jobs, most of the sample claimed they were wary of voicing their views because they would be cast as racist. Kev enumerated on how:

> Immigration is an emotive one, a tricky one. The Left jump all over you, you are not even allowed to question. The EU globalist dream is one of open borders. For me, that's a nightmare cause we would be forced out of our homes in rampaging hordes because they think this is where the money is. If they are seeking asylum, of course, why wouldn't ya? The problem we have with this immigration is slavery. You look at the boats of black lads, they have probably paid somebody to come over here, the ships that are zipping about the Mediterranean is just slavery—sex slavery, sex trafficking.

Observe how Kev also highlights how criminal actors in the Global South have taken advantage of capitalism's crises, since they have compelled vulnerable people to pay extortionate fees to cross the Mediterranean where thousands have tragically died.[53] Whilst some make it across the continent and survive, they are often compelled to undertake menial and illegal forms of work where they are deprived of basic rights and the nation's minimum wage.[54] The EU has failed to adequately ameliorate this problem, instead emphasising the importance of humanitarianism. As previously documented, exemplifying this were Angela Merkel's suggestions for open borders, which was an idea that was anathema to many respondents like Kev. Tom also claimed:

> You cannot just disperse millions of people throughout the world, and everything be okay. You need to look at the root cause, why doesn't

somebody stop the war in the Middle East? Then people wouldn't have to be dispersed—go back and rebuild. Look, we need to do our bit, but not to the detriment of our own. If people are coming from Syria and get priority, that is wrong. Put us first, our economic issues. People will say where are they going to go? I don't know, and it's bad saying that, but economically we aren't in a good position.

Zahi Zalloua claims the dominant debate about the refugee crisis plays out between the nationalist right and the liberal left. Whilst the former desires to restrict the flow of refugees entering Western nations, the latter embody 'Beautiful Souls',[55] calling for open borders and good ethics and morals. This could be identified as a hollowed-out demand since they know open borders will never happen as it would intensify anger and discontent. Indeed, focusing solely on helping refugees 'is a pharmakon; it is both cure and poison',[56] since it fails to address what Tom believes are the underlying issues, not least restructuring society so that the mass movement of vulnerable people is not a structural inevitability. By depoliticising a political economic crisis, today's liberal left fails to identify neoliberal capitalism as the fundamental issue at stake, evaporating the historical class struggle in favour of politically safe ideas like moralism, sympathy and empathy. According to Slavoj Zizek, this concealment of the politico economy ensures that capitalism generates structural crises often free from critique.[57]

Observe how Tom identifies that it is the socio-economic context exposed in the previous chapters—namely, deindustrialisation, the absence of well-paid work, underemployment and degrading working conditions—that generates reservations about accepting refugees. This need to posit cultural concerns within broader events and processes was identified by Katie:

> At the end of the day, if we are bombing the shit out of countries, we should be expected to take some people on, but why don't they stop at the first country they come across?

According to some scholars, the West's, particularly the United Kingdom and United States' intervention in the Middle East ensured Iraq is a compliant state through opening their oil reserves to international markets, though this destroyed the country's infrastructure, generated countless deaths and displaced many others.[58] Therefore, for Katie, it should not be unreasonable for some Western states to accommodate victims of the profit motive, though she ponders over why they do not stay in neighbouring states. Some suggest that refugees aim for Scandinavia and the United Kingdom because of their relatively good welfare states, better paid employment opportunities and consumer culture's spectacle of hedonistic enjoyment and material prosperity.[59] Alice, though, continues the story:

> What I am not happy with is them claiming asylum then coming through different countries and making their way over to the UK. It is outrageous. If you are looking for a safe haven, find one and stay there. They come over here because they are prioritised over our own people who need looking after. I'm not happy with it. The people working in our hospitals from all over the world—consultants, surgeons, doctors, nobody is objecting to that. We need them, and it is helpful. But illegals, I don't agree with that.

Rob agrees:

> If they have something to offer, then fine. But people who are coming here illegally, fleeing and jumping on lorries and sneaking in, like, I don't agree with that.

Rightly or wrongly, asylum seekers were perceived to favour the United Kingdom because they are treated favourably by the government. For the participants, important local issues like Teesside's industrial emaciation and the decline of the local area were neglected, whilst more and more resources and governmental attention were directed towards asylum seekers. Some have problematised the well-trodden idea that the UK government prioritises immigrants and refugees over the native working class, since the former tend to do jobs that are 'dirty, dangerous and difficult'[60] and therefore possess a shared structural experience to many participants in this study. Simultaneously, asylum seekers are principally dispersed throughout the most impoverished areas in decrepit housing. Recall how Archie claimed some asylum seekers were subjected to racist abuse in a deprived locale. Indeed, perhaps, what some of the respondents' racism embodies is the reverse side of '*amour propre*',[61] whereby the elevation of immigrants, refugees and asylum seekers comes at the expense of the working class.

These discussions often melded into issues associated with Islam, political correctness and what they believed was the stifling of important debates. The next section explores multiculturalism and the perceived attack on free speech.

Islam and political correctness

Discontent towards Islam, occasionally expressed in a racist manner, has been a relatively recent political development,[62] with some claiming that Brexit/nationalistic views are driven by a concern over more and more people converting to Islam across the European continent.[63] Although a handful of respondents expressed reservations, most claimed they did not possess much knowledge of Islam, suggesting the mainstream, right-wing media offered an inaccurate picture of the religion to drive racism. Whilst these individuals often pointed to the racism of Tommy Robinson, the former leader of the far-right political activist group the English Defence League, there was sometimes a contradictory agreement with some of his sentiments, as Claire unveils:

> People don't listen to what all the idiots are saying like Tommy Robinson. Well, I am against forced marriages, and I am against female genital mutilation (FGM), I think it is ridiculous. If it is a tradition, then it is ridiculous. But I don't know much about Islam, their beliefs and that, I can't give a proper opinion. They need to abide by the law of the country they are in. But because a few Muslims are terrorists it doesn't mean all Muslims are. Hitler was German—every German isn't a psycho.

Although Claire suggests Robinson is a bigot, she expresses discontent with many of the historical traditions associated with Islam like forced marriages and FGM. As the liberal left do not discuss these thorny and sensitive issues, it enables racists like Robinson to harness support. Nevertheless, Claire highlights a potential paradox of liberal multiculturalism, that is, the schism between liberal tolerance and adequate integration into society. Whilst people who voice reservations about Islam are often dismissed by the liberal left as Islamophobic and xenophobic,[64] such slandering ignores the socio-economic context that engenders cultural perspectives and sentiments. This was interlinked by many participants including Dave:

> There are more and more mosques, I'm not racist. We just seem to let everyone in. We can't take anymore. *It doesn't work for the youngsters as it is*, never mind accepting more.

Alice suggests:

> My views on some of it [Islam] is negative. Like the Burqa and forced marriages, which are just oppressive.

As mentioned, although the locality in Teesside that the research was conducted in is overwhelmingly white, surrounding areas are much more ethnically diverse, particularly nearby Middlesbrough. Dave also voices racist sentiments around the prevalence of mosques, without identifying why their presence is problematic. Indeed, Winlow and colleagues claim that multiculturalism is a positive cultural schema that sits alongside a negative political economy.[65] Although the former offers an image of harmony, diversity and acceptance, it has taken place in a broader climate of unprecedented economic inequality and the evisceration of once relatively thriving locales like Steel Town. Focusing solely on tolerance and acceptance serves to mask the structural backdrop, not least the area's industrial emaciation and the absence of well-paid jobs. It could be argued that focusing on acceptance and tolerance whilst neglecting economic matters enables neoliberal capitalism to redistribute wealth from the working class to the top of the social hierarchy. Such a cultural programme therefore rings rather hollow when, as numerous respondents indicated, the area was now a 'ghost town' or 'dead place'. Rather than emphasising tolerance, critical scholars claim we need more intolerance directed towards the root cause of today's cultural antagonisms—neoliberal capitalism.[66]

Indeed, dissatisfaction about political correctness was a common sentiment in the interviews, particularly in relation to discussing sensitive political topics. Most of the participants viewed political correctness negatively, suggesting it is another political tool to stifle debate. Therefore, it was generally viewed as another way to silence peoples' concerns in post-industrial areas like Steel Town—enabling the liberal left's political views to dominate. Tom outlines how:

> When I watch the news these days, I think this would have just been sorted out years ago. Now it is too politically correct. The whole thing with the Islamic lass, [Shamima Begum], just sort it out. But you can't say out because you are a racist. I think there is a lot of *you can't do this, you can't do that*. For me, that is one of the biggest things of the last few years, what you can and can't say. It is wrong.

Tom draws attention to what has been cast as multiculturalism's 'police officers of discourse'[67] and 'language patrollers'.[68] Expressing discontent about issues that appear to be problematic to some of the participants but whereby they do not mean to cause any offence are cast as racist, and thus, Tom withdraws his views on Shamima Begum re-entering the United Kingdom and attempting to retain British citizenship after joining ISIS when she was 15. Jess says:

> Well, you can't say you're English anymore, you have to say, *oh I'm British*. I just feel as though it is a shame, we were such a fantastic thing. I sound like a patriarch, don't I?

Many respondents also spoke about how, since the 2016 Brexit vote, accusations from sections of the liberal left that white working-class people are privileged have intensified. However, respondents like Kev claimed the idea of white privilege is 'bollocks'. Indeed, such a development is one of the liberal left's 'negative quilting points',[69] exacerbating the now threadbare connection between the political left and working-class people in places like Steel Town. For Kev, it makes little sense to conflate the socio-economic interests of all white people, since it covers up structural conditions and antagonisms between rich white people and working-class white people. It might be useful to ask: what sense does it make to compare Kev, a white working-class man, who left his job as a postman (on 25K annually) because of exploitative working conditions and poor relations with his managers, whilst his brother lost his job at the steelworks when it closed in 2015, to a white capitalist financier or white owner of a global corporation?

Therefore, as Owen Hodgkinson, James Treadwell and myself have recently highlighted terms surrounding privilege discourse covers up capitalism's class antagonism and its social inequalities, demanding cultural recognition within unequal structures.[70] White privilege serves to abstract structural issues and fails to reflect the material conditions that people live in. Advocates of white privilege are thus not really concerned with material privilege, they just want people to have earnt it, regardless of neoliberalism's tectonic inequalities.[71] Placing emphasis upon white privilege to combat today's antagonisms, Zahi Zalloua believes that many liberals engage in the psychosocial act of fetishistic disavowal—they know it is not adequate in dealing with racism, though they espouse it anyway to take the moral high ground.[72]

Kev also alludes to how political correctness is potentially divisive because it dwindles the ability to come together under a shared and collective political ideal. It emphasises the need to tolerate difference, rather than focusing on what unites us. As we will discuss in the final chapter, it is an imperative for the Left to focus on Sameness. Although as Mark Fisher outlined, emancipatory politics 'must make what was previously deemed to be impossible seem attainable'[73] and whilst Brexit potentially provided this historical opportunity,[74] the political Left remained attached to the status quo, espousing calls for a second referendum on EU membership.

Second referendum

The Liberal Democrat's demand to not implement the Brexit vote and instead enact a second referendum, alongside the broader political failure to implement Brexit, continued until December 2019 with the victory of the Conservative Party and the fall of the Red Wall at the 2019 general election. Although many polls suggest Leave voters had not changed their mind on EU membership, the Brexit Party emerged victorious at the 2019 European Elections, signifying a desire to implement Brexit. Whilst four participants either said yes or were undecided on another referendum, the others suggested it was a betrayal of democracy. Most expressed this is an angry manner, claiming it was yet another example of the political class not listening to working-class people. When asked about a second referendum, Emma replied with:

> Oh god, no. Definitely not. The decision has been made. We are a democracy, get on with it. It is a farce. We had the campaigns, people have decided, whether you like it or not. But they obviously feel as though people have *made the wrong decision*, so now they are up in arms about it. If they didn't want us to make the wrong decision, then why give us the choice? They [politicians] are just so wrong. It annoys me—people are so fed up.

Ultimately, the demands for a second referendum from the liberal left gave yet more evidence to the respondents' beliefs that politicians care only for themselves, are egotistical and do not serve the working-class. Awarding voters a say on European membership was cast as tolerable, though only if they voted to maintain the status quo and preserve membership of a neoliberal institution that is generally committed to enforcing capital's economic interests across the continent.[75] The democratic process was therefore cast as a façade, a hollowed-out spectacle that offered the appearance of change but where nothing would really change. Although parliamentary democracy is cast as emblematic of political freedom and choice, some argue that it places restrictions on what is regarded as politically and economically possible.[76] Like Emma, Alice also spoke angrily about a second referendum:

> Absolutely not. No chance—no. Because then what happens to democracy? How are you ever going to believe what they [politicians] say? What would happen in the future? Are they just going to say we can't implement that because we don't agree with it? You know, we can't get around this so let's just vote again, and go on and on? We were given the chance and information. It's a serious thing.

Some scholars have argued that capitalism's relationship with democracy is inconclusive.[77] Capitalo-parliamentarism functions by eliciting the appearance of political debate and freedom, now focusing extensively on micro-issues around identity, diversity and the characteristics of politicians, whilst macro-political economic questions about how to organise society are absent from politics. In this climate, capitalo-parliamentarism is faced with a prolonged antagonism, that is, class tensions and managing the socio-economic interests of capital versus working-class people. Wolfgang Streeck believes that most politicians under neoliberalism signed up to its economic logic of giving primacy to the market, and therefore, the democratic process has been eroded, though it continues to function by generating an illusion that people can bring about fundamental change if only they vote for the correct party. Indeed, Claire outlines how it perhaps favours certain ideological views:

> If Remain had won and there was talk of a second referendum, they would have a meltdown. There was a vote, the people voted. There was a decision, and that is it! You shouldn't have a second referendum or another one until they get the decision they want. I think it is wrong—not because I voted Leave, but if Remain had won and we were going on about a second referendum, there would be hell on.

Dave [non-voter] agrees:

> Whether it is right or wrong, we voted out—you've got to act on that.

Quinn Slobodian outlines how many of neoliberalism's early interlocutors were sceptical about democracy.[78] They believed it was a mechanism available to the masses which they may use to undermine market freedoms, capital's movement and the maximisation of profitability, since it may empower the working class and embolden their demands for better working conditions and socio-economic betterment. As this book previously outlined, encasing the economy in transnational institutions was deemed important in ensuring the demands of the masses did not disturb the smooth functioning of the global economy and its reallocation of wealth from the bottom to the social structure's top. Perhaps, this is emblematic of the EU, existing to enforce neoliberal ideals of market freedoms and capital movement, insulating economic policy decisions from critique and engendering feelings of political powerlessness.[79] Indeed, for Pete, a second referendum would potentially generate mass voter withdrawal; perhaps, it could be argued that this would serve an important ideological function for neoliberal capitalism, ensuring the political demands of working-class people in places like Steel Town were omitted, whilst the system continued as life's core background force.

With Parliament at a deadlock on Brexit throughout 2019, Boris Johnson called an election for 12 December 2019 and promised to exit the EU. Whilst the Labour Party's stance was rather ambiguous, it proposed to return to the EU and renegotiate a different exit deal. Richard Tuck branded this as a futile approach, given the EU possessed no incentive in allowing Britain to leave on good terms since it may incentivise other Eurosceptic nations like Italy, France and Greece to leave.[80] Ultimately, if the renegotiations failed, the Party was committed to implementing another referendum. Although the Party honoured the vote in 2017 and achieved relative electoral success, the Party suffered a historical and heavy loss in 2019. Emblematic of this was the collapse of the Red Wall, with many deindustrialised localities from South Wales to the Midlands and

Northeast of England—such as Steel Town—electing a Conservative MP for the first time in over 50 years or longer.[81]

A revealing aspect of the 2019 general election was also how all aspects of the liberal establishment, including most Liberal Democrat, Conservative and Labour Party MPs, the BBC and 'left-leaning' outlets like The Guardian closed ranks on Corbyn to try and prevent him from winning the election. Throughout his leadership reign, most right-wing newspaper outlets including The Sun, Daily Mail, Evening Standard and Daily Express principally portrayed him in a critical and antagonistic manner, who often had nothing positive to say about him.[82] A large bulk of the media stories also focused on personal attacks, mocking Corbyn's political ideas, personal life and appearance. The 2019 campaign, in particular, was also mired in accusations towards Corbyn of antisemitism. This was frequently reported in The Guardian and the BBC and eventually became an international debate.[83]

Indeed, although the research for this book finished in August 2019, I was able to get in touch with ten respondents after the collapse of the Red Wall and thus the Conservatives victory in Steel Town. Mia, Archie and Roger voted Labour and claimed they were rather surprised with Steel Town's result. They suggested that they thought it would be a very close election, though they did not expect a landslide Conservative victory. Capitalist realism, though, was deeply embedded in non-voters' psyche like Ellie and Dave—both failed to vote again. Although Dave claimed he had no desire to vote, Ellie reiterated her previous beliefs, or non-belief—nothing can change. The former ICI and steelworker Matty, who was a lifetime Labour voter and Brexit supporter, also abstained, suggesting that politicians are a 'waste of time'.

Nevertheless, Alice, Emma, Jimmy and Jess voted Conservative. As Jimmy felt betrayed and abandoned by Labour, he was happy with Boris Johnson's victory. He also suggested Labour were 'trying to scupper it [Brexit]', fomenting further feelings of political disillusionment. Indeed, Emma and Jess espoused similar views, with Jess stating: 'put it this way, I was happy with the result'. Empirical evidence outlined in this book, supported by the other relatively small body of qualitative research on the recent rise of English nationalism,[84] perhaps indicate that the historical collapse of the Red Wall was rooted in negative politics, that is, a deeply ingrained dissatisfaction with the Labour Party which had been bubbling throughout the neoliberal era. Whilst political discontent is palpable in areas like Steel Town, the Labour Party failed to take seriously, and seek to implement, the form of political backlash in Britain—Brexit.[85]

Conclusion

This chapter explored the nationalistic sentiments generated by the respondents' experience of life in post-industrial Steel Town. New Labour continued the logic of neoliberalism, not least the deindustrialisation process, rebranding the party away from the traditional working class. Dissatisfaction with New Labour blended into a broader discontent with politics, with the idea that 'they are all the same' a regular refrain throughout the research. As most of the political class adhered to neoliberalism's logic of awarding primacy to market forces, capitalist realism had hardened onto the respondents' psyche, generating a non-belief in fundamental politico-economic change. Whilst Jeremy Corbyn attempted to remedy this, many could not simply disconnect his premiership from New Labour's reign. Brexit was thus posited as a historical means to take forward the accumulative discontent about neoliberalism, as well as a demand for sovereignty and democratic renewal against what was regarded as an undemocratic and unaccountable EU.

Opinions on refugees were often conflated with immigrants and asylum seekers, though a striking characteristic was their complexity. Whilst many expressed minimal sympathy with those migrating from relatively impoverished or war-torn countries, they were chiefly viewed as an economic competitor for resources like jobs and housing in an epoch of intense competition. Therefore, a desire to regain control over peoples' lives in areas like Steel Town was ubiquitous, with liberal leftist calls for open borders and tolerance cast as baseless, omitting the reality of life in Steel Town including deindustrialisation and a lack of well-paid jobs. The demands to implement a second referendum grew for over three years after June 2016, with most people in this research viewing it as betrayal and another example of politicians not listening to some working-class people. This possessed parallels to neoliberalism's founding fathers, who were suspicious of democracy's ability to empower the working class. The book now closes with a discussion of the COVID-19 pandemic and the future, both politically and socially, speculating on how capitalism may be set for epochal change once again.

Notes

1. For example: Kotze, J (2019); Lloyd, A (2018b); Raymen, T (2018); Winlow, S & Hall, S (2015) *Revitalizing Criminological Theory: Towards a New Ultra-Realism*. Abingdon: Routledge.
2. Goodall, L (2018).
3. Jenkins, S (2007).
4. Badiou, A (2015).
5. Garthwaite, K (2016); Mendoza, K (2015); O'Hara, M (2015); Ruddy, A (2017).
6. Macdonald, R, Shildrick, T & Furlong, A (2020).
7. Crossley, S (2018) *Troublemakers: The Construction of 'Troubled Families' as a Social Problem*. Bristol: Policy Press; Shildrick, T, Macdonald, R & Furlong, A (2016); Shildrick, T (2018) *Poverty Propaganda: Exploring the Myths*. Bristol: Policy Press.
8. Harvey, D (2011) *The Enigma of Capital and the Crises of Capitalism*. London: Profile Books Ltd, p. 204.

9. Davis, J, Lister, J & Wrigler, D (2015) *NHS for Sale: Myths, Lies & Deception*. London: The Merlin Press Ltd.
10. Mitchell, W & Fazi, T (2017).
11. Hall, S (2012).
12. Eatwell, R & Goodwin, M (2018).
13. Hegel, W (1820) *Philosophy of Right*. New York: Dover Publications.
14. Fisher, M (2018), p. 663.
15. Goodhart, D (2017).
16. Embery, P (2020); Pabst, A (2019).
17. Johnston, A (2008), p. 175.
18. Shipman, T (2017).
19. Pabst, A (2019), p. 24.
20. Gupta, S & Virdee, S (2020); Pitcher, B (2019).
21. Hall, S & Winlow, S (2020); Lind, M (2020); Telford, L & Wistow, J (2020).
22. Henderson, A & Wyn Jones, R (2021).
23. Tuck, R (2020).
24. Lapavitsas, C (2019); Lind, M (2020); Tuck, R (2020).
25. Tuck, R (2020), p. 148.
26. Zizek, S (2016) *Against the Double Blackmail*. Milton Keynes: Allen Lane, p. 10.
27. Mitchell, W & Fazi, T (2017).
28. Lapavitsas, C (2019); Lind, M (2020).
29. Mitchell, W & Fazi, T (2017).
30. Pabst, A (2019), p. 14.
31. Babones, S (2018); Eatwell, R & Goodwin, M (2018); Embery, P (2020); Hall, S & Winlow, S (2020); Lind, M (2020); Mitchell, W & Fazi, T (2017); Pabst, A (2019); Winlow, S Hall, S & Treadwell, J (2017) (2019); Zizek, S (2016) (2018).
32. Hall, S & Winlow, S (2020).
33. Hall, S & Winlow, S (2020), p. 66.
34. Fisher, M (2018), p. 457.
35. Fotopoulos, T (2016).
36. Willett, J, Tidy, R, Tregidga, G & Passmore, P (2019).
37. Tinker, R (2018) *Brexit: How Will the Government Fund Its Commitment to Left-Behind Places?* York: Joseph Rowntree Foundation.
38. Tees Valley (2016) European funding in Tees Valley. *Tees Valley Combined Authority*. Available at: https://teesvalley-ca.gov.uk/wp-content/uploads/2016/03/Tees-Valley-EU-Funding-Overview-May-2016.pdf.
39. Willett, J, Tidy, R, Tregidga, G & Passmore, P (2019).
40. Ford, R & Goodwin, M (2014).
41. Shipman, T (2017).
42. Shipman, T (2017), p. 21.
43. Goodfellow, M (2019) *Hostile Environment*. London: Verso; Milkman, R (2020) *Immigrant Labour and the New Precariat*. Cambridge: Polity Press.
44. Goodfellow, M (2019).
45. Vargas-Silva, C, Markaki, I & Sumption, M (2016) *The Impacts of International Migration on Poverty in the UK*. York: Joseph Rowntree Foundation.
46. Milkman, R (2020).
47. Winlow, S, Hall, S & Treadwell, J (2017) (2019).
48. Fisher, M (2018), p. 770.
49. Zizek, S (2016) (2018).
50. Winlow, S, Hall, S & Treadwell, J (2017); Zizek, S (2016) (2017) (2018).
51. Babones, S (2018).
52. Goodhart, D (2017).

53. Tuck, R (2020).
54. Murray, D (2017).
55. Zalloua, Z (2020) *Zizek on Race: Towards an Anti-Racist Future*. London: Bloomsbury Publishing, p. 67.
56. Zalloua, Z (2020), p. 67.
57. Zizek, S (2016).
58. Callinicos, A (2010) *Bonfire of Illusions: The Twin Crises of the Liberal World*. Cambridge: Polity; Harvey, D (2011).
59. Zizek, S (2016).
60. Goodfellow, M (2019), p. 104.
61. Hall, S (2012), p. 172.
62. Winlow, S, Hall, S & Treadwell, J (2017) (2019).
63. Swami, V, Barron, D, Weis, L & Furnham, A (2018) To Brexit or not to Brexit: The roles of Islamophobia, conspiracist beliefs, and integrated threat in voting intentions for the United Kingdom European Union membership referendum. *British Journal of Psychology*. 109(1): 156–179.
64. Zizek, S (2016) (2017).
65. Hall, S & Winlow, S (2020); Winlow, S, Hall, S & Treadwell, J (2017) (2019).
66. Zalloua, Z (2020); Zizek (2016) (2017) (2018).
67. Pfaller, R (2017), p. 81.
68. Murray, D (2019) *The Madness of Crowds: Gender, Race and Identity*. London: Bloomsbury Publishing, p. 158.
69. Hall, S & Winlow, S (2020), p. 67.
70. Hall, S & Winlow, S (2020); Hodgkinson, O Telford, L & Treadwell, J (2021) A Critical Assessment of the Black Lives Matter Movement in Britain. *Journal of Contemporary Crime, Harm, Ethics*. 1(1): 88–107.
71. Hall, S & Winlow, S (2020).
72. Zalloua, Z (2020).
73. Fisher, M (2009), p. 17.
74. Tuck, R (2020).
75. Lind, M (2020); Tuck, R (2020).
76. Badiou, A (2012b) *The Rebirth of History*. London: Verso.
77. Streeck, WG (2016).
78. Slobodian, Q (2018).
79. Lapavitsas, C (2019); Mitchell, W & Fazi, T (2017); Tuck, R (2020).
80. Tuck, R (2020).
81. Embery, P (2020).
82. Cammaerts, B, DeCillia, B, Magalhaes, J & Jimenez-Martinez, C (2016) *Journalistic Representations of Jeremy Corbyn in the British Press*. LSE Report.
83. Heppell, T (2021) The British labour party and the antisemitism crisis: Jeremy Corbyn and image repair theory. *The British Journal of Politics and International Relations*. 23(4): 645–662.
84. For example, see: Davenport, H, MacLeavy, J & Manley, D (2018); Dawson, A (2018); Koch, I (2018) Bread and butter politics: Democratic disenchantment and everyday politics on an English council estate. *American Ethnologist*. 43(2): 282–294; Mahoney, I & Kearon, T (2018); McKenzie, L (2017a) (2017b); Telford, L & Wistow, J (2020); Willett, J, Tidy, R, Tregidga, G & Passmore, P (2019); Walkerdine, V (2020); Winlow, S, Hall, S & Treadwell, J (2017) (2019).
85. Tuck, R (2020).

Chapter 7

The past, present and future

The past

Before outlining some thoughts on the COVID-19 crisis and the future, it is necessary to briefly recap the book's central arguments. This book has, so far, empirically investigated the rise of nationalistic sentiments in post-industrial Steel Town in Teesside. It has drawn upon historical processes, biography and current structural conditions to attempt to offer a nuanced analysis of English nationalism in a deindustrialised place. It explicated how capitalism's historical mutations transformed Steel Town and the surrounding area throughout their history. The area owes its existence to the industrial revolution, forming a core part of the industrial age in the nineteenth century and parts of the twentieth century. Systemic shocks in the Victorian age, not least the 1929 Great Depression, the First and Second World Wars and myriad inequalities meant the system embarked upon an anomalist phase, placing working-class interests like socio-economic betterment at the centre of its modus operandi, since a 'pistol pointed to the head of liberal capitalism'[1] throughout the post-war epoch. Wages rose on a regular basis, and relatively powerful trade unions provided industrial workers with a defence mechanism against exploitative employers.

Data outlined in this book revealed that this epoch was recalled fondly by many respondents, offering them a degree of stability, security and coherency. ICI and the steelworks were regarded earnestly as they equipped many people and their significant other with remunerative pay, pensions and longevity. Worries about paying the bills or what the future holds for their children were dispensed from their psyche; they possessed a degree of optimism that things would continue to improve. As Leave voter Katie outlined earlier, the readily availability of industrial employment meant some workers would be able to respond to exploitation at work by telling their employers: 'f*ck you mate, I'm off'. Of course, the abundance of work was not capitalism's normal functioning but a defence mechanism that occurred within a broader regulatory straitjacket to elicit working-class support for a system which was rapidly losing its legitimacy. Nonetheless,

DOI: 10.4324/9781003198666-8

this awarded many people in Steel Town material and psychic comfort, often building important global landmarks. As North asserted: 'the world owed much to Teesside—for it produced the bulk of the rails not only for Great Britain's railways but those in many other countries such as Belgium, France and India'.[2]

Although Steel Town and Teesside were underpinned by industrial labour markets, the former was also a popular coastal resort. Its closeness to the sea meant it was popular with day trippers, whilst many local people flocked to the area, particularly in the summer months, to take advantage of its cultural amenities. People were tethered to social class, community and reciprocity in post-industrial Steel Town, with many people spending time with those in their local community including their neighbours. However, capitalism has utilised its internal crises to implement epochal change.[3] Structural crises in the 1980s enabled the system to abandon the transient class compromise and generate a new socio-economic arrangement based upon individualism, competition and primacy to market forces.[4] Deindustrialisation has been a key component of this process, with capital shifting to countries where the profit motive can be given more freedom to exploit workers.[5] Symbolising this in Teesside was the closure of ICI and the steelworks, with the latter identified as the final chapter in the area's industrial history.

As industrial production shifted from the West to the East, a service economy constituted by relatively lesser paid jobs in retail, leisure and call centres, amongst others, emerged in Teesside.[6] Many failed to ascertain the same sense of social purpose and pride from these employment roles, whilst many others encountered a joblessness to insecure employment cycle. Targets and overworking were another contributor to working-class discontent, individualising and atomising the workforce. This constitutive context meant the locality was now cast as a ghost town, populated by empty and abandoned stores in which the town was perceived to offer little social substance.

This is the context into which the new English nationalism emerged in left-behind places like Steel Town, whereby Brexit was cast as a unique opportunity to stymie the established orthodoxy and pursue fundamental political, economic and cultural change. The EU was regarded as further eroding the working-class ability to yield social change, whilst immigrants were generally cast as an economic competitor for resources. Whilst the liberal left often casts some working-class peoples' desire for 'community and political solidarity as nostalgic sentimentalism',[7] such a dismissal was heightened with the rise of English nationalism; as revealed, many scholars cast Brexit as a desire to return to the imperial age, mere racism and stupidity.[8] Most of these academics, though, have not actually spoken to those that espouse nationalistic sentiments; rather, they based their knowledge claims on rather distant quantitative methods.

However, statistical methods often omit history, contextual conditions, biography and the subjectivity of human actors. Indeed, Brian Salter asked about the academic failure to predict the vote to Leave, since it 'came as a large and very unwelcome surprise to most British university intellectuals'.[9] The rich qualitative data in this book point to how this is potentially because of the dependence on statistical methodologies. As documented, they tend to posit peoples' lives as linear and bereft of nuance. The depths of history and how it continues to shape working-class peoples' attitudes, which was a striking aspect of this book, are absent. Whilst they offer empirical points for further exploration, their causation claims confuse symptoms, correlations and fundamental causes; therefore, perhaps, they cannot offer a comprehensive understanding of what life is like in places like post-industrial Steel Town.

As this book has spent some time exploring historical processes, it seems fitting that it now outlines capitalist crises brought by the COVID-19 pandemic, its impact upon society and how the system may be set to mutate once again.

The present—coronavirus!

Any discussion of the future must consider the COVID-19 pandemic, which emerged several months after the historical collapse of the Red Wall. First identified in Wuhan, China, towards the end of 2019, the virus spread rapidly across continents and generated myriad social distress in its wake. On 31 January 2020, England's first COVID-19 case was reported in the city of York, 54 miles south of Steel Town, whilst by March 2020, the World Health Organisation had declared a global pandemic and thus an international emergency.[10] Whilst many of the respondents' sentiments about society and politics had been characterised by capitalist realism and thus the non-belief in profound social change, the pandemic compelled the government to instigate unprecedented and rapid changes to social life, not least the implementation of national lockdowns on 23 March 2020, 5 November 2020 and 6 January 2021. Other non-pharmaceutical interventions including social distancing, mask wearing and working from home where possible also became the norm. Not witnessed since the Second World War, myriad restrictions have been placed upon peoples' movement, often with a focus on staying locally and avoiding unnecessary travel. At the time of writing, these measures have been applied at varying grades of intensity for nearly two years. Of course, it might be argued that such measures have 'drastically altered the very fabric of human existence, banning most forms of social interactions and requiring individuals to rapidly adapt to completely different daily routines'.[11]

As part of the measures, people were ordered to 'stay at home, save lives, protect the NHS',[12] though the NHS ought to exist to protect the health of the nation's citizens,[13] not the other way around. The systemic failings of neoliberal capitalism were exposed as a marketised, fragmented, under-resourced and underfunded health system, made worse by austerity measures in the preceding years, struggled to cope with heightened demand for its services.[14] As COVID-19 fatalities primarily consist of the elderly—the average age of death in England is 82[15]—care homes were particularly vulnerable to the disease; however, much of the care sector had been privatised throughout neoliberalism, with working conditions degrading and poorly paid, and thus, many did not have the capacity to deal with the virus. Staff in some care homes have spoken about how the intensification of work generated anxiety, depression and hopelessness, whilst the prohibition on family visits meant the poor health of many elderly residents, particularly those with dementia, worsened and perhaps contributed to their sudden decline.[16]

The just-in-time delivery model of neoliberal globalisation, whereby the state and companies primarily import commodified objects from the Global South rather than manufacturing them domestically, meant the healthcare system was left with a shortage of personal protective equipment (PPE), putting many peoples' lives needlessly at risk.[17] However, as mentioned, capital has always sought to profit from moments of crises, and the pandemic has proved no exception with various acts of potential corruption littering capitalo-parliamentarianism. As Lee Jones and Shahar Hameiri outline, the dearth of PPE provided profitability opportunities for the private sector, with many large companies with no experience of manufacturing PPE, but who possessed links to various Lords or government ministers, were awarded multimillion-pound contracts.[18] Harvey's revolving door of the state-finance nexus has thus been potentially exposed again, with nearly £11 billion of contracts granted without competitive tendering.

My recent collaborative work exposed how the lockdowns have potentially generated an array of unintentional social consequences.[19] Though they reduce transmission and potentially contain COVID-19 mortalities, as they transiently suspend much economic activity and confine people to their homes, they have also impacted upon rising unemployment levels, mental ill health, domestic violence, child abuse and widened the gap between the world's super rich and poor. Unemployment is now rising across much of the OECD, with young people particularly hard hit by the pandemic. With the capitalist system in crises, many right-wing politicians suggested that the nation state should enact policies briefly orientated around welfare to save capitalism.[20] Potentially embodying this is the Conservative government's myriad economic intervention in the form of a generous furlough scheme, instigated on 20 March 2020 and involving the state paying 80% of peoples' wages up to £2,500 a month. Indeed, by the end of 2020, nearly 29,600 workers in Teesside were furloughed.[21] Without this scheme, it is possible that 'the crisis would have immediately spiralled beyond all control',[22] though the scheme ended in September 2021.

Whilst the UK government has often claimed that 'we are all in this together', Slavoj Zizek noted that 'the pandemic functioned as a kind of detonator that exploded already existing tensions in our societies',[23] particularly health inequalities. Those who are particularly vulnerable to SARS-CoV-2 include people with underlying health conditions and, indeed, socially, and economically deprived locales often contain more health problems such as asthma, diabetes, heart and liver disease, cancer and obesity.[24] Moreover, jobs at the lower ends of the social structure tend to be more associated with respiratory problems, meaning people living in areas that are materially disadvantaged and contain various health issues are more at risk of dying if they contract COVID-19.[25] Accordingly, those locales with the highest levels of deprivation and poorly paid jobs are associated with higher mortality rates from the disease.[26] In fact, rather early into the pandemic Middlesbrough in Teesside was identified as a locality at particular risk of both high COVID-19 cases and excess fatalities.[27]

Of course, Teesside has been impacted by the pandemic, enduring a rise in joblessness, with nearly 7% of local people looking for employment by January 2021, an increase of 2.7% in comparison to the previous year.[28] There has also been 'unprecedented levels of demand for Universal Credit', that is, a welfare payment for those on low incomes to cover their living costs, which has increased by over 3% from March to May 2020 and stagnated thereafter. 9.7% of 16- to 24-year-olds in Teesside are now claiming unemployment benefits, which is 2.7% higher than the rest of the United Kingdom. Whilst the Teesside region was identified as one of the places in England whereby people were least likely to comply with the restrictions, it also possessed comparably high infection rates throughout the pandemic.[29]

With such social insecurity and uncertainty about the present and the future, it is no surprise that many peoples' mental ill health has been exacerbated during the pandemic. The NHS is arguably dealing with a mental health crisis, since the number of under 17s taking prescribed drugs like antidepressants has reached a historical high, rising by 40% during the pandemic.[30] Recent research ascertained that many adults increased their alcohol consumption during the lockdowns, particularly those aged between 18 and 34, contributing to their higher prevalence of mental ill-health such as depression.[31] Other research also identified an intensification of many mental health problems in young people across England, particularly anxiety and depression, combined with an increase in both loneliness and alcohol consumption.[32] It is not surprising that many children in Teesside have reported the degradation of their mental health; in fact, the Middlesbrough mayor suggested the locale is enduring a pandemic of mental health problems amongst children.[33] Relatedly, The Nuffield Foundation's research with people in the Northeast of England discerned how nearly 40% of participants claimed they are financially worse off than before the pandemic emerged, with many people reporting higher levels of loneliness, isolation and self-harm.[34] Other research documented how well-being levels differed across society, with those labouring in lowly paid and poorly skilled jobs reporting the lowest rates of well-being during the pandemic, particularly those working in construction, food and retail,[35] intensifying already existing inequalities in the neoliberal era.

Whilst the inadvertent harms of the pandemic/lockdowns continue to accumulate, there has perhaps been a striking consensus throughout much of the pandemic on the lockdowns and the accompanying restrictive measures. As mentioned, the political world before the pandemic emerged was defined by post-politics, that is, the reduction of politics to the mere administration of what exists and the absence of belief in an alternative social world. Most politicians acted as enforcers of neoliberal logic, stifling contestation on the need for a different political order. Perhaps, this is why lockdowns were presented as a fait accompli by capitalo-parliamentarianism, with little debate occurring over the social and economic costs of the policy response, and if the benefits outweighed the potential harm.[36] Indeed, contestation on COVID-19 in both the media and politics has been confined within a narrow set of parameters—such as, not locking down 'hard' enough or 'quick' enough. Lockdown's efficacy, which many have questioned,[37] and/or exploring alternative approaches, such as those adopted in Sweden and Belarus who both did not lockdown,[38] have been given very little political attention. 'Harder' lockdowns involving tougher restrictions on peoples' movement for longer periods of time were also generally dismissed, as well as a zero-COVID-19 strategy which was seen as unrealistic even by many liberals who were content with a steady and manageable death rate.

Those that provided some opposition to the lockdowns have been in a minority, particularly the backbench and vocal critics, Tory MPs Sir Charles Walker and Desmond Swayne, who claim that the core governmental response has engendered myriad harm to the economy and many peoples' lives, particularly those at the bottom of the social structure. Meanwhile, though, inarticulate political dissatisfaction is growing, with anti-lockdown protests occurring at various points in 2021, including on 26 June in London, which attracted thousands of people from across England, though perhaps this merely formed the background noise to lockdown logic, failing to disrupt the political consensus. Such discontent has been fuelled by various political scandals, involving senior government officials who have often not obeyed the restrictions that they helped devise. Embodying this is Conservative MP Matt Hancock. He was compelled to resign on 26 June 2021 after sizable public pressure, as video footage emerged of Hancock breaking social distancing rules and having an affair with his aide Gina Coladangelo,[39] perhaps intensifying the widespread sense of political cynicism, scepticism and fatalism that exists in England's left-behind locales.

While many countries are now emerging out of the pandemic,[40] the harm caused by the SARS-CoV-2 pandemic and the lockdowns upon the economy and social life are likely to be long lasting, meaning it is possible that the state will pursue a different form of political economy to remedy the intensification of societal inequalities. After over 40 years of neoliberal hegemony and its depoliticisation of social life, it is possible that history is about to begin again. Given the tectonic problems that litter society today, not least global warming, an unprecedented gap between the world's super rich and impoverished, myriad private indebtedness, post-social relations and the rise of political dissatisfaction, the need for change is more important than ever. In this context, though, as James Bridle outlines, when we think about the future, or what he terms the 'new dark age', it is fair to say that:

> Writing about the new dark age, even if I can leaven it with networked hope, is not pleasant. It requires saying things that we would rather leave unsaid, thinking things that we would rather keep unthought. Doing so often leaves one with a hollow feeling in the gut, a kind of despair. And yet to fail to do so will be to fail to acknowledge the world as it is, to continue to live in fantasy and abstraction[41].

Accordingly, the book now closes with a discussion of the future, speculating on what potentially lies ahead, including climate breakdown and the possibility of a Green Industrial Revolution.

The future: what lies ahead?

Politically, it is plausible that the Conservative government may keep the Labour Party out of office for the next ten years. The current Labour Party leader, Keir Starmer—a London-centric, ardent Remainer who ignores class-based politics—will not win over the hearts and minds of working-class people in post-industrial locales like Steel Town in Teesside. We are in the midst of historical political change, which is unlikely to end just yet. Whilst parts of the Red Wall have collapsed, there are sizable chunks that may still shift to the Conservatives at the next general election. This includes Yvette Cooper's seat in Normanton, Pontefract and Castleford in West Yorkshire, where Labour held the seat in 2019 by 1,276 votes; John Healey's seat in Wentworth and Dearne in South Yorkshire, where Labour witnessed a 24.7% drop in their overall vote share in 2019; and Olivia Blake's seat in the Sheffield Hallam constituency, which won in 2019 by a mere 712 votes.

Since the empirical research for this book came to an end, the Labour Party have learnt very little from their previous electoral humiliation. Rather than being gracious in defeat and utilising it to reflect on what went wrong, the shift away from the socio-cultural and economic interests of the working class towards identity politics and its focus on minority issues has intensified. Whilst these issues are important, they are not electorally popular[42] and should not displace placing capitalism's core antagonism—social class—at the core of the party's modus operandi. Indeed, Matt Goodwin insists that Keir Starmer is unelectable, in part because the party is now dominated by social liberals and thus culturally detached from those across the fallen Red Wall, who it needs support from to win the next election in May 2024.[43] Similarly, prominent left-wing activist and trade unionist Paul Embery claimed that the party is now 'for the woke, the toytown revolutionary and Twitter',[44] viewing working-class people as culturally regressive, backword looking and nostalgic for an age that cannot return, focusing instead on winning the votes of those who are perceived as more cosmopolitan and liberal.

Given Labour's intake of MPs during the last several elections have often been individuals focused on surface-level identity issues rather than class and how those identities intersect, it is likely that this shift in emphasis will remain for some time. It might be argued that these understandings of identity politics are an impotent political force. As mentioned, it relegates capitalism's historical class struggle to the historical dustbin, favouring a multitude of singular political causes, all vying for recognition within a profoundly unequal and harmful socio-economic system, rather than attempting to construct a new form of political economy.[45] Therefore, it does not pose a threat to capitalism's underlying economic forces: competition, the maximisation of profitability, market expansion and the inevitable social inequalities that these combined forces engender. It might be argued therefore that focusing solely on the cultural field allows crisis-ridden neoliberal capitalism to continue unhinged, stifling the emergence of a coherent political project.[46]

Surface-level understandings of identity politics have little to say about the core issues that matter to local people in places like deindustrialised Steel Town; areas that Labour must win back if it is to be electorally successful again. As Adrian Pabst recently outlined, politics must be about the search for the collective good, a striving to repair England's broken towns, labour markets and communal domains like its high streets.[47] It must, therefore, be concerned with the good life for all. What identity politics does is stymie commitment to a shared ideal, something that is often central to successful political projects.[48] The seemingly unstoppable force of 'neoliberal progressivism'[49] continues to take in much of society and its social institutions, whereby the only structural antagonism often omitted from consideration is social class.

This hollowing out of the party has perhaps signalled the death knell of Labour, a process that began in the 1990s with the election of New Labour. However, as tentatively mentioned, the evisceration of organised, working-class politics was always a dream of the early neoliberals, who viewed the working class as a 'disease'.[50] They cast the working class as a threat to their utopia of a world governed by the impersonal hand of the market. This is because they would ask for entitlements that would disrupt the functioning of the market economy, not least fair wages, trade union representation, economic stability and social security in both young and old age. Therefore, the symbiotic relationship between neoliberal capitalism and the liberal left is there for all to see—both groups tend to view the working class in a condescending manner, and both view them as disposable.[51]

Whilst the task ahead of Labour is tectonic, the political discontent expressed across its former Red Wall seats like Steel Town is pliable and can be channelled into a new political project. A partial issue, however, is to turn subjects of non-belief into subjects of belief again; to further shatter capitalist realism and construct a new political economy with positive and clear messages. The Labour Party and its associated Leftist groups must return to the *Same*. Whilst many working class people express discontents towards immigration and refugees, they too have more in common with minority social groups. All groups are subjected to the vagaries of the market. All are deemed superfluous.

Emphasising Sameness is not 'class essentialism',[52] but a political awareness that an electorally significant number of people, particularly across the Red Wall, endure uncertain and unstable employment, an incursion on their pay and rights at work, the absence of comprehensible trajectories and worry about both the present and the future.[53] Focusing on a common struggle and shared interests enables relatively trivial cultural differences to be overcome. As the cause of peoples' distress is recognised—neoliberal capitalism—cultural antagonisms will recede. Neoliberalism will reveal itself as not natural and immovable, but another political economic programme amongst many possibilities.

As many scholars have identified, the coronavirus crisis provides an opportunity to rethink our current political economy[54]; therefore, it provides a chance for the Left to put forward some bold socio-economic policies to help steer the English citizenry through a post-pandemic world. Indeed, Modern Monetary Theory (MMT) is a marginal economic framework that has been gaining traction in some intellectual circles in recent years,[55] and it might equip the Left with an economic narrative that enables them to diminish their appearance of economic incompetence and harness electoral support. Throughout the neoliberal era, most policy proposals by the Left have been met with the inevitable response of 'how will you pay for it'? The Left's response often involves more taxation for the richest members of society, thus hinging upon the idea that taxation pays for government spending. However, proponents of MMT suggest this well-trodden notion is a myth. Instead, MMT indicates that sovereign states hold the monopoly on the printing of their currency—they are the currency issuer and not like a household who are the currency user and thus fiscally constrained.

Whilst the neoliberals often cast Left-leaning policy proposals as too expensive, which would only serve to bankrupt the country, leave the next generation with unsustainable debt or increase the deficit, MMT indicates that sovereign states can never run out of money because they issue it. The economic narrative that has dominated throughout neoliberalism— that the state is constrained in its spending—resonates with the citizenry because they must live within their means and can go bankrupt if they do not. However, a sovereign state does not have to manage a currency like this, it has the economic tools at its disposal to implement policies for the benefit of working-class people. Whilst being a 'taxpayer' often enables people to feel as though they are contributing productively to society, a Left that utilises MMT can still inform people that taxes are important, though not for the reasons espoused by the political Right. Taxation serves numerous purposes, including being a powerful economic tool to shape the distribution of wealth in society and thereby dwindle inequalities, not least the unprecedented gap between the rich and poor which has been exacerbated during the pandemic.[56] Utilising this core insight from MMT might shift the economic debate, enabling the Left to outmanoeuvre its political opponents.

Of course, the importance of work to working-class life cannot be understated.[57] As the industrial age demonstrated, work can be a source of pride, social purpose and fulfilment; it can foster feelings of belonging, place and community. A state-funded job guarantee might be a useful means to ameliorate unemployment, the accompanying social distress and ensure what John Crudas recently casts as the dignity of labour once again.[58] Through the scheme, a job paid at the living wage would be available to all jobless citizens, at both part-time and full-time hours. Whilst the emotional toil and psychological pain of searching for work would individually dissipate, it would also help revive locales like post-industrial Steel Town, transforming peoples' lives, their families and their local community. This is because unemployment often engenders myriad social damage or 'scarring effects',[59] including mental health problems, criminal activity, deficient health and well-being, alcohol misuse and higher rates of suicide. Perhaps, a state-backed job guarantee would also shift the debate on what constitutes acceptable working conditions, compelling capital to increase wages in poorly paid jobs.[60] It might also engender an attitude that a job should be a human right, rather than people often having to feel lucky that they possess one.

A job guarantee has been proposed by some Leftist intellectuals as part of a broader Green New Deal.[61] The latter is a bold policy framework, involving a paradigm shift away from fossil fuels towards greener forms of energy to address global warming. Given the historical and urgent need to do this, and the tens of thousands of green jobs it could create, scholars claim it could form part of a transformative governmental commitment to full employment,[62] though as we previously encountered, the political elite oppose such a policy since it undermines their ability to discipline the workforce. As many working-class people have often been cynical towards green agendas, in part because they view them as an attack on their livelihoods, it is important to place jobs, livelihoods and relative prosperity at the centre of a Green New Deal. This would involve unprecedented investment in green infrastructure, including a *degrowth* of the fossil fuel industry and a sizable growth in the green/renewable energy industries such as wind, solar and biomass. It would also involve mass reforestation projects to capture carbon alongside carbon capture technologies, as well as myriad regulations imposed on corporations that emit a large amount of pollution.[63]

Indeed, there are various signs that the Conservative government may potentially seek to tackle global warming by shifting away from neoliberalism towards a different form of political economy. Whilst the 2008 global financial crash dealt a hammer blow to neoliberalism, the rise of nationalism combined with the coronavirus crisis means it is likely that the system is set to change again. Francis Fukuyama's (1992) thesis offered the notion of the End of History, whereby capitalism's historical ideological opponent—communism—was invariably discredited both by the horrors that occurred under its watch across the world, and by the fall of the Berlin Wall in 1989 as the Soviet Union collapsed. Subsequently, it felt like neoliberal capitalism, its depoliticisation of social life and the emergence of its naturalised logic—capitalist realism—were all that existed. Nothing could occur beyond these narrow confines. However, it is possible that we are now approaching the end of end of history.[64]

At the Ditchley Annual Lecture in July 2020, Government minister Michael Gove suggested that we are immersed in myriad crises, drawing parallels to the 1929 Great Depression and claiming we are set for the Fourth Industrial Revolution[65] which would involve a transformation of social life. Relatedly, a recent Build Back Better (from the pandemic) document from the government also offered terms such as the 'Green Industrial Revolution', outlining the need for myriad investment across society, particularly in green energy and economically abandoned areas to 'level up' England.[66] This involves the target of net zero emissions by 2050, with the state taking a leading role in shaping the new form of political economy whilst allowing the private sector to innovate. Governmental proposals include a ban on the sale of new petrol and diesel vehicles by 2030, accompanied by a £1.3 billion investment in charge point infrastructure, £12 billion support package for carbon capture and the development of eight freeports and net zero clusters in England's emaciated industrial domains. Whilst we have heard some of this rhetoric from the Conservative Party a far back as 2017, when former prime minister Theresa May spoke about the need to tackle climate breakdown and social inequalities,[67] the need to remedy a broken social order has only intensified with the COVID-19 pandemic. Moreover, as this book frequently highlighted, at various historical moments social forces combine to compel governments to instigate epochal change, and perhaps, this is the juncture we are now approaching.

Indeed, a core part of the net zero 2050 plan is for Teesside to form the UK's first decarbonised industrial cluster, with carbon-intensive businesses subject to decarbonising by as early as 2030. Known as the 'Net Zero Teesside' project, the initiative seeks to provide the carbon capture infrastructure required to store carbon under the nearby North Sea, potentially creating 5,500 jobs directly and many more in the local supply chain.[68] The project is comprised of five core members including BP and Shell and is also supported by the government. Another core development for the transition to a greener economy is H2Teesside.[69] Led by the energy company BP, the project would involve building the UK's largest blue hydrogen plant by 2030 near the old steelwork's site. The plant would capture up to two million tonnes of carbon dioxide annually, and work could start in 2027. Moreover, work is currently underway to demolish the steelworks plant in Steel Town, which is part of a £113 million plan to clean up the site to make it ready for new investments as part of the energy transition. The Conservative Teesside or 'Tees Valley' Mayor, Ben Houchen, has been central to this, securing Freeport status in Teesside in March 2021. The Freeport is the largest in the United Kingdom and it is estimated that it could potentially create around 18,000 jobs and boost the local economy by £3.2 billion within the next five years,[70] which would provide a welcome economic boost to Steel Town and the surrounding locales. However, some scholars have suggested infrastructural projects might be useful to level up the country, though they are unlikely to be transformative and their job creation projections may be rather optimistic.[71]

Whilst the future could herald a shift to a green economy, with Teesside potentially being at the centre of a green industrial revolution, it is still possible that the idea of building back better and levelling up will amount to little. Many scholars have suggested that the latter idea is more about electoral calculation rather than a genuine understanding of how to remedy social inequalities; it remains poorly conceptualised as it is politically expedient for it to be so in what is the most unequal country in Europe.[72] Of course, it is also possible that the new dark age will engender structural conditions akin to the dystopian fictional movie *Children of Men*, whereby civilisation is on the brink of collapse in part due to global infertility and the state has been stripped back to its authoritarian functions.[73] As Slavoj Zizek outlines, the citizenry desperately wants the pandemic to end, but perhaps it 'will not end: it is reasonable to see the ongoing pandemic as announcing a new era of ecological troubles'.[74] If we fail to move away from neoliberalism and implement changes such as a Green New Deal, then tectonic problems await in the near future. Of course, the forging of the Paris climate agreement (COP 21) in December 2015 was viewed as a landmark moment, as it followed various other international conferences on climate change like the Copenhagen conference in 2011 that failed to generate agreement and change.[75] COP 21 relies upon voluntary pledges from 197 countries to avoid global warming of over two degrees, since anything above this would be catastrophic.

However, we are set to pass four degrees warming by the end of this century, which would basically leave the North Pole with no ice for the first time in three million years and lead to the extinction of animals like the polar bears.[76] Climate scientists thus agree that the shift to a green economy needs to occur immediately, since the West Antarctic ice sheet is melting rapidly with over 100 metres of ice lost already due to the warming of the ocean.[77] This loss is currently doubling every ten years, and the loss of the West Antarctic ice sheet could engender sea levels rise by 5 metres, ensuring coastal regions across the world as well as whole countries like Bangladesh and the Maldives would be submerged under water. Soaring temperatures also mean large parts of South Asia, the Middle East and Africa will be uninhabitable in the near future.[78]

Rising global temperatures will likely mean that extreme weather events like floods, hurricanes, droughts and forest fires will become more common. Perhaps, a clear indicator of this was the bushfires that raged across Australia in 2019 and early 2020, with millions of hectares of land burned.[79] This attracted worldwide media and political attention, as the fires burned for several months, destroying forests, animals, insects and causing individual, social, economic and cultural harm. Over 300 million tonnes of carbon dioxide were released into the atmosphere and the economic cost of ameliorating the damage was over £100 billion. Other impacts of soaring temperatures include soil degradation, destruction of ecosystems, reduced fresh-water capacity and the acidification of various oceans, causing further global instability and insecurity.[80] Many countries may also become war zones as people fight for resources like food and water, which is already happening in some impoverished nations of the Global South.[81] Global warming also increases the risk of new infectious diseases emerging.[82] Floods, for example, risk microbiological water pollution, whilst the heating of the water can more easily transmit waterborne pathogens as the environment becomes more suitable for bacterial growth.[83] Concerns also exist amongst scientists that the melting of the polar ice caps will engender viruses and diseases that have not circulated for millions of years, which will wreak havoc upon our immune systems.[84]

These conditions will likely lead to the mass movement of vulnerable people from the Global South to the West, with around 330 million people potentially being displaced by 2050, fuelling social tensions and divisions.[85] As documented, we have already witnessed signs of this across Europe with the refugee crisis, as millions of people have fled war torn and impoverished countries, often in the Middle East, to seek refuge upon the shores of the West. Whilst many make a life-threatening journey across the seas in dilapidated boats, where thousands have tragically died, others try desperately to hide through other means, including in lorries and even in the bonnets of cars.[86] For those that make it across, they are often met with depersonalised and inhumane border crossings that include huge metal walls with barbed wire erected across the top, coupled with an unwelcoming political atmosphere whereby some politicians attempt to stir further division rather than seek to remedy the root causes of the problem.

Another issue that conjures up a future like *Children of Men*, specifically of a childless world, is the global decline in human fertility, with estimates suggesting that by 2045 the median sperm count could be zero.[87] Essentially, the male sperm count has been declining throughout the neoliberal era, whilst the number of children that people have been having has also been declining.[88] A core driver of this are toxic chemicals that impact detrimentally on hormones and fertility, which exist in an abundance of consumer products, particularly those that are plastic based. It is estimated that, if unchecked, most couples will require assisted reproduction to try and have a child by 2045. Considering the above, it is potentially fair to suggest that: 'We are swiftly approaching the endgame for humanity, the point at which we pass a point of no return'.[89]

Influential bodies like the World Economic Forum have thus documented the need for fundamental change, with deglobalisation being a core aspect of the shift away from neoliberalism, not least because it is environmentally unsustainable to continually import products from thousands of miles away,[90] whilst it also leaves states vulnerable in moments of crises like pandemics. They have also highlighted the need for more people to work from home, potentially giving workers more freedom and autonomy whilst dwindling the amount of environmental pollution generated by lengthy commutes to the office. They claim the condition of the working classes will be a central question for many nation states in the near future, with many working-class people likely to witness socio-economic betterment in their wages and working conditions, in part to defuse ongoing political dissatisfaction and the rise of new nationalisms.

However, history tells us that for progressive gains to be made, societies often must pass through a period of prolonged social turmoil and, indeed, myriad distress continues to grow. The early twentieth century tells us that we cannot rule out the rise of extreme political ideologies under such structural conditions.[91] Nonetheless, as mentioned, a unified political project that displays a commitment to a shared ideal can harness working-class dissatisfaction and construct a post-neoliberal social order. If fragments of the future lie scattered in the present,[92] then it appears as though it will be the political Right and not the Left that will steer us into this brave new world. Given we are potentially immersed in the preliminary stages of this epochal political shift, critical analysis and reflection are more important than ever, particularly on the present moment, where we are going, the world that is yet to emerge and the challenges and catastrophes that potentially lie ahead. Ultimately, the future is yet to be determined.

Notes

1. Streeck, WG (2016), p. 190.
2. North, G (1975), p. 21.
3. Fisher, M (2009); Harvey, D (2005) (2011).
4. Hall, S, Winlow, S & Ancrum, C (2008).
5. Winlow, S & Hall, S (2013).
6. Lloyd, A (2013) (2018); Telford, L & Wistow, J (2020); Telford, L & Lloyd, A (2020); Warren, J (2018).
7. Hall, S (2012), p. 170.
8. For example, see: Bell, D & Vucetic, S (2019); Bhambra, G (2017); Gupta, S & Virdee, S (2020); Pitcher, B (2019).
9. Salter, B (2018), p. 467.
10. Blakeley, G (2020) *The Corona Crash: How the Pandemic Will Change Capitalism*. London: Verso.
11. Maekalae, M, Reggev, N, Dutra, N, Tamayo, R, Silva-Sobhrino, R, Klevjer, K & Pfuhl, G (2020) Perceived efficacy of COVID-19 restrictions, reactions and their impact on mental health during the early phase of the outbreak in six countries. *Royal Society Open Science*. 7: 1–23.
12. Briggs, D, Ellis, A, Lloyd, A & Telford, L (2020).
13. Briggs, D Telford, L Lloyd, A & Ellis, A (2021) Working, living, and dying in Covid times: Perspectives from frontline residential adult social care workers in the United Kingdom. *Safer Communities*. 20(3): 208–222.
14. Jones, L & Hameiri, S (2021) COVID-19 and the failure of the neoliberal regulatory state. *Review of International Political Economy*: 1–25. Online First: https://doi.org/10.1080/09692290.2021.1892798; Sparke, M & Williams, O (2022) Neoliberal disease: COVID-19, co-pathogenesis and global health insecurities. *EPA: Economy and Space*. 54(1): 15–32.
15. Briggs, D, Ellis, A, Lloyd, A & Telford, L (2021).
16. Briggs, D, Telford, L, Lloyd, A & Ellis, A (2021).
17. Jones, L & Hameiri, S (2021).
18. Jones, L & Hameiri, S (2021).
19. See, for example: Briggs, D, Ellis, A, Lloyd, A & Telford, L (2020); Briggs, D, Ellis, A, Lloyd, A & Telford, L (2021); Briggs, D, Telford, L, Lloyd, A & Ellis, A (2021); Ellis, A, Briggs, D, Lloyd, A & Telford, L (2021) A ticking time bomb of future harm: Lockdown, child abuse and future violence. *Abuse: An International Impact Journal*. 2(1): 37–48.
20. Blakeley, G (2020).

21. Tees Valley Combined Authority (2021) *Monthly Unemployment Update—February 2021*. Stockton-on-Tees: Tees Valley Mayor.
22. Blakeley, G (2020), p. 59.
23. Zizek, S (2021) *Pandemic 2! Chronicles of a Time Lost*. Cambridge: Polity Books, p. 132.
24. Bambra, C, Riordan, R, Ford, J & Matthews, F (2020) The COVID-19 pandemic and health inequalities. *Journal of Epidemiology and Community Health*. 74: 964–968.
25. Bambra, C, Riordan, R, Ford, J & Matthews, F (2020).
26. Rose, T, Mason, K, Pennington, A, McHale, P, Buchan, I, Taylor-Robinson, D & Barr, B (2020) Inequalities in COVID19 mortality related to ethnicity and socio-economic deprivation. *MedRxiv*; Whitehead, M, Barr, B & Taylor-Robinson, D (2020) Covid-19: We are not 'all in this together'—less privileged in society are suffering the brunt of the damage. *The British Medical Journal*.
27. Franklin, B (2020) Covid-19 local area health risk rating. *Centre for Progressive Policy*, 5 May 2020. Accessed on 24/06/2021. Available at: https://www.progressive-policy.net/publications/covid-19-local-area-risk-rating.
28. Tees Valley Combined Authority (2021).
29. NHS North Tees and Hartlepool (2020) Teesside key workers on COVID-19 'This isn't over. . .'. Accessed on 25/06/2021. Available at: www.nth.nhs.uk/news/teesside-key-workers-on-covid-19-this-isnt-over/.
30. Donnelly, L (2021) Number of children taking antidepressants hits all-time peak during pandemic. *The Telegraph*. Accessed on 25/06/2021. Available at: www.telegraph.co.uk/news/2021/06/23/number-children-taking-antidepressants-hits-all-time-peak-pandemic/.
31. Jacob, L, Smith, L, Armstrong, N, Yakkundi, A, Barnett, Y, Butler, L, McDermott, D, Koyanagi, A, Shin, J, Meyer, J, Firth, J, Remes, O, Lopez-Sanchez, G & Tully, M (2021) Alcohol use and mental health during COVID-19 lockdown: A cross-sectional study in a sample of UK adults. *Drug and Alcohol Dependence*. 219: 1–5.
32. Evans, S, Alkan, E, Bhangoo, J, Tenenbaum, H & Ng-Knight, T (2021) Effects of the COVID-19 lockdown on mental health, wellbeing, sleep, and alcohol use in a UK student sample. *Psychiatry Research*. 298: 1–7.
33. *Middlesbrough Gov* (2020) Mayor backs charity call for mental health support in schools. Accessed on 25/06/2021. Available at: www.middlesbrough.gov.uk/news/mayor-backs-charity-call-mental-health-support-schools.
34. Fancourt, D, Bu, F, Mak, J & Steptoe, A (2020) *Covid-19 Social Study: Results Release 25*. London: Nuffield Foundation.
35. Chen, D & Wang, Y (2021) Inequality-related health and social factors and their impact on well-being during the COVID-19 pandemic: Findings from a national survey in the United Kingdom. *International Journal of Environmental Research and Public Health*. 18: 1–9.
36. Briggs, D Telford, L Ellis, A Lloyd, A & Kotze, J (2021) *Lockdown: Social harm in the covid-19 era*. London: Palgrave Macmillan.
37. See, for instance: Allen, D (2021) Covid lockdown cost/benefits: A critical assessment of the literature; Bhattacharya, J, Gupta, S & Kulldorff, M (2020) Focused protection: The middle ground between lockdowns and 'let it rip'. *The Great Barrington Declaration*. Accessed on 27/06/2021. Available at: https://gbdeclaration.org/focused-protection/; Chin, V, Ioannidis, J, Tanner, M & Cripps, S (2020) Effects of non-pharmaceutical interventions on COVID-19. *A Tale of Three Models*: 1–45; Ioannidis, J, Cripps, S & Tanner, M (2020) Forecasting for COVID-19 has failed. *International Journal of Forecasting*: 1–16; Melnick, E & Ioannidis, J (2020) Head to head: Should governments continue lockdown to slow the spread of covid-19? *British Medical Journal*. 369: 1–3.
38. Baral, S, Chandler, R, Prieto, R, Gupta, S, Mishra, S & Kulldorff, M (2021) Leveraging epidemiological principles to evaluate Sweden's COVID-19 response. *Annals of*

Epidemiology. 54: 21–26; Josefsson, K (2021) Perspectives of life in Sweden during the COVID-19 pandemic. *Journal of Clinical Sport Psychology.* 15: 80–86; Karath, K (2020) Covid-19: How does Belarus have one of the lowest death rates in Europe? *British Medical Journal.* 370: 1–2.

39. Harrison, E (2021) Matt Hancock quits as health secretary after breaking social distance guidance. *BBC News.* Accessed on 27/06/2021. Available at: www.bbc.co.uk/news/uk-57625508.
40. Blakeley, G (2020); Briggs, D, Ellis, A, Lloyd, A & Telford, L (2021); Malm, A (2020) *Corona, Climate, Chronic Emergency.* London: Verso; Zizek, S (2020) (2021).
41. Bridle, J (2020) *New Dark Age: Technology and the End of the Future.* London: Verso, p. 16.
42. Eatwell, R & Goodwin, M (2018); Hall, S & Winlow, S (2020).
43. Goodwin, M (2021) Why Keir Starmer is doomed. *Unherd.* Available at: https://unherd.com/2021/04/why-keir-starmer-is-doomed/.
44. Embery, P (2020), p. 136.
45. Zalloua, Z (2020).
46. Hall, S (2012); Hall, S & Winlow, S (2013); Winlow, S, Hall, S & Treadwell, J (2017).
47. Pabst, A (2021).
48. Winlow, S, Hall, S & Treadwell, J (2017).
49. Fraser, N (2019).
50. See Slobodian, Q (2018).
51. Hall, S & Winlow, S (2020); Hall, S, Winlow, S & Treadwell, J (2017) (2019).
52. Zizek, S (2017), p. 232.
53. Lloyd, A (2018b); Mahoney, I & Kearon, T (2018); McKenzie, L (2017a); Mitchell, W & Fazi, T (2017); Streeck, WG (2017); Winlow, S, Hall, S & Treadwell, J (2017).
54. Blakeley, G (2020); Briggs, D, Ellis, A, Lloyd, A & Telford, L (2021); Pabst, A (2021); Zizek, S (2020) (2021).
55. Briggs, D, Ellis, A, Lloyd, A & Telford, L (2021); Kelton, S (2020) *The Deficit Myth.* London: John Murray; Lloyd, A (2018b); Mitchell, W & Fazi, T (2020).
56. Briggs, D, Ellis, A, Lloyd, A & Telford, L (2021).
57. Cruddas, J (2021) *The Dignity of Labour.* Cambridge: Polity; Embery, P (2020).
58. Cruddas, J (2021).
59. Tcherneva, P (2020), p. 37.
60. Tcherneva, P (2020).
61. Blakeley, G (2020); Tcherneva, P (2020).
62. Chomsky, N & Pollin, R (2020) *Climate Crisis and the Global Green New Deal.* London: Verso.
63. Chomsky, N & Pollin, R (2020).
64. Hochuli, A, Hoare, G & Cunliffe, P (2021) *The End of the End of History: Politics in the Twenty-First Century.* Winchester: Zero Publishing.
65. Gove, M (2020) 'The privilege of public service' given as the Ditchley annual lecture. Accessed on 12/07/2021. Available at: www.gov.uk/government/speeches/the-privilege-of-public-service-given-as-the-ditchley-annual-lecture.
66. HM Treasury (2021) *Build Back Better: Our Plan for Growth.* Accessed on 12/07/2021. Available at: https://assets.publishing.service.gov.uk/government/uploads/system/uploads/attachment_data/file/968403/PfG_Final_Web_Accessible_Version.pdf.
67. Pabst, A (2021).
68. Net Zero Teesside (2021) *The UK's First Decarbonised Industrial Cluster.* Teesside: Net Zero Teesside.
69. BP (2021) BP plans UK's largest hydrogen project. *BP.* Accessed on 13/07/2021. Available at: www.bp.com/content/dam/bp/business-sites/en/global/corporate/pdfs/news-and-insights/press-releases/bp-plans-uks-largest-hydrogen-project.pdf.

70. Tees Valley Combined Authority (2021) *Teesside Freeport*. Accessed on 13/07/2021. Available at: https://teesvalley-ca.gov.uk/teesside-freeport/.
71. Connolly, J, Pyper, R & Zwet, A (2021) Governing 'levelling-up' in the UK: Challenges and prospects. *Contemporary Social Science*: 1–15; Jennings, W (2020) Last word: The future of towns. *Political Insight*. 44.
72. Connolly, J, Pyper, R & Zwet, A (2021); Jones, M (2019) *Cities and Regions in Crisis: The Political Economy of Sub-National Economic Development*. Cheltenham: Edward Edgar; Leyshon, A (2021) Economic geography I: Uneven development, 'left behind places' and 'levelling up' in a time of crisis. *Progress in Human Geography*: 1–14; Martin, R, Gardiner, B, Pike, A, Sunley, P & Tyler, P (2022) *Levelling Up Left Behind Places*. Abingdon: Routledge.
73. Fisher, M (2009).
74. Zizek, S (2021), p. 12.
75. Clemencon, R (2016) The two sides of the Paris climate agreement. *Journal of Environment and Development*. 25(1): 3–24.
76. Chomsky, N & Pollin, R (2020).
77. Chomsky, N & Pollin, R (2020).
78. Klein, N (2015) *This Changes Everything: Capitalism vs the Climate*. London: Penguin.
79. Lockie, S (2020) Sociological responses to the bushfire and climate crises. *Environmental Sociology*. 6(1): 1–5.
80. Klein, N (2015).
81. See Parenti, C (2011) *Tropic of Chaos: Climate Change and the New Geography of Violence*. Nashville: Nation Books.
82. Gale, P, Brouwer, A, Ramnial, V, Kelly, L, Kosmider, R, Fooks, A & Snary, E (2010) Assessing the impact of climate change on vector-borne viruses in the EU through the elicitation of expert opinion. *Infection and Epidemiology*. 138(2): 214–225.
83. Rossati, A (2017) Global warming and its health impact. *The International Journal of Occupational and Environmental Medicine*. 8(1): 7–20.
84. Briggs, D (2021).
85. Briggs, D (2021).
86. Briggs, D (2021).
87. Swan, S (2021) *Count Down: How Our Modern World is Threatening Sperm Counts, Altering Male and Female Reproductive Development, and Imperilling the Future of the Human Race*. New York: Simon & Schuster.
88. Swan, S (2021).
89. Briggs, D (2021), p. 153.
90. Briggs, D, Ellis, A, Lloyd, A & Telford, L (2021); Schwab, K & Malleret, T (2020) *Covid 19: The Great Reset*. Switzerland: World Economic Forum.
91. Pabst, A (2021).
92. Zizek, S (2017) (2018).

Index

abstracted empiricism 55
anxiety 35–37, 42, 91, 140–141
apprenticeships 21, 35, 70, 77, 94
asylum seekers 46, 122, 125, 127
austerity 9, 13, 17–18, 24, 32, 38, 42–44, 47, 51–52, 54, 56, 62, 67, 99, 110, 115, 117, 120

Brexit 5–6, 10, 47, 51–62, 114–121, 127, 130, 132–134

capital 13, 21, 25–26, 32–35, 39, 41, 44, 56, 69–70, 72–73, 76–78, 89, 92, 102, 109, 111, 117
capitalism 13, 17, 19–20, 33–38, 71–73, 76–78, 98, 138; laissez faire 17, 24, 68; neoliberal 6, 8, 32, 113, 126, 144–145; post-war 6, 22, 67–70, 89, 103
capitalist realism 10, 101, 111–113, 133–134, 145
class compromise 9, 24, 98, 138
coastal 13, 15, 17, 138, 149
communism 17, 68, 147
community 4–5, 38–39, 67, 73–76, 86–87, 120, 138; ghost town 1, 4, 129
Conservative Party 39, 42, 110, 118, 121
consumerism 37–38, 41, 46
coronavirus 139–143, 145, 147
corruption 140
crime 27, 35, 44, 96
cynicism 143

deaptation 114
debt 32, 37–38, 42, 46, 95, 146
deindustrialisation 45, 57, 76–87, 138
depoliticisation 109, 119, 143, 147
deprivation 16, 18, 26, 35, 68, 141

education 57, 94–95, 124
Empire 5, 53–54
employment 15, 22, 26–27, 43, 67–76, 90–103, 119–120; full employment 20–22, 25, 46, 71, 80, 92, 147
ethnographic 60–61
European Union (EU) 5, 39–40, 51–60, 114–121; four freedoms 39–40, 117
exploitation 35, 37, 98, 125, 137

Farage, Nigel 52, 114, 121
fascism 17–19
fetishistic disavowal 82, 130
financial crisis/crash 38–42, 117; great depression 17–18, 68
free market 34, 108

globalisation 38, 107, 140
global warming 84, 143, 147, 149

human 7, 58, 89, 103, 122, 139, 146, 150

ICI 16, 18, 20, 26, 69–70, 77–78, 94
identity politics 144; political correctness 129–130
immigration 39–40, 52, 55–56, 60, 121–127
individualism 21, 33–35, 83
industrial revolution 14; green industrial revolution 147–149
interviews 58, 60–61
Islam 127–129

Johnson, Boris 11, 52, 132–133

Labour Party 18, 20, 24, 38–39, 42–43, 46, 107–114
left behind 44, 54, 111, 138, 143

liberal left 118–119, 122, 124, 126,
    128–129, 131; Liberal Democrats
    41–42, 110, 130
lockdown 142

media 6, 22–23, 52, 54, 56–57, 110, 115,
    121, 123, 128, 133
Mediterranean 125
Middle East 40, 46, 62, 108, 126,
    149–150
Modern Monetary Theory (MMT)
    145
multiculturalism 55, 128

nationalisation 19, 27, 56
nationalism 51–60, 106–134
nation state 20, 33–35, 42, 111, 140
neoliberalism 24–26, 32–47, 78–80,
    82–83, 92–93, 95–96, 145; founding
    fathers 33, 134
nihilism 55, 125
non-voting 46, 111

overwork 101–102

pandemic 3, 35, 92, 139–143, 147–149
politicians 14, 19–20, 42, 47, 54,
    107–114, 131, 142
poverty 26–27, 54, 68, 110
privatisation 25, 33, 40, 43–44, 53,
    78, 117
privilege 36, 129–130
protests 28, 42, 45, 78–79, 142

qualitative research 57, 59, 60–62, 66
quantitative 8, 55, 58–60

race riots 22
racism 53–54, 57–58, 60, 74, 115,
    127–128, 130
red wall 5, 46, 59–60, 130, 132–133,
    143–155
refugees 40, 122, 124, 126–127
reserve army 35–36, 82–84, 92
resilience 82
restoration 24, 32, 87, 89

second referendum 130–133
Second World War 18–20, 38, 55, 68, 75, 139
security 22, 24, 27, 67–76, 87, 94, 102
sleep 72, 102
social club 61, 81, 90
social democratic 5, 20, 24, 39, 75
sovereignty 8, 117, 119, 134
steelworks 19, 23, 26, 28, 67, 69–74;
    closure 19, 23, 26, 28, 67, 69–74
strike 21, 24, 26, 28, 71, 76

targets 27, 44, 99–101
trade unions 7, 24, 27, 34, 40, 54, 71, 76

unemployment 15, 17, 26, 36, 97–98,
    140, 146
United Kingdom Independence Party
    (UKIP) 8, 47, 52, 114, 121

xenophobia 8, 47